Asking Questions

Norman M. Bradburn
Seymour Sudman
Brian Wansink

Asking Questions

The Definitive Guide to
Questionnaire Design—
For Market Research, Political Polls,
and Social and Health Questionnaires,
Revised Edition

JB JOSSEY-BASS™

A Wiley Brand

Published by Jossey-Bass
A Wiley Imprint
989 Market Street, San Francisco, CA 94103-1741   www.josseybass.com

Jossey-Bass books and products are available through most bookstores. To contact Jossey-Bass directly call our Customer Care Department within the U.S. at 800-956-7739, outside the U.S. at 317-572-3986, or fax 317-572-4002.

Jossey-Bass also publishes its books in a variety of electronic formats. Some content that appears in print may not be available in electronic books.

Library of Congress Cataloging-in-Publication Data

Bradburn, Norman M.
  Asking questions : the definitive guide to questionnaire design—for market research, political polls, and social and health questionnaires / Norman M. Bradburn, Brian Wansink, Seymour Sudman.—Rev. ed.
     p. cm.
  Earlier ed. by Sudman and Bradburn with Sudman named first.
  Includes bibliographical references (p.) and index.
  ISBN 978-0-7879-7088-8 (alk. paper)
  1. Social sciences—Research. 2. Questionnaires. I. Wansink, Brian.
II. Sudman, Seymour. III. Title.
  H62.B63 2004
  300'.72'3—dc22   2004001683

FIRST EDITION
PB Printing   20 19 18 17 16 15 14 13 12 11 10

Contents

*This book is dedicated to the memory of our colleague
and coauthor Seymour Sudman who died tragically
while we were in the midst of writing this book.
His spirit and wisdom have continued to inspire
us as we brought this manuscript to press.
He lives on in this book.*

Preface

This book is a revised and updated edition of *Asking Questions: A Practical Guide to Questionnaire Design*, first published in 1982. It focuses on the type of question asking that social science researchers and market researchers use in structured questionnaires or interviews. Many of the principles of effective formalized questioning we focus on in this book are useful in other contexts. They are useful in informal or semistructured interviews, in administering printed questionnaires in testing rooms, and in experimental studies involving participant evaluations or responses.

We intend this book to be a useful "handbook" for sociologists, psychologists, political scientists, evaluation researchers, social workers, sensory scientists, marketing and advertising researchers, and for many others who have occasion to obtain systematic information from clients, customers, or employees.

In the past two decades, two major changes in the practice of survey research prompted us to produce a revised edition. First, there has been a revolution in research on question asking brought about by the application of cognitive psychology to the study of questionnaire design. We now have a conceptual framework for understanding the question-answering process and the causes of the various response effects that have been observed since the early days of social scientific surveys. This work has helped move questionnaire construction from an art to a science.

Second, there has been a technological revolution in the way computers can be used to support the survey process. Computer-assisted survey information collection (CASIC) refers to a variety of specialized programs used to support survey data collection—for example, CAPI (computer-assisted personal interviewing) or CATI (computer-assisted telephone interviewing), to name the most common forms of CASIC. The greater use of computer technology at every stage of data collection in surveys has made many of the suggestions in our earlier edition obsolete and necessitated a thorough reworking of discussion that was predicated on traditional paper-and-pencil questionnaires. We are also beginning an era of Web-based surveys. Although there is still much to learn about this new method of conducting surveys, we have tried to incorporate what we know at this time into our discussions where relevant.

We have tried to make the book self-contained by including major references. Some readers, however, may wish to refer to our earlier books, *Response Effects in Surveys: A Review and Synthesis* (Sudman and Bradburn, 1974); *Improving Interview Method and Questionnaire Design: Response Effects to Threatening Questions in Survey Research* (Bradburn, Sudman, and Associates, 1979); *Thinking About Answers* (Sudman, Bradburn, and Schwarz, 1996); and *Consumer Panels*, (Sudman and Wansink, 2002), for more detailed discussion of the empirical data that support our recommendations.

This book is specifically concerned with questionnaire construction—not with all aspects of survey design and administration. Although we stress the careful formulation of the research problems before a questionnaire is designed, we do not tell you how to select and formulate important research problems. To do so requires a solid knowledge of your field—knowledge obtained through study and review of earlier research, as well as hard thinking and creativity. Once the research problem is formulated, however, this book can help you ask the right questions.

The book is divided into three parts. In Part I we discuss the social context of question asking. We present our central thesis, namely that questions must be precisely worded if responses to a survey are to be accurate; we outline a conceptual framework for understanding the survey interview and present examples to illustrate some of the subtleties of language and contexts that can cause problems. We also discuss some of the ethical principles important to survey researchers—the right to privacy, informed consent, and confidentiality of data.

Part II is devoted to tactics for asking questions. In Chapters Two through Nine we consider the major issues in formulating questions on different topics, such as the differences between requirements for questions about behavior and for questions about attitudes. We also consider how to ask questions dealing with knowledge and special issues in designing questions that evaluate performance, measure subjective characteristics, and measure demographic characteristics.

In Part III we turn from the discussion of the formulation of questions about specific kinds of topics to issues involved in crafting the entire questionnaire. We discuss how to organize a questionnaire and the special requirements of different modes of data collection, such as personal interviewing, telephone interviewing, self-administration, and electronic surveying. We end with a set of frequently asked questions and our answers.

Throughout the book we use terms that are well understood by survey research specialists but that may be new to some of our readers. We have therefore provided a glossary of commonly used survey research terms. Many of the terms found in the Glossary are also discussed more fully in the text. In addition, we have included a list of academic and not-for-profit survey research organizations in Appendix A.

The chapters in Part II are introduced with a checklist of items to consider. The checklists are intended as initial guides to the major points made and as subsequent references for points to keep in mind during the actual preparation of a questionnaire.

Readers new to designing surveys should read sequentially from beginning to end. Experienced researchers and those with specific questionnaire issues will turn to appropriate chapters as needed. All readers should find our detailed index of use.

In this book we have distilled a vast amount of methodological research on question asking to give practical advice informed by many years of experience in a wide variety of survey research areas. But much is still not known. We caution readers seeking advice on how to write the perfect questionnaire that perfection cannot be guaranteed. For readers who wish to do additional research in questionnaire design, much interesting work remains to be done.

Acknowledgments

While we were in the process of writing this new edition, Seymour Sudman died tragically. His vast knowledge of the research literature, deep experience, and wise judgment continue to enrich this volume. We miss him greatly.

This edition builds on its predecessor and all those who contributed to it. We are indebted to many colleagues at the Survey Research Laboratory (SRL), University of Illinois, and at the National Opinion Research Center (NORC), University of Chicago. These colleagues include Herbert Jackson, who compiled the material for Chapter Twelve, and Matthew Cheney, Sarah Jo Brenner, and Martin Kator, who helped in manuscript preparation by compiling and summarizing recently published findings in the area of survey design.

At Jossey-Bass, Seth Schwartz and Justin Frahm: We are grateful for their patience with the sometimes distracted authors and for their inventive solutions to the inevitable challenges that arose in turning a manuscript into an aesthetically pleasing book. Readers, as do we, owe them all a deep debt of gratitude.

Norman Bradburn
Arlington, Virginia

Brian Wansink
Urbana, Illinois

August 2003

The Authors

Norman M. Bradburn (Ph.D. Harvard University, 1960) is the Margaret and Tiffany Blake Distinguished Service Professor emeritus in the Department of Psychology and the Harris Graduate School of Public Policy Studies at the University of Chicago. He has written widely, often with Seymour Sudman, on topics in survey methodology. He was a pioneer in the application of cognitive psychology to the design of survey questionnaires. For a number of years, he was the director of the National Opinion Research Center at the University of Chicago. He is currently the assistant director for social, behavioral, and economic sciences at the National Science Foundation.

Seymour Sudman (Ph.D. University of Chicago, 1962) was the Walter H. Stellner Distinguished Professor of Marketing at the University of Illinois (Urbana-Champaign) from 1968 until his death in 2000. Through a lifetime of active research, he contributed immeasurably to the area of survey design, sampling, and methodology. He was actively involved in providing guidance to the U.S. Census Bureau, and he served as deputy director and research professor of the Survey Research Laboratory at the University of Illinois.

Brian Wansink (Ph.D. Stanford University, 1990) is the Julian Simon Research Scholar and professor of marketing, of nutritional science, of advertising, and of agricultural and consumer economics at the

University of Illinois (Urbana-Champaign) and is an adjunct research professor at Cornell University and at Wageningen University in the Netherlands. He directs the Food and Brand Lab, which focuses on psychology related to food choice and consumption (www.FoodPsychology. com). Prior to moving to Illinois, he was a marketing professor at Dartmouth College and at the Wharton School at the University of Pennsylvania. He coauthored *Consumer Panels* with Seymour Sudman.

Asking Questions

Part One

Strategies for Asking Questions

Chapter One

The Social Context
of Question Asking

The precise wording of questions plays a vital role in determining the answers given by respondents. This fact is not appreciated as fully as it should be, even in ordinary conversation. For example, a colleague mentioned that he needed to pick out granite for a kitchen countertop. The only day he could make the trip was the Saturday before Labor Day. Although he called on Friday to make certain the store was open, he arrived at the store on Saturday only to find a sign on the door that said "Closed Labor Day Weekend." When asked if he remembered what question he had asked the clerk at the store, he said, "I asked him what hours he was open on Saturday, and he replied 'Nine to five.'"

This story illustrates the basic challenge for those who engage in the business of asking questions. It illustrates not only the importance of the golden rule for asking questions—Ask what you want to know, not something else—but also, more important, the ambiguities of language and the powerful force of context in interpreting the meaning of questions and answers. Our colleague had unwittingly asked a perfectly ambiguous question. Did the question refer to Saturdays in general or the next Saturday specifically? The clerk obviously interpreted the question as referring to Saturdays in general. Our colleague meant the next Saturday and did not think his question could mean anything else until he arrived at the store and found it closed.

In everyday life, these types of miscommunications happen all the time. Most of the time they are corrected by further conversation or by direct questions that clarify their meaning. Sometimes they only get corrected when expected behavior does not occur, as was the case when the store turned out to be closed. But the stylized form of question asking used in surveys does not often provide feedback about ambiguities or miscommunications. We must depend on pretesting to weed out ambiguities and to help reformulate questions as clearly as possible—to ask about what we want to know, not something else.

The thesis of this book is that question wording is a crucial element in surveys. The importance of the precise ordering of words in a question can be illustrated by another example.

> Two priests, a Dominican and a Jesuit, are discussing whether it is a sin to smoke and pray at the same time. After failing to reach a conclusion, each goes off to consult his respective superior. The next week they meet again. The Dominican says, "Well, what did your superior say?"
>
> The Jesuit responds, "He said it was all right."
>
> "That's funny," the Dominican replies. "My superior said it was a sin."
>
> The Jesuit says, "What did you ask him?"
>
> The Dominican replies, "I asked him if it was all right to smoke while praying."
>
> "Oh," says the Jesuit. "I asked my superior if it was all right to pray while smoking."

Small Wording Changes that Made Big Differences

The fact that seemingly small changes in wording can cause large differences in responses has been well known to survey practitioners since the early days of surveys. Yet, typically, formulating the questionnaire is thought to be the easiest part of survey research and often receives too little effort. Because no codified rules for question asking exist, it might appear that few, if any, basic principles exist to differentiate good from bad questions. We believe, however, that many such principles do exist. This book provides principles that novices and experienced practitioners can use to ask better questions. In addition, throughout the book we present examples of both good and bad questions to illustrate that question wording and the question's social context make a difference.

Loaded Words Produce Loaded Results

Suppose a person wanted to know whether workers believed they were fairly compensated for their work. Asking "Are you fairly compensated for your work?" is likely to elicit a very different answer than asking "Does your employer or his representative resort to trickery in order to defraud you of part of your earnings?" One would not be surprised to find that an advocate for improving the situation of workers asked the second question. Clearly the uses of words like "trickery" and "defraud" signal that the author of the question does not have a high opinion of employers. Indeed, this was a question asked by Karl Marx on an early survey of workers.

Questionnaires from lobbying groups are often perceived to be biased. A questionnaire received by one of the authors contained the following question: "The so-called 'targeted tax cuts' are a maze of special interest credits for narrow, favored groups. Experts agree the complex, loophole-ridden tax code makes it easy for Big Government liberals to raise taxes without the people even realizing it. Do you feel a simpler tax system—such as a single flat rate or a national sales tax with no income tax—would make it easier for you to tell when politicians try to raise your taxes?"

Even an inexperienced researcher can see that this question is heavily loaded with emotionally charged words, such as "so-called," "loophole-ridden," and "Big Government liberal." The authors of this questionnaire are clearly interested in obtaining responses that support their position. Although the example here is extreme, it does illustrate how a questionnaire writer can consciously or unconsciously word a question to obtain a desired answer. Perhaps not surprisingly, the questionnaire was accompanied by a request for a contribution to help defray the cost of compiling and publicizing the survey. Surveys of this type, sometimes called frugging (fund-raising under the guise) surveys, are often primarily intended to raise funds rather than to collect survey information. The American Association for Public Opinion Research has labeled fundraising surveys deceptive and unethical, but they are unfortunately not illegal.

Wording questions to obtain a desired answer is not the only type of problem that besets survey authors. Sometimes questions are simply complex and difficult to understand. Consider this example from a British Royal Commission appointed to study problems of population (cited in Moser and Kalton, 1972): "Has it happened to you that over a long period of time, when you neither practiced abstinence, nor used birth control, you did not conceive?" This question is very difficult to understand, and it is not clear what the investigators were trying to find out.

The Nuances of Politically Charged Issues

Yet even when there are no deliberate efforts to bias the question, it is often difficult to write good questions because the words to describe the phenomenon being studied may be politically charged. The terms used to describe the area of concern may be so politically sensitive that using different terms changes the response percentages considerably. A question asking about welfare and assistance to the poor from the 1998 General Social Survey (Davis, Smith, and Marsden, 2000) produced quite different opinions.

> We are faced with many problems in this country, none of which can be solved easily or inexpensively. I am going to name some of these problems, and for each one I'd like you to tell me whether you think we're spending too much money on it, too little money, or about the right amount. Are we spending too much money, too little money or about the right amount on . . .

	"Welfare" (N = 1,317)	*"Assistance to the Poor"* (N = 1,390)
Too little	17%	62%
About right	38%	26%
Too much	45%	12%
Total	100%	100%

Not all wording changes cause changes in response distributions. For example, even though two old examples of questions about government responsibility to the unemployed were worded differently, 69 percent of respondents answered "yes." Perhaps this is because the questions were fairly general. One question, from a June 1939 Roper survey, asked, "Do you think our government should or should not provide for all people who have no other means of subsistence?" (Hastings and Southwick, 1974, p. 118).

A differently worded question, this one from a Gallup poll of January 1938, asked, "Do you think it is the government's responsibility to pay the living expenses of needy people who are out of work?" (Gallup, 1972, p. 26).

Respondents are less likely to agree as questions become more specific, as illustrated by three Gallup questions from May to June 1945:

Do you think the government should give money to workers who are unemployed for a limited length of time until they can find another job? (Yes 63%)

It has been proposed that unemployed workers with dependents be given up to $25 per week by the government for as many as 26 weeks during one year while they are out of work and looking for a job. Do you favor or oppose this plan? (Favor 46%)

Would you be willing to pay higher taxes to give people up to $25 a week for 26 weeks if they fail to find satisfactory jobs? (Yes 34%)

Note that introducing more details—such as specifying actual dollars, specifying the length of the support, and reminding respondents that unemployment benefits might have to be paid for with increased taxes—changed the meaning of the question and produced a corresponding change in responses. In later chapters we will discuss in more detail how wording affects responses, and we will make specific recommendations for constructing better questionnaires.

Questioning as a Social Process

A survey interview and an ordinary social conversation have many similarities. Indeed, Bingham and Moore (1959) defined the research interview as a "conversation with a purpose." The opportunity to meet and talk with a variety of people appears to be a key attraction for many professional interviewers. By the same token, a key attraction for many respondents appears to be the opportunity to talk about a number of topics with a sympathetic listener. We do not know a great deal about the precise motivations of people who participate in surveys, but the tenor of the evidence suggests that most people enjoy the experience. Those who refuse to participate do not refuse because they have already participated in too many surveys and are tired; characteristically, they are people who do not like surveys at all and consistently refuse to participate in them or have experienced bad surveys.

Viewing Respondents as Volunteer Conversationalists

Unlike witnesses in court, survey respondents are under no compulsion to answer our questions. They must be persuaded to participate in the interview, and their interest (or at least patience) must be maintained throughout. If questions are demeaning, embarrassing, or upsetting, respondents may terminate the interview or falsify their answers. Unlike the job applicant or the patient answering a doctor's questions, respondents have nothing tangible to gain from the interview. Their only reward is some measure of psychic gratification—such as the opportunity to state their opinions or relate their experiences to a sympathetic and nonjudgmental listener, the chance to contribute to public or scientific knowledge, or even the positive feeling that they have helped the interviewer. The willingness of the public to participate in surveys has been declining in recent years for many reasons, one of which is the tremendous number of poor and misleading surveys that are conducted. It is therefore doubly important for the survey researcher to make sure that the questionnaire is of the highest quality.

Although the survey process has similarities to conversations, it differs from them in several respects: (1) a survey is a transaction between two people who are bound by special norms; (2) the interviewer offers no judgment of the respondents' replies and must keep them in strict confidence; (3) respondents have an equivalent obligation to answer each question truthfully and thoughtfully; and (4) in the survey it is difficult to ignore an inconvenient question or give an irrelevant answer. The well-trained interviewer will repeat the question or probe the ambiguous or irrelevant response to obtain a proper answer. Although survey respondents may have trouble changing the subject, they can refuse to answer any individual question or break off the interview.

The ability of the interviewer to make contact with the respondent and to secure cooperation is undoubtedly important in obtaining the interview. In addition, the questionnaire plays a major role in making the experience enjoyable and in motivating the respondent to answer the questions. A bad questionnaire, like an awkward conversation, can turn an initially pleasant situation into a boring or frustrating experience. Above and beyond concern for the best phrasing of the particular questions, you—the questionnaire designer—must consider the questionnaire as a whole and its impact on the interviewing experience. With topics that are not intrinsically interesting to respondents, you should take particular care to see that at least some parts of the interview will be interesting to them.

Why Some Sensitive Topics Aren't Sensitive

Beginning survey researchers often worry about asking questions on topics that may be threatening or embarrassing to respondents. For many years, survey researchers believed that their interviews could include only socially acceptable questions. In the 1940s it was only with great trepidation that the Gallup poll asked a national sample of respondents whether any member of their family suffered from cancer. Today surveys include questions about a whole host of formerly taboo subjects, such as religious beliefs, income and spending behavior, personal health, drug and alcohol use, and sexual and criminal behavior.

Popular commentators and those not familiar with survey research sometimes note that they would not tell their best friends some of the things that surveys ask about, such as sexual behavior or finances. The fact that the interviewer is a stranger and not a friend is part of the special nature of the situation. People will disclose information to strangers that they would not tell their best friends precisely because they will never see the stranger again and because their name will not be associated with the information. When you tell a friend about your potentially embarrassing behavior or intimate details about your life, you may worry about the repercussions. For example, Roger Brown, a well-known social psychologist, noted in the introduction to his autobiographical memoir that he deliberately did not have his longtime secretary type the manuscript of the book, although she had typed all his other manuscripts, because he did not want her to be shocked or distressed by the revelations about his personal life. He preferred to have the typing done by someone who did not have a personal connection with him (Brown, 1996). With proper motivation and under assurances of confidentiality, people will willingly divulge private information in a survey interview.

Most respondents participate voluntarily in surveys. They will wish to perform their roles properly, that is, to give the best information they can. It is your responsibility to reinforce respondents' good intentions by designing the questionnaire effectively. If the questionnaire requires respondents to recall past events, the question should give them as many aids as possible to achieve accurate recall. (Techniques for designing the recall type of question are discussed in Chapter Two.)

Dealing with the Social Desirability Bias

In general, although respondents are motivated to be "good respondents" and to provide the information that is asked for, they are also motivated to be "good people." That is, they will try to represent themselves to the interviewer in a way that reflects well on them. Social desirability bias is a significant problem in survey research. This is especially the case when the questions deal with either socially desirable or socially undesirable behavior or attitudes. If respondents have acted in ways or have attitudes that they feel are not the socially desirable ones, they are placed in a dilemma. They want to report accurately as good respondents. At the same time, they want to appear to be good people in the eyes of the interviewer. Techniques for helping respondents resolve this dilemma on the side of being good respondents include interviewer training in methods of establishing rapport with the respondent, putting respondents at their ease, and appearing to be nonjudgmental. (Question-wording techniques that can help reduce social desirability bias are discussed in Chapter Three.)

Viewing the interview as a special case of ordinary social interaction helps us better understand the sources of error in the questioning process. Conversations are structured by a set of assumptions that help the participants understand each other without having to explain everything that is meant. These assumptions have been systematically described by Paul Grice (1975), a philosopher of language. (See Sudman, Bradburn, and Schwarz, 1996, chap. 3 for a full discussion.) According to Grice's analysis, conversations are cooperative in nature and are governed by a set of four maxims that each participant implicitly understands and shares. The maxim of

What are the 4 maxims

1

quality says that speakers will not say anything they know to be false. The maxim of relation indicates that speakers will say things that are relevant to the topic of the ongoing conversation. The maxim of quantity enjoins speakers to make what they say as informative as possible and not to be repetitive. The maxim of manner requires speakers to be clear rather than ambiguous or obscure. If the questionnaire makes it difficult for respondents to follow these maxims, an uncomfortable interaction between the interviewer and respondent can result. Respondents' answers can also be distorted. (The importance of these principles for questionnaire design is discussed in Chapters Four and Five.)

Investigators should try to avoid asking respondents for information they do not have. If such questions must be asked, the interviewer should make it clear that it is acceptable for the respondent not to know. (Particular problems relating to knowledge questions are discussed in Chapter Six.)

The standard face-to-face interview is clearly a social interaction. The self-administered mailed questionnaire or those conducted electronically via the Web are much less of a social encounter, although they are not entirely impersonal. Personal interviews conducted by telephone provide less social interaction than a face-to-face interview but more than a self-administered questionnaire. To compensate for the lack of interaction, the self-administered questionnaire, whether paper-and-pencil or electronic, must depend entirely on the questions and written instructions to elicit accurate responses and motivate the respondent to participate in the study. The interviewer does not have the opportunity to encourage or clarify, as would be possible in a face-to-face interview and to some extent in a telephone interview. (Differences among these modes of asking questions are discussed in Chapter Ten.)

Ethical Principles in Question Asking

Discussions of ethical problems in survey research have centered on three principles: the right of privacy, informed consent, and confidentiality. Survey research is intrusive in the sense that the privacy of respondents is violated when they are selected to participate in the survey and then asked a series of questions. It is critically important to be aware of respondents' right of privacy. Westin (1967, p. 373) defines right of privacy as "the right of the individual to define for himself, with only extraordinary exceptions in the interest of society, when and on what terms his acts should be revealed to the general public." For the purpose of survey research, we would extend Westin's definition to include attitudes, opinions, and beliefs, in addition to actions.

Why the Right of Privacy Is Not Absolute

Several aspects of the right of privacy have implications for the ethics of survey research. First, privacy is not viewed as an absolute right. The interests of society are recognized in extraordinary circumstances as sometimes justifying a violation of privacy, although the presumption is in favor of privacy. Second, the right of privacy with regard to information refers to people's right to control data about themselves that they reveal to others. They can certainly be asked to reveal data about themselves that may be highly sensitive, but they have the right to control whether they voluntarily answer the question. There is no presumption of secrecy about a person's activities and beliefs. Rather, people have the right to decide to whom and under what conditions they will make the information available. Thus, the right of privacy does not prevent someone from asking questions about someone else's behavior, although under some conditions it may be considered rude to do so. The right of privacy does, however, protect respondents from having to disclose information if they do not wish to. And it requires that information revealed under conditions of confidentiality must be kept confidential.

With regard to confidentiality of information, norms may vary from situation to situation. In some cases, such as with medical or legal information, explicit authorization is needed to communicate the information to a third party (for example, "You may tell X"). In other situations, such as during ordinary conversations, the implicit norm is to permit communication about the contents of the conversation to third parties unless there is an explicit request for confidentiality (for example, "Keep this confidential"). One of the reasons for routine explicit assurance of confidentiality in research interviews is to overcome the natural similarity between research interviews and everyday conversations with strangers, which have the implicit norm of nonconfidentiality.

What's Informed Consent?

The term *informed consent* implies that potential respondents should be given sufficient information about what they are actually being asked and how their responses will be used. The intent is for them to be able to judge whether unpleasant consequences will follow as a result of their disclosure. The assumption is that people asked to reveal something about themselves can respond intelligently only if they know the probable consequences of their doing so. The standards by which procedures for obtaining informed consent are evaluated usually refer to the risks of harm to respondents who provide the requested information or participate in a particular research activity. What it means to be "at risk" thus becomes crucial for a discussion of the proper procedures for obtaining informed consent.

When is consent "informed"? Unfortunately, there does not appear to be agreement on the answer to this question. It is generally thought that the amount of information supplied to the respondent should be proportional to the amount of risk involved. You must ask yourself, then: "How much risk is actually involved in the research? How completely can I describe the research without contaminating the data I am trying to obtain? How much will a typical respondent understand about the research project? If respondents do not understand what I am telling them, is their consent to participate really informed?"

These questions and variations on them plague researchers as they try to define their obligations to respondents.

The Important Role of Institutional Review Boards

Research conducted today within a university or medical research setting that receives support from federal grants requires that protocols for informing research participants about their participation risks and for ascertaining their informed consent must be approved by an Institutional Review Board (IRB) composed of both peers and lay members of the community. Although the motivating force to establish IRBs was to ensure that participants in biomedical experiments or clinical trials were adequately informed about the risks to their health in taking part in the experiment, the review procedures have been extended little by little to include all research involving human participants whether it involves health or not and whether it is supported by the federal government or not. Many IRBs now require review even of pilot tests and focus groups that are intended to pretest a survey instrument prior to its use in the field.

Fortunately, most IRBs have a special procedure to expedite review of protocols for surveys that do not involve sensitive topics or that involve respondents who are not in a special risk category. (Respondents who might be in a special risk category include minors or those participating in drug treatment programs.) In some cases, however, IRBs whose members are not familiar with social research have placed requirements on survey researchers for written consent forms that are more appropriate for biomedical research projects than for population-based surveys. As noted earlier, obtaining an interview requires a delicate negotiation between the interviewers (and researcher) and the selected respondents. The negotiation must balance privacy and confidentiality issues against the benefits of participating in the survey. If the requirements for elaborate signed consent forms become excessive or inappropriate to the risks of participating, participation rates will fall to levels that may not be high enough to justify the research.

Respondents in the vast majority of surveys are not "at risk," where risk is thought of as the possibility that harm may come to respondents as a consequence of their answering questions. However, some surveys do ask about illegal or socially disapproved of behavior that could constitute a nonphysical risk. In such cases, respondents' answers, if revealed to others, might result in social embarrassment or prosecution. For those surveys extra care is taken to ensure confidentiality and security of the responses.

In other instances a survey may contain questions that will make some respondents anxious and uncomfortable. A recent study asked World War II veterans to respond to questions regarding how their combat experience influenced subsequent attitudes and long-term behaviors (Sudman and Wansink, 2002). Even though the events occurred more than fifty years ago, many individuals chose to skip the section related to their combat experiences. If these studies are being conducted with personal interviews, carefully and thoroughly training interviewers can help remove such anxiety and discomfort. Professional interviewers are excellent at creating an environment in which respondents can talk about personal matters without embarrassment. In fact, this professional, nonjudgmental questioning is one of the ways that survey interviews differ from ordinary conversations. If questions elicit anxiety from respondents for personal reasons, however, the interviewer can do little other than inform the respondent as fully as possible about the survey's subject matter.

Interviewers typically inform respondents of the general purpose and scope of the survey, answering freely any questions the respondents ask. If the survey contains questions that might be sensitive or personal, respondents should be told that such questions will be in the interview schedule and that they do not have to answer them if they do not wish to do so. Written consent is not typically obtained because it is usually clear that participation is voluntary. If the interviewer will have to obtain information from records as well as directly from the respondent—for example, if a respondent's report about an illness must be checked against hospital records—written permission to consult the records must be obtained. For many interviews with minors, written permission from parents or legal guardians must be obtained.

Helping Guarantee Anonymity

Does informed consent imply that the respondent must be explicitly told that participation in the survey is voluntary? Many practitioners feel that informing the respondent of the general nature of the survey and assuring confidentiality make it sufficiently clear that participation is voluntary. In some cases, informing respondents about the general nature of the survey can be as simple as saying, "This survey will ask you about your shopping behaviors" or "We will be asking you about your attitudes toward various leisure activities." To go beyond the ordinary norms of such situations is to raise the suspicions of respondents that something is not quite right about this survey. For example, Singer (1978) found that even a request for a signature reduced the response rate for the questionnaire as a whole. In another study (Wansink, Cheney, and Chan, 2003), a split-half mailing that asked five hundred people to write their name and address on the back of a survey yielded a 23 percent decrease in response.

Under certain circumstances merely asking a question might be harmful to respondents. For example, if you were conducting a follow-up survey of individuals who had been in a drug or alcohol rehabilitation program, the very fact that respondents were approached for an interview would indicate that they had been in the program. If they did not want that fact known to family or friends, any contact and attempt to ask questions might give rise to mental stress. Here problems of privacy, consent, and confidentiality are thoroughly entwined. In such cases it is important to protect the respondents' privacy, to ensure that they will not be "at risk," and to keep information confidential. To do so, great attention must be given to research procedures to ensure the respondent (or his or her relationship with friends, families, or employers) is not harmed.

This attention needs to begin prior to the first attempt to contact respondents and must continue through to the completion of the research.

Except in special cases of some surveys involving substance abuse and other topics collected under a "shield law," individual responses to surveys are not protected from subpoena by law enforcement officials or attorneys if the individuals are involved in a lawsuit. The fact that the researcher has promised confidentiality to the respondents will not protect the researcher from having to produce the individual records if required by legal action. As a matter of prudence, judges often deny requests from attorneys or legal officers for access to individual records, but they balance the requirements of justice in each case against the public good of protecting the confidentiality of research records. The only way researchers can be sure to keep individual data confidential—if it is not protected by a shield law—is to destroy the names and addresses of respondents and any links between the responses and names.

Unless the names and addresses are required for follow-up interviews in a longitudinal study, it is best to destroy as soon as possible any data that could potentially identify the respondent. In some cases, this can also include data on variables that could be used to infer an individual's identity, such as birth dates, treatment dates, and other detailed information. In cases where names and addresses are needed for longitudinal studies, two separate files should be established, one for the names and one for the location data, with a third file containing the code necessary to link the two files. The identifier files can be kept in a separate and secure site that has the maximum protection possible. In one case, there was reason to expect that the identifier files might be subpoenaed and misused in a way that would reveal the identities of all individuals in the file. In this case, the identifier files were kept in a country where they are not subject to U.S. subpoena. The intent of such seemingly exceptional measures is to protect the privacy of respondents by making it as difficult as possible to link individual identifier data with the substantive data. Besides protecting the trust under which the data were collected, this also helps avoid inadvertent disclosure and makes the cost of obtaining the linked data very high for those who might be fishing for something useful in a legal case.

How Much Do Respondents Need to Know?

Most survey researchers limit themselves to rather general descriptions of the subject matter of the survey. Most respondents' refusals occur before the interviewers have had time to explain fully the purposes of the survey. For the vast majority of sample surveys, the question is not really one of informed consent but, rather, one of "uninformed refusal." Participation in surveys is more a function of the potential respondents' general attitude toward surveys than of the content of a specific survey. Sharp and Frankel (1981) found that people who refuse to participate in surveys are more negative about surveys in general, more withdrawn and isolated from their environment, and more concerned about maintaining their privacy, regardless of the purpose of the survey. Today, refusals may also occur simply because of an increased amount of perceived or actual time pressure.

In sum, it is your ethical responsibility as a researcher to inform the respondent as fully as is appropriate about the purposes of the survey, to explain the general content of the questions, and to answer any questions the respondent may have about the nature of either the scholarship or the sponsorship of the research and how the data will be used. In addition, you should inform respondents about the degree to which their answers will be held confidential. Although you must make every effort to ensure that that degree of confidentiality is maintained, you must not promise a higher degree of confidentiality than you can in fact achieve. Thus, for example, if the conditions of the survey do not allow you to maintain confidentiality against subpoenas, you should not so promise your respondents.

The Research Question Versus the Actual Question Being Asked

In discussing questionnaire development, we must distinguish between the research question and the particular questions that you ask respondents in order to answer the research question. The research question defines the purposes of the study and is the touchstone against which decisions are made about the specific individual questions to be included in the questionnaire. The research question is most often general and may involve abstract concepts that would not be easily understood by the respondents being surveyed. For example, you may want to determine the attitudes of the American public on gun control, the effects of a particular television program on health information and health practices of those who view it, or whether an increase in automation is resulting in an increase in worker alienation.

Articulating the Specific Purpose of the Study

Regardless of whether the purpose of the research is to test a social scientific theory or to estimate the distribution of certain attitudes or behaviors in a population, the procedures for questionnaire construction are similar. First you will need to identify the concepts involved in the research question. Then you will formulate specific questions that, when combined and analyzed, will measure these key concepts. For example, if you are interested in the attitudes of potential voters toward a particular candidate, you will have to decide which attitudes are important for the topic at hand: attitudes about the particular positions the candidate holds, attitudes about the candidate's personality, or attitudes about the candidate's likability. The more clearly formulated and precise the research question, the more easily the actual questions can be written and the questionnaire designed.

The process of trying to write specific questions for a survey helps clarify the research question. When there are ambiguities in question wording or alternative ways of wording questions, decisions about formulating questions must be consistent with the original purposes of the survey. Often the purposes themselves may not be very clear and must be further refined before a final choice can be made. For instance, if you were conducting a survey with the purpose of deciding whether a potential candidate should run for a particular office, you might be interested in how much respondents know about the person, what political views they identify with that person, and what they are looking for in a good candidate. In contrast, if you were conducting a survey for a candidate who had already declared her intention to run for office, you might be more interested in what respondents think about the candidate's stand on particular issues and whether they intend to vote for that candidate.

Writing Questions that Relate to the Purpose of the Study

Even when surveys are being conducted on the same topic, very different questions might be asked depending on the specific purpose of the study. For example, most surveys ask about the educational level of the respondent. If, for the purposes of your survey, a grouping of respondents into three or four levels of education will suffice, then a simple question like "What is the highest grade you completed in school?" with three or four response categories may well serve the purpose. If, however, the purposes of your survey require that the educational level of the population be precisely estimated, you would need considerably more detail about education—making distinctions, for example, between degrees granted and years of education started but not completed. Because the way in which questions are asked is intimately tied to the purposes of the survey, there is no "standard" way to ask about personal characteristics, such as education and income. (See the discussion in Chapter Nine.)

As a general rule, when constructing a questionnaire, you must continuously ask "Why am I asking this question?" and must, in each instance, be able to explain how the question is closely related to the research question that underlies the survey. Our training as researchers has always led us to believe that more information is good. Unfortunately, it becomes costly if we lose our focus when constructing a survey. The problem usually begins with someone saying, "Wouldn't it be interesting to know. . . ?" The problem is that when the resulting cross-tabs, bar charts, or pie charts are presented, a great deal of time and money has been spent and we may not be much wiser than prior to the research. It is critical to keep focused on the basic research question.

Suggestions for Beginners

The process of writing questions is fun, and well-written questions can quickly engage the interest of the participants. Competition develops among the question writers to see who can come up with the cleverest or most interesting questions. Given our biases toward more information, a game of "Wouldn't it be nice to know?" can quickly ensue, and soon there are many more questions than the budget can afford or than respondents can endure. Too often questionnaire writers are so caught up in the excitement of question writing that they jump rapidly into writing questions before they have adequately formulated the goals of the research and thoroughly understood the research questions. Many questionnaires constructed by inexperienced people look as if the researchers did not know what they were trying to find out until they saw what they had asked.

To develop a good questionnaire, observe the following rules:

1. Resist the impulse to write specific questions until you have thought through your research questions.

2. Write down your research questions and have a hard copy available when you are working on the questionnaire.

3. Every time you write a question, ask yourself "Why do I want to know this?" Answer it in terms of the way it will help you to answer your research question. "It would be interesting to know" is not an acceptable answer.

Use Questions from Other Surveys

It is always useful before creating new questions to search for questions on the same topic that have been asked by other researchers. This can justify your questions and provide an important point of comparison. In academic research, using validated scales is critical for research to be publishable in key journals.

Yet satisfactory existing questions are unlikely to cover all the research questions of a study. Most questionnaires consist of some questions that have been used before and some new questions, although even the new questions may be adapted from earlier ones. Using existing questions will shortcut the testing process and may also allow you to compare results across studies. For studies done with similar populations and in similar contexts and where there is no reason to expect changes, using identical questions allows you to estimate response reliability. Over longer time periods or where changes are expected, using the same question permits estimates of trends.

Some researchers have ethical concerns about using another person's questions, but the replicating nature of social science research in general and survey research in particular not only permit but encourage the repetition of questions. Normally, no permission from the originator of the question is required or expected. You may, however, want to communicate with the question originator to learn whether there were any difficulties with the question that were not discussed in the published sources. If you want to use items from a questionnaire that has been copyrighted, permission from the publisher, and probably the payment of a small fee, would be required.

Generally, in any given report, it will be important to acknowledge the source of any questions that are asked. However, researchers are becoming increasingly aware that simply replicating questions might not be so simple as it seems on the surface. Attention must also be paid to the context within which particular questions are asked, since responses to some questions are sensitive to the context defined by the questions asked prior to them (Schuman and Presser, 1981; Sudman, Bradburn, and Schwarz, 1996). If you are interested in the trend in responses to a question over time, pay particular attention to the preceding questions asked in the studies where the question was previously used. (The order of questions in a questionnaire is discussed in Chapter Ten.) Once you start looking, you will be surprised at the variety of sources that can provide examples of earlier questions on a topic. The two major sources of survey questions are published material and data archives. Although we list a few of the major sources and archives, the list is intended to be suggestive rather than complete. Getting help from an available research librarian or information specialist can be very helpful.

Finding Good Questions from Other Surveys

We assume that a careful literature search has been conducted to help define the research questions. When a reference is a complete book, a copy of the questionnaire will often be included as an appendix. In journal articles, however, the questionnaire will usually be omitted due to lack of space. In this case it is appropriate to write to the author of the study and ask for a copy of the questionnaire. More general sources of questions include the following:

Gallup, G. H. *The Gallup Poll: Public Opinion, 1935–1971.* (3 vols.).

Gallup, G. H. *The Gallup Poll. Public Opinion, 1972–1977.* (2 vols.)

Hastings, E. H., and Hastings, P. K. (eds.). *Index to International Public Opinion, 1978–1979.*

National Opinion Research Center. *General Social Surveys, 1972–2002: Cumulative Codebook.*

New York Times/CBS News polls, as indexed in *The New York Times Index.*

Opinion Roundup section of the Public Opinion Polls section of *Public Opinion Quarterly*.

Robinson, J. P., Rusk, J. G., and Head, K. B. *Measures of Political Attitudes*.

Robinson, J. P., and Shaver, P. R. *Measures of Social Psychological Attitudes*. (Rev. ed.)

Roper Public Opinion Research Center. *Survey Data for Trend Analysis: An Index to Repeated Questions in U.S. National Surveys Held by the Roper Public Opinion Research Center*.

Some of the largest American archives of survey research data are listed next. (Refer also to the Appendix for a list of the major not-for-profit survey research labs in North America and Europe.) There will normally be some charge for locating and reproducing questions and results. In addition, government, university, and other nonprofit survey organizations will usually make their questions and questionnaires available to others, even if they have no formal archives.

Data and Program Library Service, University of Wisconsin, 4451 Social Science Building, Madison, WI 53706

Institute for Research in Social Science, Manning Hall, University of North Carolina, Chapel Hill, NC 27514

Inter-university Consortium for Political and Social Research, University of Michigan, Ann Arbor, MI 48106 (Institute for Social Research archives are at the same address.)

National Opinion Research Center, University of Chicago, 6030 South Ellis Ave., Chicago, IL 60637

Roper Public Opinion Research Center, 341 Mansfield Road, Unit 1164, University of Connecticut, Storrs, CT 06269

Survey Research Center, University of California, Berkeley, CA 94720

Survey Research Lab, University of Illinois, Champaign, IL 61820

This search for existing questions sometimes becomes tedious and time-consuming, but it is time well spent. Even if you ultimately use only a few existing questions, the search generally helps you sharpen the research question and improve the quality of the new questions that you write.

Consider the following caveats when adapting questions from other sources. Very small changes in wording or in the response categories offered can result in large differences in results. Within a year of each other, three polls (see Figure 1.1) asked representative samples of Americans about who they believed to be the greatest male athlete of the twentieth century (closed-ended), the greatest male or female athlete living at any point in the twentieth century (open-ended), and the greatest active athlete in the world of sports today (open-ended). Although all were taken within one year of each other, there is very little correspondence between the three. This underscores the importance of making certain any questions that are borrowed or replicated from another source specifically identify the issue that is of primary interest to your research question.

Sources of Error in Responses

Since questionnaires are designed to elicit information from respondents, the quality of a question can be measured by the degree to which it elicits the information that the researcher desires. This criterion is called validity. Directly measuring the validity of questions is often difficult and depends on the nature of the question.

Different Types of Questions Have Different Errors

We find it useful to divide questions into the following three groups: (1) those that ask about behavior or facts, (2) those that ask about knowledge, and (3) those that ask about psychological states or attitudes. Behavioral or factual questions ask about characteristics of people, things people have done, or things that have happened

Figure 1.1. Who is the World's Greatest Athlete?

	NBC News/ Wall Street Journal, Sept. 9-12, 1999 (N = 1,010)	Gallup/CNN/ USA Today, Dec. 20-21, 1999 (N = 1,031)	The Gallup Poll, Aug. 24-27, 2000 (N = 1,019)
	"Which one of the following do you consider to be the greatest American male athlete of the 20th century?" (closed-ended)	"What man or woman living anytime this century do you think was the great- est athlete of the century, in terms of their athletic performance?" (open-ended)	"In your opinion, who is the greatest athlete active in the world of sports today?" (open-ended)
	%	%	%
Michael Jordan	35	23	4
Babe Ruth	13	4	0
Muhammad Ali	11	0	0
Jim Thorpe	11	4	0
Jesse Owens	10	3	0
Jackie Robinson	7	0	0
Jack Nicklaus	2	0	0
Johnny Unitas	1	0	0
Mark McGwire	n/a	9	3
Walter Payton	n/a	2	0
Jackie Joyner-Kersee	n/a	2	0
Tiger Woods	n/a	0	30
Cal Ripken	n/a	0	2
Other	1*	27*	26*
No Opinion, Not Sure, or None	9	26	35

*1% or less apiece

to people that are, in principle, verifiable by an external observer. That is, behavioral questions concern characteristics, events, or acts that are external to the individual and could be observed by a third party. (To say that they are in principle verifiable does not mean, of course, that it would be easy to verify them or, in some cases, that it is even legal or ethically permissible to verify them, such as with voting records or sexual behavior.)

Questions about knowledge measure respondents' knowledge about a topic of interest or their cognitive skills. In sample surveys, knowledge questions are often combined with attitude or behavior questions to gauge the saliency of an issue or the outcome of a program. Questions that have the form of knowledge questions are sometimes used as disguised attitude questions. More rigorous forms of measuring knowledge, as in knowledge tests, are frequently used to survey schooling outcomes. The field of psychometrics deals with the sophisticated statistical techniques for the reliable and valid measurement of knowledge. Discussion of these techniques is beyond the scope of this book. Researchers interested in the serious measurement of knowledge should consult with a psychometrician in developing their questionnaires.

Questions about psychological states or attitudes are not verifiable even in principle, since states or attitudes exist only in the minds of the individuals and are directly accessible, if at all, only to the individuals concerned. Psychological states or attitudes are not available to an external observer. For behavior, the notion of validity has an intuitive meaning, as the value that would be agreed on by several external observers observing the same event. For attitudes, the intuitive meaning of validity is not clear. Should the measure of validity be what respondents tell about themselves in moments of privacy with their most intimate friends, or should it be what has a strong relationship to actual behavior? The answer lies more in one's theoretical conceptualization of attitudes than in generally agreed-on criteria.

Even though one may not have a clear idea about validity criteria for attitude questions, it is nonetheless certain that differing ways of asking questions may produce quite different answers and that questions about some attitudes are more susceptible to question-wording differences than others. We do not yet know the detailed mechanisms that produce such changes, but we are beginning to understand the cognitive processes involved. (See Sudman, Brad-burn, and Schwarz, 1996, and Tourangeau, Rips, and Rasinski, 2000, for a more complete discussion.) It is clear, however, that some attitudes are more variable in their measurement than others.

The Difference Between Bias and Variability

In our thinking about these issues, we have used the concept of response effect to include components of bias and variability. Bias refers to an estimate that is either more or less than the true value. Variability is measured by the susceptibility of measurements to differences in question wording. This variability is sometimes called the reliability of a measure, since random errors may arise from the form of the measurement itself (rather than from systematic error due to a sample bias or some other aspect of the measurement instrument).

In order to clarify the sources of response effects, let us look at a particular behavioral question. A common question in surveys is "What was your total family income from all sources last year?" There is a true answer to this question, even though we may never know what it is since even income tax records, assuming that we had access to them, contain their own source of error. However, even though there is a true answer to this question, we may get an erroneous answer because the respondent simply forgot about certain amounts of income, particularly those from less obvious sources (such as dividends from a stock or interest on a savings account), or because the respondent may attribute income to the wrong year.

The incorrect placement of events in a particular time period is called telescoping. In forward telescoping, the respondent includes events from a previous time period in the period being asked about; in backward telescoping, the respondent pushes events backward into a time period previous to the one being asked about. Forward telescoping typically results in overreporting of events; backward telescoping typically results in underreporting. Both forward and backward telescoping may occur with the same frequency in a survey, so that the two may cancel each other out. However, studies show that forward telescoping is more common, resulting in a net overreporting of the telescoped material in most surveys.

Motivated and Unmotivated Biases

Another form of error would be the deliberate or motivated nonreporting of income that the respondent wishes to conceal—for example, illegal income or income not reported to the IRS. Another source of error arises from the deliberate overstating or understating of income in order to make an impression on the interviewer. Generally this type of error shows in income inflation, but some respondents, particularly in the upper income ranges, may deflate their reported incomes. Yet another source of error stems from the respondent's failure to understand the question in the way the researcher intended. For example, the respondent may fail to report gift income, even though this type of income was intended by the researcher to be included. Finally, respondents may simply be ignorant of some income (perhaps income received by family members) about which they are asked to report.

This rather involved collection of errors can be identified by four basic factors related to response error: memory, motivation, communication, and knowledge. Material may be forgotten, or the time at which something happened may be remembered incorrectly. Respondents may be motivated not to tell the truth because of fear of consequences or because they want to present themselves in a favorable light. Respondents may not understand what they are being asked, and answer the question in terms of their own understanding. Finally, they may just not know the answer to the question, and answer it without indicating their lack of knowledge. In the chapters that follow, these factors and the way they affect the business of asking questions will be explored in greater detail.

Additional Reading

Consult the references listed in this chapter (in the section on "Suggestions for Beginners") for additional examples of questionnaire wordings and their effect on responses. The Polls section of *Public Opinion Quarterly* is especially useful. It summarizes questions on different topics in each issue. In addition, the following readings may be useful.

The Psychology of Survey Response (Tourangeau, Rips, and Rasinski, 2000) and *Thinking About Answers* (Sudman, Bradburn, and Schwarz, 1996) present conceptual frameworks and extensive scientific evidence for understanding response effects in surveys. They are recommended to the reader who wishes to pursue the conceptualization and literature behind the recommendations given in this book.

Part Two

Tactics for
Asking Questions

Chapter Two

Asking Nonthreatening Questions About Behavior

The most direct and probably the most common questions asked of respondents relate to their behavior. It is hard for a novice question writer to see any problems with a question like "Do you own or rent your place of residence?" or "What brand of coffee did you buy the last time you purchased coffee?" Nevertheless, such questions are not so simple and straightforward as they might first appear. Questions about behavior may be viewed as threatening and may result in biased reports. Clearly, it is more difficult to ask a question about child abuse or spousal abuse than about owning a television set. But even questions about such topics as voting in a recent election or owning a library card may be threatening enough to disrupt the smooth interaction between the interviewer and the respondent. This interruption may come about because the question causes respondents some discomfort or because the respondents believe that the truthful answer to the question will put them in a bad light and cause the interviewer to think less well of them.

We defer the topic of asking threatening questions to the next chapter and limit the discussion here to questions that are not threatening (or, at least, not very threatening). Such questions may relate, for instance, to work activities, ownership or purchases of consumer goods, some forms of health-related behavior, social interactions with others, or vacation and travel behavior. Questions on household composition, income, employment, and other demographic characteristics might be discussed here but are deferred to Chapter Nine, where standard wordings are suggested.

As we shall see later, both threatening behavior questions (Chapter Three) and attitude questions (Chapter Five) are very sensitive to question wording. Although nonthreatening behavior questions are less sensitive to wording changes than other questions, they are influenced by comprehension and memory. When these questions are correctly comprehended, the most serious problem with nonthreatening behavioral questions is that human memory is fallible and depends on the length and recency of the time period and on the saliency of the topic. In this chapter we discuss what is known about memory errors and then suggest a series of strategies for reducing these errors.

Checklist of Major Points

1. Decide whether the question is or is not threatening. If threatening, see also Chapter Three.

2. When asking a closed-ended question about behavior, make sure that all reasonable alternative answers are included. Omitted alternatives and answers that are lumped into an "Other" category will be underreported.

3. Aided-recall procedures may be helpful if the major problem is underreporting of behavior.

4. Make the question as specific as possible. More reliable information is obtained when you ask about behavior in an exact time period instead of asking generally about respondents' usual behavior. If the goal, however, is simply to group respondents into categories rather than precisely measure their behavior, such questions do not have to be so precisely worded.

5. The time period of the question should be related to the saliency of the topic. Periods of a year (or sometimes even longer) can be used for highly salient topics, such as purchase of a new house, birth of a child, or a serious auto accident.

Large chunk of time periods

Periods of a month or less should be used for items with low saliency, such as purchases of clothing and minor household appliances. Periods that are too short, however, should be avoided, since forward telescoping (remembering the event as having occurred more recently than it did) can cause substantial overreporting of behavior.

6. For regular, frequent behavior, respondents will estimate the number of events by using the basic rate they have stored in memory. Accuracy of these estimates can be improved by asking about exceptions to respondents' regular behavior.

7. The use of secondary records (where available), household observation, and bounded recall will reduce or eliminate telescoping and also improve the reporting of detailed information.

8. Where detailed information on frequent, low-salience behavior is required, providing diaries will result in more accurate results than memory.

9. Use words that virtually all respondents will understand. Do not use special terms or vocabulary unless all members of the sample would be expected to know them or the term is explained in the question.

10. Increasing the length of the question by adding memory cues may improve the quality of reporting. Do not assume that the shorter questions are necessarily better.

11. Recognize that, for nonthreatening behavior, respondents will generally give more accurate information about themselves than about relatives, friends, or coworkers. If cost is a factor, however, informants can provide reasonably accurate information about others, such as parents about children, and spouses about each other.

Ten Examples of Behavioral Questions

We start with examples of questions used by various government and other survey agencies for collecting information about behavior.

These questions represent the work of professional questionnaire designers. All have undergone careful review and pretesting. Nevertheless, they are not immune from the memory and other problems that we discuss later in this chapter.

Outdoor Recreational Activities

Figure 2.1 illustrates a series of questions about outdoor recreational activities. Part 1, which asks only whether the respondent ever did an activity during the last twelve months, is considerably easier to answer than Part 2, which asks for the number of times the respondent participated. Limiting participation to that in the State of Illinois makes the question still more complex. As we shall discuss later in the chapter, it is highly likely that respondents who frequently engage in an activity will not count individual episodes but will estimate. The period for activities is extended to a year because many of these activities are seasonal; a survey conducted in the winter would get no data on summer sports.

Jogging

There are several interesting wording uses in the Gallup question on jogging, shown in Figure 2.2. The use of the words "happen to" in the question "Do you happen to jog, or not?" is intended to reduce or eliminate social desirability biases. Although jogging appears to be a nonthreatening topic, some respondents who do not jog might be tempted to report that they did, because jogging is popular and associated with health and fitness. Similarly, adding the words "or not" is intended to give equal weight to both the positive and the negative answer. Although the responses to this question from the 1996 Gallup Poll might not differ substantially from those to the simpler question "Do you jog?" the additional words are intended to ensure the accuracy of the results.

Figure 2.1. Outdoor Recreation Survey.

1. First, I'd like to get a general idea about the specific kinds of things you do for recreation or to relax. I have a list of activities people sometimes do. Please think back over the past month, since _____.

   As I read each activity, please tell me whether or not you have done it this past month. Did you . . .

	Yes	No
A. Go to a movie?	☐	☐
B. Dine at a restaurant for pleasure?	☐	☐
C. Go window shopping?	☐	☐
D. Go to a theater or concert?	☐	☐
E. Go on a picnic?	☐	☐
F. Go hunting or fishing?	☐	☐
G. Read for pleasure?	☐	☐
H. Take a ride in an automobile for pleasure?	☐	☐
I. Do gardening for pleasure?	☐	☐
J. Participate in a civic or religious organization or club?	☐	☐
K. Go for a walk or a hike?	☐	☐
L. Go to a professional, college, or high school sports event?	☐	☐

2. Now, I have some questions about sports. Please think back over the past year, since _____. Did you . . .
   (Enter date 1 year ago today)

	Yes	No
A. Play badminton?	☐	☐
B. Play basketball?	☐	☐
C. Go bowling?	☐	☐
D. Play football?	☐	☐
E. Play golf?	☐	☐
F. Play racketball, handball, paddleball, or squash?	☐	☐
G. Play softball or baseball?	☐	☐
H. Swim?	☐	☐
I. Play tennis?	☐	☐

Source: National Opinion Research Center, 1975.

Note also the explanations given in the body of Question 1. Respondents may not know what is meant by the word "regularly." Some might assume that it meant monthly or weekly, and some might ask the interviewer to clarify the word, which could then force the interviewer to decide what the word meant. By specifying "on a daily basis," the question removes or reduces the uncertainty. Respondents who miss an occasional day may still be uncertain, but most respondents will not be. Also, in earlier surveys some respondents had answered "yes" to this question because they believed that their job helped to keep them physically fit. By excluding work "at a job," the question makes it clear that only non-work-related activities are to be considered here.

Health Services

Figure 2.3 presents a condensed series of questions on the source and on the frequency of medical care (Survey Research Laboratory [SRL], 1993, 1978). (Attitudinal questions that were part of this series have been omitted.) The first question asking about visits to a medical doctor in the last year is widely used and seems straightforward, but it may be difficult for some respondents to know what is meant. Should they or shouldn't they include visits to the doctor's office for an allergy shot? Does it matter if the shot is given by the doctor or a nurse?

The series of questions about the usual source of medical care does not directly ask about one or more specific events; instead, the respondent is asked to first perform a series of memory tasks and to then perform a series of comparison and averaging tasks. Thus, these questions appear to be difficult. Nevertheless, virtually all respondents were able to answer these questions, and the answers were sufficiently accurate to distinguish between respondents who had medical care readily available, those who had difficulty in obtaining care, and those who had no source of care.

Figure 2.2. Questions on Exercise.

1. Aside from any work you do here at home or at a job, do you do anything regularly—that is, on a daily basis—that helps you keep physically fit?

   ☐ Yes

   ☐ No

2. a. Do you happen to jog, or not?

   ☐ Yes

   ☐ No

   b. On the average, how far do you usually jog in terms of miles or fractions of miles?

   _____ miles

Source: Gallup, 1978.

Figure 2.3. Questions on Health Care.

1. During the last year, how many times did you see or talk to a medical doctor?

   _____ times

2. Is there one particular person or place where you usually go for health care?

   ☐ Yes

   ☐ No *(Skip to Q. 7.)*

3. Have you been using this person or place as your usual source of health care for . . .

   ☐ Less than 6 months

   ☐ 6 months to 1 year

   ☐ More than 1 year but less than 3 years

   ☐ 3 to 5 years, or

   ☐ More than 5 years?

Source: Survey Research Laboratory, 1993.

Household Health Diary

Another procedure for obtaining health information is the use of a diary for recording events as they occur. Figure 2.4 illustrates a sample page from such a diary, including instructions, and sample entries inserted in the blanks.

The diary also includes sections on "felt ill but went to work or school," "visited or called a doctor," "went to a hospital," "obtained medical supplies," and "paid doctor or hospital bills." Although it would have been possible to ask about the details of the illness, such as why did the person feel ill, and what medicine or treatment was used, this information would be difficult to recall, especially for minor illnesses such as colds and headaches.

Childrearing Practices

Two comments can be made about the questions on childrearing shown in Figure 2.5. The first question is an open-ended, field-coded question (SRL, 1978). That is, respondents are not given the answers, but the interviewers have a list of categories into which to put the answers. (If the response is ambiguous, this procedure may introduce an additional source of error. This problem is especially important for attitude questions. Field coding is discussed in greater detail in Chapter Six.)

Note that multiple answers are allowed but are not actively sought. Question 4 is a two-part question with skip instructions. The B part would be asked only if a "yes" is obtained in part A. Both the numbering and the skip instructions help guide the interviewer in asking questions of the respondents.

Religious Practices

Figure 2.6 illustrates that the Gallup Poll's wordings on religious questions (2001) are similar to its wordings on the jogging question in Figure 2.2. It might be argued that membership in a church or

Figure 2.4. Household Health Diary.

STAYED HOME FROM WORK OR SCHOOL OR COULD NOT DO USUAL HOUSEHOLD TASKS

List all illnesses during this month to all household members who had to stay home from school, work, or could not do their usual job.

If the same person starts off a little sick, but goes to work for two days and then stays home for two more days until he is recovered, you would report the first two days on page 5 and the last two days on page 3.

SAMPLE

Date first stayed home	Date resumed usual activities	Who in the family? (First name)	Why did they stay home? (Headache, cold, cramps, sprained ankle, etc.)	Did they stay in bed all or part of the day? (Check one)		What medicine or treatment was used? (Check one)		
				Yes	No	None	Prescription (Name, if known)	If other, what?
Oct. 7	Oct. 9	John	Flu	X				Aspirin
Oct. 13	Oct. 14	Mary	Stomach cramps	X		X		
Oct. 14	Oct. 19	John Jr.	Dislocated shoulder	X			Plaster cast	

Source: Survey Research Laboratory, 1976.

Figure 2.5. Questions on Childrearing.

1. Where does your son/daughter regularly play or spend his/her free time? (Check all codes that apply.)
   - ☐ At home
   - ☐ In school
   - ☐ In someone else's house
   - ☐ Just outside the house or in the yard
   - ☐ In the street
   - ☐ In a playground or park
   - ☐ In a community building or community center
   - ☐ Other *(Specify)* _____
   - ☐ Don't know

2. Does your son/daughter have a place at home where he/she can read or study in quiet?
   - ☐ Yes
   - ☐ No

3. Do you have any special time you set aside for being with children?
   - ☐ Yes
   - ☐ No

4. a. Do any of the following ever take care of your children?

Neighbors	☐ Yes	☐ No
Relatives	☐ Yes	☐ No
Friends	☐ Yes	☐ No
Teenagers	☐ Yes	☐ No
Daycare center	☐ Yes	☐ No
Nursery school	☐ Yes	☐ No

   Something else *(Specify)* _____

   (If all "No," skip to Q. 7.)

   b. In an average week, how many hours are your children/is your child taken care of by someone other than yourself/you or your husband?

   _____ hours

Source: Survey Research Laboratory, 1978.

synagogue is a deliberate event and does not just happen. The same question asked in the General Social Survey simply asks, "Are you, yourself a member of a church or synagogue?"

Readers may wonder whether religion is a sensitive topic. For several decades the U.S. Census and other government sample surveys have not asked about religion because of concerns about the separation between church and state. Nevertheless, nongovernmental survey organizations have uniformly found that religion is not a sensitive topic and that reports of religious behavior are easy to obtain. In behavior questions the word *you* may often be confusing, since it may refer to the respondent or to all the members of the household. To avoid this confusion, use of "you, yourself" is often helpful when there may be ambiguity.

Figure 2.6. Questions on Religion.

A. Do you happen to be a member of a church or synagogue, or not?
  ☐ Member
  ☐ Not a member *(Skip to Q. 2)*

B. Did you, yourself, happen to attend church or synagogue in the last seven days?
  ☐ Yes
  ☐ No

Source: Gallup, 2001.

Lawyers' Survey

Special problems arise in non-household surveys. The lawyers' survey (Figure 2.7) was conducted by mail. This may well be an advantage for questions such as 3B and 3C, which ask for information on number of attorneys and other employees in the firm.

In large firms the respondent would probably not have this information at hand and would need to spend a little time getting the count. Many business surveys are done by mail, so that respondents have a chance to collect the information. An alternative is to

Figure 2.7. Questions in Lawyers' Survey.

1. In what year were you first admitted to the practice of law in any state?

   _____

2. a. Are you currently engaged in the practice of law?
      - ☐ Yes, in private practice *(Go to Q. 3a.)*
      - ☐ Yes, in nonprivate practice *(Answer Q. 2b.)*
      - ☐ No, retired *(Go to Q. 4.)*
      - ☐ No, in non-lawyer occupation *(Go to Q. 4.)*

   b. Which one of the following best describes your legal occupation?
      - ☐ Business legal staff
      - ☐ Government attorney
      - ☐ Legal aid attorney or public defender
      - ☐ Member of the judiciary
      - ☐ Law faculty
      - ☐ Other *(Specify)* _____

      (If not in private practice, go to Q. 4.)

3. a. Are you a sole practitioner, a partner, a shareholder, or an associate?
      - ☐ Sole practitioner
      - ☐ Partner or shareholder
      - ☐ Associate

   b. How many other attorneys practice with your firm?
      - (1) _____ Partners or shareholders
      - (2) _____ Associates

   c. How many employees other than attorneys work for your firm as . . .
      - (1) _____ Secretaries?
      - (2) _____ Legal assistants/Paralegals?
      - (3) _____ Other?

Source: Survey Research Laboratory, 1975.

send the questionnaire ahead by mail, so that necessary information may be collected, but to obtain the final answers in a personal interview so that ambiguous answers can be clarified. This survey uses specialized language such as "sole practitioner," "partner," "associate," and "paralegals." The specialized language causes the lawyer respondents no difficulty, although these are not meaningful terms to most non-lawyers.

Farm Innovation Study

The same use of specialized language is seen in Figure 2.8, dealing with farm practices (SRL, 1974). Again, these terms did not cause the surveyed farmers any serious difficulties. The most problematic questions in this series are those asking "How many years ago did you first do (have) this?" Farmers who have been following these practices for many years will have trouble remembering the beginning date unless it corresponds to an important anchor point, such as the year the respondent started farming this particular land. It should be possible, however, to distinguish between farmers who adopted a practice in the last year or two and those who adopted it more than ten years ago.

Business Expenditures

Sometimes the questions ask for more specificity than respondents can provide. Figure 2.9 gives such an example from the 1997 Economic Census. In the survey used to generate this form, the representative of a hotel was asked to report sales for detailed merchandise and receipt lines, such as for distilled spirits, wine, and beer and ale. Many hotels do not keep records at this level of detail and are unable to report this information, even though estimation is permitted.

Both the questionnaire writer and the data analyst (if these are not the same person) must take a balanced view to questions that put such a substantial strain on the respondent's memory or records, even when the results are aggregated. On the one hand, questions

Figure 2.8. Questions on Farm Practices.

1. Did you operate a farm last year?
   - ☐ Yes
   - ☐ No *(End interview)*

2. Farmers often find that some farm practices are more suitable for their own farm than other practices. Here are some practices we'd like to ask you about.

		Yes	No	(If Yes) How many years ago did you first do (have) this?
a.	Do you use the futures market for selling grain?	☐	☐	_____
b.	Do you dry corn on the farm?	☐	☐	_____
c.	Do you use forward contract to sell crops?	☐	☐	_____
d.	Do you have narrow crop rows, 36" or less?	☐	☐	_____
e.	Do you use a large planter, 6 or 8 rows?	☐	☐	_____
f.	Do you have a chisel plow?	☐	☐	_____
g.	Do you use extension or USDA economic outlook information in planning farm business?	☐	☐	_____
h.	Do you have a program to regularly test the soil to determine fertilizer applications?	☐	☐	_____
i.	Do you keep farm records for reasons other than income tax?	☐	☐	_____
j.	Do you use reduced tillage?	☐	☐	_____

3. a. Do you use contour farming?
   - ☐ Yes
   - ☐ No *(Skip to Q. 4.)*
   b. How many years ago did you first do this? _____
   c. Have you ever received money from the government for using contour farming?
   - ☐ Yes
   - ☐ No

Source: Survey Research Laboratory, 1974.

Figure 2.9. 1997 Economic Census: Traveler Accommodations.

U.S. DEPARTMENT OF COMMERCE
BUREAU OF THE CENSUS

FORM
RT-7001

1997 ECONOMIC CENSUS
TRAVELER ACCOMMODATIONS

OMB No. 0607-0826: Approval Expires 08/31/99

RT-7001

DUE DATE ▶ FEBRUARY 12, 1998

If you have questions about completing this report, please call or write the Census Bureau. In any communication, be sure to refer to the 11-digit Census File Number (CFN) printed in the label to the right. Please return your completed report to:

BUREAU OF THE CENSUS
1201 East 10th Street
Jeffersonville, IN 47134-0001

Toll-free assistance, 8:00 a.m. to 8:00 p.m., eastern time, Monday through Friday:

1-800-233-6136

Please read the accompanying instructions before answering the questions.

Census use

(Please correct any errors in name, address, and ZIP Code.)

YOUR RESPONSE IS REQUIRED BY LAW. Title 13, United States Code, requires businesses and other organizations that receive this questionnaire to answer the questions and return the report to the Census Bureau. By the same law, **YOUR CENSUS REPORT IS CONFIDENTIAL.** It may be seen only by Census Bureau employees and may be used only for statistical purposes. Further, copies retained in respondents' files are immune from legal process.

Item 1. EMPLOYER IDENTIFICATION NUMBER

Is the Employer Identification Number (EIN) shown in the label the same as the one used for this establishment on its latest 1997 Employer's Quarterly Federal Tax Return, Treasury Form 941?

094   1 ☐ Yes   2 ☐ No – *Report current EIN below*

(9 digits)

Item 2. PHYSICAL LOCATION

a. Is this establishment's physical location the same as the address shown in the label? (P.O. box and rural route addresses are not physical locations)

093   1 ☐ Yes   2 ☐ No – *Report physical location below*

Number and street

City, town, village, etc. | State | ZIP Code

b. Is this establishment physically located inside the legal boundaries of the city, town, village, etc.?

095   1 ☐ Yes   3 ☐ No legal boundaries
      2 ☐ No   4 ☐ Do not know

c. In what type of municipality is this establishment physically located?

096   1 ☐ City, village, or borough
      2 ☐ Town or township
      3 ☐ Other – *Specify* _____
      4 ☐ Do not know

d. In what county (e.g., Dade County) is this establishment physically located?

Item 3. OPERATIONAL STATUS

a. How many months during 1997 was this establishment actively operated?   002 Number of months

b. Which of the following best describes this establishment's status at the end of 1997? Mark (X) only ONE box.

001   1 ☐ In operation   Figures only
      2 ☐ Temporarily or seasonally inactive   Month | Year
      3 ☐ Ceased operation – *Give date at right*
      4 ☐ Sold or leased to another operator –
          Give date at right AND enter name, etc., below

Name of new owner or operator

Number and street

City | State | ZIP Code

HOW TO REPORT DOLLAR FIGURES

Dollar figures should be rounded to thousands of dollars.
Example: If a figure is $1,125,628.79

	Millions (000)	Thousands (000)	Dollars (000)
• *Preferred* report	1	126	
Acceptable	1	126	629

Item 4. DOLLAR VOLUME OF BUSINESS

	Mil.	Thou.	Dol.
Sales of merchandise and other operating receipts for 1997 (Exclude sales or other taxes collected) 010			

Item 5. PAYROLL

Payroll in 1997, BEFORE DEDUCTIONS

	Mil.	Thou.	Dol.
a. Annual 030			
b. First quarter (January–March) 031			

Item 6. EMPLOYMENT

Number of paid employees for pay period including March 12, 1997 (Include both full- and part-time employees)   032   Number

Item 7. KIND OF BUSINESS

What was this establishment's PRINCIPAL kind of business in 1997? Mark (X) only ONE box.

070

Hotel with 25 or more guestrooms . . . . ☐ 7011601
Hotel with less than 25 guestrooms . . . . ☐ 7011801
Motel . . . . ☐ 7011311
Motor hotel . . . . ☐ 7011401

Bed and breakfast inn with 25 guestrooms or more . . . . ☐ 7011701

Bed and breakfast inn with with less than 25 guestrooms . . . . ☐ 7011901

Casino hotel (gambling) with guestrooms for lodging . . . . ☐ 7011501

Casino (gambling) without guestrooms for lodging . . . . ☐ 7999051

Ski area or resort with guestrooms for lodging . . . . ☐ 7011603

Ski area or resort without guestrooms for lodging . . . . ☐ 7999031

Hotel operated by membership organization:
  With rooms open to the general public . . . . ☐ 7011602
  With rooms limited to members only . . . . ☐ 7041101

Lodging house operated by membership organization:
  With rooms open to the general public . . . . ☐ 7021002
  With rooms limited to members only . . . . ☐ 7041201

ITEM 7 CONTINUED ON PAGE 2

PENALTY FOR FAILURE TO REPORT

CONTINUE ON PAGE 2

Figure 2.9. 1997 Economic Census: Traveler Accommodations, *continued*.

Page 2

Item 7. KIND OF BUSINESS – Continued

070

Rooming and boarding house	☐ 7021001
Tourist court or cabin	☐ 7011321
Dormitory (commercially operated)	☐ 7021003
Hostel	☐ 7011322
Sporting or recreation camp (fishing camp, dude ranch, etc.)	☐ 7032001
Trailer park, recreational vehicle park, or campground (except residential)	☐ 7033001
Bar or restaurant operated by social or fraternal organization for members	☐ 8641101
Bar, tavern, pub, or other drinking place (selling alcoholic beverages for consumption on premises)	☐ 5813001
Full-service restaurant (patrons order through waiter/waitress service and pay after eating)	☐ 5812121
Limited-service restaurant (patrons pay before eating; including delivery-only locations)	☐ 5812802
Hotel/motel real estate owner (owning land or building but not the lodging business)	☐ 6512919
Apartment building operator	☐ 6513003
Other kind of business – *Describe*	☐ 7777777

Item 8. Not applicable to this report

Item 9. Not applicable to this report

Item 10. MERCHANDISE/RECEIPT LINES

Report sales for each merchandise/receipt line sold by this establishment, either as a dollar figure or as a whole percent of total sales. *(See HOW TO REPORT DOLLAR FIGURES on page 1 and HOW TO REPORT PERCENTS below)*

HOW TO REPORT PERCENTS	If figure is 38.76% of total sales:	Mil.	Thou.	Dol.	Percent
	• *Report whole percents* →				39
	Not acceptable →				38.76

Merchandise/receipt lines	Census use	ESTIMATES are acceptable. Report dollars OR percents.			
		Mil.	Thou.	Dol.	Percent
		230	231		232
1. Guestroom or unit rentals (exclude occupancy taxes)	0010				
2. Camp tuition or fees	0020				
3. Telephone service charges	0030				
4. Gaming receipts (include receipts from the operation of casino games, slot machines, etc. by this establishment)	0040				
5. Rental of public rooms (e.g., conference/convention meeting rooms)	0050				
6. Membership dues and fees	0060				
7. Meals, unpackaged snacks, sandwiches, nonalcoholic beverages generally served for immediate consumption (include ice cream and yogurt served for immediate consumption)					
a. Food/nonalcoholic beverages prepared for carryout and consumption off the premises	0121				
b. Food/nonalcoholic beverages prepared for consumption on the premises	0122				
c. Sum of lines 7a and 7b	0120				

Item 10. MERCHANDISE/RECEIPT LINES – Continued

Merchandise/receipt lines	Census use	ESTIMATES are acceptable. Report dollars OR percents.			
		Mil.	Thou.	Dol.	Percent
8. Alcoholic drinks (served at this establishment)					
a. Distilled spirits	0131				
b. Wine	0132				
c. Beer and ale	0133				
d. Sum of lines 8a through 8c	0130				
9. Packaged liquor, wine, and beer	0140				
10. Groceries and other food items for human consumption off the premises (include bottled, canned, or packaged soft drinks; candy; gum; packaged snacks; etc.)	0100				
11. Tobacco products and accessories (exclude sales from vending machines operated by others)	0150				
12. All other merchandise (Report receipts for services on line 13)	9810				
(Specify principal lines and estimated sales below) 076					
a. 077	9811				
b. 078	9812				
c.	9813				
13. All other nonmerchandise receipts (include receipts from rentals, storage, and other services provided to customers) EXCLUDING SALES AND OTHER TAXES	9980				
14. TOTAL (Should equal item 4 if reporting in dollars)	9990				100%

Item 11. SPECIAL INQUIRIES

The number of guestrooms, units, or quarters consists of the number which can be rented as single units. Suites of rooms which cannot be subdivided should be counted as a single unit.

	Number as of December 31, 1997
Number of rooms, units, or quarters, by type	380
a. Primarily rented as residential quarters or units (occupied as one's primary residence)	381
b. Primarily rented as transient guestrooms or units	382
c. TOTAL (Sum of lines a and b)	

Item 12. Not applicable to this report

Item 13. LEGAL FORM OF ORGANIZATION

Which of the following best describes this establishment's legal form of organization during 1997? *Mark (X) only ONE box.*

003

1 ☐ Individual owner (sole proprietorship)
2 ☐ Partnership
3 ☐ Cooperative association (taxable)
4 ☐ Cooperative association (tax-exempt)
5 ☐ Government – *Specify* _____
0 ☐ Corporation *(Do not mark if any form of cooperative association)*
9 ☐ Other – *Specify* _____

FORM RT-7001

CONTINUE ON PAGE 3

Form RT-7001   Page 3

If not shown, please enter your 11-digit Census File Number from the address label on page 1

Census File Number

Item 14.   OWNERSHIP, CONTROL, AND LOCATIONS OF OPERATION

a. Is the FIRST DIGIT of your Census File Number (shown in the address label immediately after "CFN") a zero?

1 ☐ Yes – *Complete this Item*
2 ☐ No – *Skip to Item 15*

b. Is this company owned or controlled by another company?

Enter name, address, and EIN of the owning or controlling company

097   1 ☐ Yes ⟶
2 ☐ No

EIN (9 digits)

c. Does this company own or control any other company or companies?

Enter name, address, and EIN of the owned or controlled company

096   1 ☐ Yes ⟶
2 ☐ No

EIN (9 digits)

d. How many establishments operated under the Employer Identification Number shown in the label (or as corrected in item 1) AT THE END of 1997?

Number

079

If more than one, provide the **physical location** address and other information indicated below for each establishment. The headquarters location should be first, followed by all other locations. If more room is needed, continue in the same format in REMARKS or on a separate sheet of paper.

Estimates are acceptable if book figures are not available.

Name			1997	Mil.	Thou.	Dol.
Number and street			Sales or receipts	081		
City	State	ZIP Code	Annual payroll	082		
Kind-of-business description			Paid employees for pay period including March 12 083			
Hotels/motels and other lodging facilities – number of guestrooms ⟶	084		Census use 086			

Name			1997	Mil.	Thou.	Dol.
Number and street			Sales or receipts	081		
City	State	ZIP Code	Annual payroll	082		
Kind-of-business description			Paid employees for pay period including March 12 083			
Hotels/motels and other lodging facilities – number of guestrooms ⟶	084		Census use 086			

Name			1997	Mil.	Thou.	Dol.
Number and street			Sales or receipts	081		
City	State	ZIP Code	Annual payroll	082		
Kind-of-business description			Paid employees for pay period including March 12 083			
Hotels/motels and other lodging facilities – number of guestrooms ⟶	084		Census use 086			

REMARKS – *Please use this space for any explanations that may be essential in understanding your reported data.*

Item 15.   CERTIFICATION – This report is substantially accurate and has been prepared in accordance with instructions.

Period covered by this report	FROM:	Mo.	Year	TO:	Mo.	Year	Name of person to contact regarding this report – *Print or type*
Telephone	Area code		Number		Extension		Title

Signature of authorized person

Date

PLEASE PHOTOCOPY THIS FORM FOR YOUR RECORDS

Source: U.S. Bureau of the Census, 1997.

should not be summarily omitted because precise information cannot be obtained; ballpark information can sometimes be very valuable. On the other hand, analysts should avoid making precise analyses of such loose questions. It is a serious but unfortunately common error to use powerful multivariate procedures carried to three decimal points with questions where even the first significant figure is in doubt.

Consumer Expenditure Survey

Shown as Figure 2.10 are questions on ownership and purchasing of major household equipment items. (Only the first page is shown.) This was a panel study, and these questions were asked twice, one year apart. Asking questions at two different time periods has the major advantage of reducing error in the date of purchase, by a procedure called bounded recall. (Bounded recall will be discussed in greater detail later.) Note also that the accuracy of reports about ownership is increased because the interviewer and the respondent have the opportunity to examine both furniture and appliances. On this survey and on similar surveys, researchers are not interested merely in ownership or possession but in information more difficult to recall, such as that involving brand and price.

How to Tell if a Question Is Threatening

There is no standard method to determine whether a question is threatening or not. Some questions that are not threatening in general may be threatening to particular individuals for idiosyncratic reasons; they might remind the respondent of a recent painful event or they might be mistakenly interpreted as referring to something that is unique to that individual. The best we can do is determine whether a question is likely to be threatening to a large number of respondents. The easiest way to determine the threat of a question is to ask ourselves whether we believe respondents will feel there is a right or wrong answer to it. Certain behaviors are seen by many people as socially desirable and therefore may be overreported. Examples follow.

- Being a good citizen
    Registering to vote and voting
    Interacting with government officials
    Taking a role in community activities
    Knowing the issues
- Being a well-informed and cultured person
    Reading newspapers, magazines, and books and using libraries
    Going to cultural events such as concerts, plays, and museum exhibits
    Participating in educational activities
- Fulfilling moral and social responsibilities
    Giving to charity and helping friends in need
    Actively participating in family affairs and childrearing
    Being employed

In contrast, the following are some examples of conditions or behavior that many people underreport in an interview:

- Illnesses and disabilities
    Cancer
    Sexually transmitted diseases
    Mental illness
- Illegal or contra-normative private behavior
    Committing a crime, including traffic violations
    Tax evasion
    Drug use
- Consumption of alcoholic products
- Sexual practices

Figure 2.10. Questions on Major Household Items.

Section 6 – APPLIANCES, HOUSEHOLD EQUIPMENT, AND OTHER SELECTED ITEMS

FIELD REPI

▶ **Part A – Purchase of Household Appliances**   8 06 02 6 →

a	b	c	d	e
Information Booklet, page 16 **1.** Since the 1st of *(month, 3 months ago)*, have you (or any members of your CU) purchased or rented any of the following items for your CU, or for someone outside your CU? *Do not list any appliance previously reported in section 5B, item 7. If an appliance is reported in both section 5 and section 6, probe to verify that they are not duplicated.*	**What type did you purchase or rent?** *Enter a brand name or a brief description of item.*	PROCESSING USE ONLY	**ENTER ITEM CODE** *from column a* **Was this –** **1 – Purchased for own use?** **2 – Rented?** Go to column g. **3 – Purchased for someone outside your CU?** Mark (X) box	**When did you purchase it?**

	ITEM CODE	YES	NO							Month
MICROWAVE OVEN ..	120									
COOKING STOVE, RANGE, OR OVEN ...	/////									
Electric	100				[0010]		1☐ 2☐ 3☐			
Gas	110				[0020]		1☐ 2☐ 3☐			
Other	130				[0030]		1☐ 2☐ 3☐			
REFRIGERATOR	140				[0040]		1☐ 2☐ 3☐			
HOME-FREEZER	150									
DISHWASHER	/////				[0050]		1☐ 2☐ 3☐			
Built-in	160				[0060]		1☐ 2☐ 3☐			
Portable	170									
GARBAGE DISPOSAL .	180				[0070]		1☐ 2☐ 3☐			
CLOTHES WASHER ..	190				[0080]		1☐ 2☐ 3☐			
CLOTHES DRYER	200									
RANGE HOOD	210				[0090]		1☐ 2☐ 3☐			
Combination of any of the above items	220 /////				[0100]		1☐ 2☐ 3☐			
2. FIELD REPRESENTATIVE CHECK ITEM *Mark (X) box if there are no entries recorded in columns b–j.*	1 06 01 3 ↓ [0010] 999 ☐ Go to Part B				[0110]		1☐ 2☐ 3☐			
					[0120]		1☐ 2☐ 3☐			
NOTES					[0130]		1☐ 2☐ 3☐			
					[0140]		1☐ 2☐ 3☐			
					[0150]		1☐ 2☐ 3☐			
					[0160]		1☐ 2☐ 3☐			
					[0170]		1☐ 2☐ 3☐			

Section 6

f	g	h	i	j	PRE		
					1	2	3
What was the purchase price after any trade-in allowance?	If code 2 in column d – What was the total rental expense since the 1st of (month, 3 months ago), excluding the current month?	Did this include sales tax?	Were there any extra charges for installation? If "Yes" – How much?	Did you purchase or rent any other...? If "No" go to next item in column a.	Description from column b and section 5B item 7	Month from column e	Cost from column f or column g and section 5B item 7
		YES | NO	NO	YES | NO		Month	
$ |.00	$ |.00	1☐ | 2☐	0☐ |$ |.00	☐ | ☐			$ |.00
$ |.00	$ |.00	1☐ | 2☐	0☐ |$ |.00	☐ | ☐			$ |.00
$ |.00	$ |.00	1☐ | 2☐	0☐ |$ |.00	☐ | ☐			$ |.00
$ |.00	$ |.00	1☐ | 2☐	0☐ |$ |.00	☐ | ☐			$ |.00
$ |.00	$ |.00	1☐ | 2☐	0☐ |$ |.00	☐ | ☐			$ |.00
$ |.00	$ |.00	1☐ | 2☐	0☐ |$ |.00	☐ | ☐			$ |.00
$ |.00	$ |.00	1☐ | 2☐	0☐ |$ |.00	☐ | ☐			$ |.00
$ |.00	$ |.00	1☐ | 2☐	0☐ |$ |.00	☐ | ☐			$ |.00
$ |.00	$ |.00	1☐ | 2☐	0☐ |$ |.00	☐ | ☐			$ |.00
$ |.00	$ |.00	1☐ | 2☐	0☐ |$ |.00	☐ | ☐			$ |.00
$ |.00	$ |.00	1☐ | 2☐	0☐ |$ |.00	☐ | ☐			$ |.00
$ |.00	$ |.00	1☐ | 2☐	0☐ |$ |.00	☐ | ☐			$ |.00
$ |.00	$ |.00	1☐ | 2☐	0☐ |$ |.00	☐ | ☐			$ |.00
$ |.00	$ |.00	1☐ | 2☐	0☐ |$ |.00	☐ | ☐			$ |.00
$ |.00	$ |.00	1☐ | 2☐	0☐ |$ |.00	☐ | ☐			$ |.00
$ |.00	$ |.00	1☐ | 2☐	0☐ |$ |.00	☐ | ☐			$ |.00

Source: U.S. Bureau of the Census, 2001.

Many behavioral questions, however, are not at all threatening, or are only mildly threatening. Of the questions given in the previous examples, only a few (those dealing with childrearing in Figure 2.5) might be considered threatening, and even here the threat may not be serious. In some ways, social changes over the past several decades have made the survey researcher's task easier. It is now possible to ask questions about cancer, drug use, and sexual behavior that could not have been asked earlier. Only a few respondents will refuse to answer these questions. Unfortunately, this does not mean that such questions are no longer threatening.

Not all respondents will find a particular question threatening. Thus, a question about smoking marijuana will not be threatening to those who have never smoked or to those who feel that there is absolutely nothing wrong with smoking marijuana. It will be threatening, however, to respondents who smoke but are afraid that the interviewer will disapprove of them if they admit it.

If you are in doubt about whether a question is potentially threatening, the best approach is to use previous experience with the same or similar questions. If no previous experience is available, a small pilot test can be informative. (See the discussion in Chapter Eleven. If the question is threatening or possibly threatening, see Chapter Three.)

Eight Ways to Make Behavioral Questions Easier to Answer

In the past decade we have gained a better understanding of the methods respondents use to answer questions about behavioral frequencies and numerical quantities, such as "How many times have you done (behavior) in the past two weeks?" or "How many aunts, uncles, and cousins do you have?" It is now well recognized that for many such questions respondents do not attempt to answer by counting individual episodes or units. Instead they often simply make an estimate based on rates that are either stored in memory as schema or computed on the spot from a sample of available data.

A general finding is that as the number of experiences of an event increases above five, respondents are more likely to estimate than to count (Blair and Burton, 1987). When behaviors are regular and similar, such as brushing one's teeth or eating breakfast, estimation will result in more accurate responses than counting (Menon, 1997). The selection of the time period influences whether respondents count or estimate. Data users unfamiliar with cognitive processes often believe they can obtain much more information by increasing the length of the time period that a question covers, but this belief is illusory.

If the behavior is frequent, irregular, and relatively unimportant, such as making a telephone call or buying gasoline for one's car, respondents asked about a short time period will simply count and report the number of events retrieved. Respondents asked about a longer time period, will typically count for a short time period and then compute an answer based on this rate. Not only does the longer time period not provide additional information, it may increase the possibility of a computation error when the respondent is required to extrapolate.

If the behavior is regular, respondents will already have a rate stored in memory and will simply retrieve this rate and apply it to whatever time period is specified. It is obvious that increasing the time period for regular behaviors has no effect on the amount of data obtained. For example, if respondents are asked how many times they brush their teeth in a given period of time, they would simply multiple their daily rate by the number of days in the time period they are asked to report. Only for infrequent, irregular behavior, such as buying consumer durables or going to the doctor, does increasing the length of the time period increase the amount of information retrieved. There are eight proven methods for improving the quality of reporting if respondents count.

⚡ Use Aided Recall

In its most general sense, an aided-recall procedure is one that provides one or more memory cues to the respondent as part of the question. The questions in Figure 2.1 illustrate one form of aided recall. Rather than asking "What do you do for outdoor recreation?" the questions focus on specific activities and sports. Another form of this method is to put examples into the question, such as "How many organizations do you belong to—for example, unions, churches, fraternal organizations?"

Similarly, respondents may be shown a card containing a list of books, magazines, and newspapers and asked which they have read in the past month. Aided recall may also be used with knowledge questions and with cards listing well-known persons, products, or organizations. This use is discussed in Chapter Six.

A final form of aided recall is the household inventory conducted jointly by the respondent and the interviewer. These household inventories can be used to determine the presence of furniture, appliances, books and magazines, and goods such as food, soap, and cleaning products. Unless the product has been totally consumed, its presence is a memory aid. Aided-recall procedures produce higher levels of reported behavior than unaided procedures do (Sudman and Bradburn, 1974), since they can help respondents remember events that would otherwise be forgotten.

Precautions When Using Aided Recall. Certain precautions must be observed, however, when aided recall is used. First, the list or examples provided must be as exhaustive as possible. As shown in general research on memory and in magazine readership and television viewing studies, behaviors not mentioned in the question or mentioned only as "Other (Specify)" will be substantially underreported relative to items that are mentioned specifically.

If your questions concern media, products, and organizations, lists are almost certainly available from published directories. For other types of behaviors, where outside lists are not available, earlier studies may provide information on the types of behaviors to include on the list. If such studies are not available, you would have to conduct a pilot study to obtain the necessary information. It is usually a mistake for a single researcher or even a group of researchers to develop a list of behaviors based only on personal experience. Personal experience is limited, and the inevitable consequence of relying on it is an incomplete and flawed listing.

If the number of alternatives in a category is too great, your list may be restricted to a limited number of the most likely alternatives. Unfortunately, no estimate can then be made of the excluded behaviors. You could also include an "All Other" category in such aided-recall questions. Such a category is useful for rapport building because it gives respondents who otherwise would not have been able to respond positively an opportunity to answer. However, the data from this "All Other" category cannot be combined with the listed data. Moreover, if the list is not exhaustive, you cannot make an estimate of total behavior—although, by summing up only the listed behavior, you can make a minimum estimate.

In some cases you can proceed in two stages, asking first about groups and then about specific cases. A list of all published magazines, for example, might be almost infinite in length. But you can group these into a dozen or so categories, giving examples for each category. For example, you might ask, "Do you regularly read any news magazines like *Time* or *Newsweek*? Any sports publications? Household or family magazines? Personal health and self-improvement magazines? Electronics or auto or hobby magazines?" This may be good enough if you merely want to code specific magazines into such groups anyway. But you can also ask for the names of particular magazines read within any or all categories the respondent reports reading.

When a list becomes large, the order of the list may become important, especially when the respondent reads the list. Items at the top or at the bottom of a long list will be read or listened to more carefully and will receive more positive responses than items in the middle. For long lists, careful researchers use two or more different forms and randomize the order of the items on both forms. Another procedure, shown in Figure 1.1, requires the interviewer to read all items to the respondent and obtain a "yes" or "no" answer for each item. This procedure is now widely used in telephone interviewing, where the respondent cannot be handed a card to read. It also has the advantage of removing or reducing list order effects, although both the interviewer and the respondent may become bored if the list is too long.

Order effects are sensitive to the mode of administration. Because of primacy effects, items appearing early in the list are often over-selected when the questionnaire is administered in person with show cards or when it is self-administered. On the other hand, because of recency effects, items appearing at the end of the list are over-selected, particularly when the questionnaire is administered by telephone and the respondents can only hear the list read.

Dealing with Long Lists. Another problem with aided recall develops from the use of long lists. Imagine respondents have been given a list of fifty activities and asked which of these they have done in a specified time period. If they have done none of these activities, the question is likely to make them uncomfortable, even if the topic is nonthreatening. They will feel that the interviewer expects at least some "yes" answers from among a long list of activities. Such respondents are likely to report some activities, either by deliberately fibbing or by unconsciously misremembering the date when a behavior occurred.

  ° You should anticipate this problem and avoid it by using two techniques. The first, illustrated in Figure 1.1, is to make the list so extensive that virtually all respondents will be able to answer "yes" to some items. The second way is to start with a screening question such as "Did you happen to have read any magazines in the past two weeks, or not?"—before showing the respondent a list of magazines.

The long list example typifies the most serious problem with aided recall—the implicit expectation that a respondent needs to provide positive responses. If a behavior is reasonably salient and the reporting period reasonably short, aided-recall procedures may lead to substantial overreporting and should not be used, or should be used only in conjunction with other procedures that reduce overreporting. (The exceptions to this rule are the socially undesirable behaviors discussed in Chapter Three, where aided-recall methods help compensate for the general tendency of respondents to underreport.)

The short screener question—"Did you happen to read any magazines in the past two weeks, or not?"—may have the opposite effect. If such a screener is used several times in the interview, respondents may learn that they can skip out of a whole series of questions by saying "no." In general, it is better to vary question formats where possible, to make the interview more engaging for the respondent and also to decrease the chances of respondent anticipation.

Make the Question Specific

One simple reason for making each question as specific as possible is to make the task easier for the respondent, which, in turn, will result in more accurate reports of behavior. General questions, if they are answered conscientiously, require substantial effort by the respondent. Consider a seemingly straightforward question such as "What brand of soft drink do you usually buy?" If the question is taken seriously, the respondent must first decide on the appropriate time period, and then what conditions to include. For instance, are purchases at work, in restaurants, at sporting events, and at movies to be included? Or are only store purchases for home use to be counted? The respondent must next decide on the meaning of the word *you*. Does it refer only to the respondent or to all members of the household? How are purchases by one household member for other household members to be treated? A final question to be resolved is the definition of a soft drink. Are lemonade, iced tea, fruit punch, and mineral water to be included or not?

A few respondents who are highly consistent in their behavior may nearly always choose the same brand. They can answer this question with little or no difficulty. But most respondents who buy several brands will have to do some cognitive work in order to answer this question. Some will respond with the first brand name that comes to mind. That is, they will change a behavior question into one dealing with brand awareness and salience. This leads to a substantial overreporting of purchases of widely advertised brands, such as Coca-Cola and Pepsi Cola. Only a few respondents will answer that they don't know or ask the interviewer for more information. Thus, a small percentage of "don't know" answers does not ensure that the question is answered accurately. As Payne (1951) points out, the researcher should behave like a newspaper reporter and ask the five W's: who, what, where, when, and sometimes why.

Whose Behavior? For behavior questions it should always be clear whether respondents are reporting only for themselves, for other household members, or for the entire household in total. The word *you* can be either singular or plural and is often a source of confusion. We suggest using "you, yourself" when information is wanted only from the respondent; "you or any member of this household" when the survey is attempting to determine whether any household member performed a given behavior; and "you and all other members of this household" when the survey is attempting to obtain total household behavior. Exactly the same system can be used if the interview takes place in an organizational or industrial setting. Just replace the word "household" with "company," "firm," or "organization," as appropriate.

What Behavior? Question 1 in Figure 2.2 illustrates a clarification of what behavior to report because it excluded all job-related activities. In a question about gasoline purchasing, you would want to specify whether or not purchases while on vacation or other trips should be included. Similarly, in questions about food and drink consumption, it is necessary to specify whether out-of-home consumption is to be included or excluded.

When Did it Happen? The "when" question should specify the time period by using actual dates instead of terms such as "last week" or "last month." If an interview is conducted on June 28 and the respondents are asked about last month, some will consider the time period from June 1 to June 28 as the last month, and others will consider the period from May 28. Typical wordings that can be used are "In the past two weeks, that is, since June 14 . . ." or "in the past month (or thirty days) since May 21 . . ." It is generally less precise to ask "When was the last time you did something?" Even if respondents could remember accurately, this form gives equal weight to those who do something often and those who do it rarely. Analyses and conclusions based on such data are likely to be confusing and misleading. In addition, the memory task is more difficult for those who do it rarely, so that their answers are subject to much greater memory errors.

Limiting the time period means that some (possibly many) respondents will report none of the specified behavior during the time period. This will bother researchers who are attempting to maximize the amount of information they get. However, from a perspective of total survey quality, it is better to minimize the number of erroneous or potentially erroneous responses.

Asking Why and When Questions. This chapter is not the place to discuss "why" questions. It is also difficult to discuss "what" questions in general terms, since the "what" questions depend on the purpose of your research. You must have a clear idea of why your study is being done before you start to write questions. Although a few researchers are able to keep the aims of their study in mind without formal procedures, most—especially beginning researchers—cannot. Before you write any questions it is a good idea to put down on paper the aims of the study, hypotheses, table formats, and proposed analyses. These aims should not become absolute, but they should provide some useful guidelines and boundaries.

Even if you are clear on what is wanted, the respondent may still be uncertain, since respondents do not have your perspective on a topic. Belson (1981) demonstrates widespread misunderstanding of survey questions and such words as *usually, have, weekday, children, young people, generally, regularly,* and *proportion.* He hypothesizes that respondents will interpret broad terms or concepts less broadly than the researcher intended. He also suggests that respondents distort questions to fit their own situations or experience. Although one cannot ensure that all respondents will understand all questions exactly as intended, the use of specific questions will help reduce respondent differences in interpretation. If general or global questions are used, they should be tested to determine what respondents think they mean.

Select an Appropriate Time Period to Ask About

The basic idea to consider in determining a time period is that a person's accurate recall of a behavior is directly related to the amount of time elapsed and to the salience of the behavior (Sudman and Bradburn, 1974). The more important the event, the easier it is for the respondent to remember. Although research on saliency is limited, there appear to be three dimensions that distinguish between events that are more and less salient: (1) the unusualness of the event, (2) the economic and social costs or benefits of the event, and (3) the continuing consequences of the event.

Longer Time Periods for Highly Salient Events. Events that occur rarely in one's life—such as graduating from high school, getting married, buying a house, having a baby, or having a serious motorcycle accident or surgery—are likely to be remembered almost indefinitely. Historical events can have the same saliency. Almost anyone who was old enough can remember exactly what they were doing when Pearl Harbor was attacked, when President Kennedy was assassinated, or when the World Trade Center collapsed on September 11, 2001. In contrast, habitual events, such as all the things that one did at home and work, would be difficult to remember for even a day or two.

In general, the greater the cost or benefit of an activity, the more one is likely to remember it. Winners of $100,000 in a state lottery will remember the details better than will the winners of $25. The purchase of a $500 microwave oven is easier to remember than the purchase of a $.69 potato peeler. Juvenile shoplifters will remember the time they were caught and forget the details of successful shoplifting efforts. Finally, some events result in continuing reminders that the event happened. The presence of a house, car, or major appliance is a reminder that the purchase was made. The presence of children is a reminder of their births.

Many behavioral events are salient along two or three dimensions. Thus, buying a house is a unique event; it requires payment of a very large sum of money, and the presence of the building acts as a continuing reminder. On the other hand, the purchase of a food item is a low-cost, habitual act with no continuing consequences.

Within this framework, memory about highly salient events is satisfactory for periods of a year or possibly more. Unfortunately, little work has been done on periods much longer than a year. However, for highly salient events, such as major accidents or illnesses, periods of two or three years appear to be possible. Periods of two weeks to a month seem to be appropriate for low-salience events. For behaviors of intermediate saliency, periods of one to three months are most widely used. Choosing an optimum time period does not mean that the data will be error free, but only that errors will be minimized if recall procedures are used.

Longer Time Periods for Summary Information. When summary information is available, longer time periods can be used. Many respondents can give fairly reliable estimates of total medical expenditures, expenses for vacations, or income received in the past calendar year, even if they are unable to remember the details of how or why the money was spent or obtained. The best explanation of this is that they obtained summary information for another purpose, such as tax records, or because they budgeted a specified amount of money for a vacation.

If summary information is likely to be available from records and is all that is required, you should use that information instead of taking data for a much shorter time period and calculating the yearly amount. Ordinarily, however, you will be interested in both the summary data and the details of individual events. In this case, both summary questions and detailed questions for a short time period should be asked. Comparing the summary results with those obtained from extrapolating the data from the shorter period allows you to check the reliability of responses.

How to Minimize Telescoping. An appropriate time period is also important if you are to minimize backward telescoping, or remembering events as happening more recently than they did. Suppose that a national sample of households are asked to report the amount of coffee they purchased in the past seven days and that this total is then compared with shipments of all coffee manufacturers or observed sales in retail outlets. These comparisons usually show that the amount reported is more than 50 percent higher than the amount manufactured and sold. What is happening is a process called telescoping.

Telescoping results when the respondent remembers that the event occurred but forgets the exact date. In the past, most researchers were not concerned about telescoping because they believed that errors in the dates would be randomly distributed around the true date. However, recent research indicates that, as time passes, respondents are more uncertain about dates. As a result, respondents typically round their answers to conventional time periods, such as ten days ago, one month ago, or three months ago. The result of these two processes is to produce an overstatement of the reported events. Thus, an overstatement of coffee purchasing occurs because respondents who bought coffee two or three weeks ago are likely to report that they purchased it in the last ten days or two weeks.

Telescoping Biases Increase with Short Time Periods. Unlike simple omissions, which increase with the length of the time period, telescoping biases increase as the time period between the interview and the event is reduced. The worst problems with telescoping are for very short periods—yesterday, the last three days, last week. The reason is evident. Respondents who misremember by only a day will overreport by 100 percent if asked about yesterday, will overreport by about 7 percent if asked about the past two weeks, and will overreport by only 1 percent if asked about the last three months. For longer periods, absolute deviations from the correct date increase, but the relative deviations become smaller.

If the behavior is highly salient, so that the percentage of omissions is small, substantial overstatements will occur if the time period is too short. In this case the researcher's desire for a longer time period to obtain more data coincides with the selection of a time period to obtain the most accurate recall. Since both telescoping and omissions are occurring simultaneously, and since the effects of time work in the opposite directions for these two forms of forgetting, there is some time period at which the opposite biases cancel and the overall levels of reported behavior are about right. (See Sudman and Bradburn, 1974, for fuller discussion.) For many kinds of behavior—such as grocery shopping, leisure activities, and routine medical care—this period appears to be between two weeks and one month. Even when an optimum time period is selected, however, the details of the behavior still may not be correct for particular individuals.

Use Bounded Recall

Bounded-recall procedures, as developed by Neter and Waksberg (1963, 1964, 1965), involve repeated interviews with the same respondents (a panel study). The initial interview is unbounded, and the data are not used for this period. At all subsequent interviews, however, the respondent is reminded of behaviors reported previously. The interviewer also checks new behaviors reported with those reported earlier, to make sure that no duplication has occurred. Thus, to prevent errors on dates, the earlier interviews "bound" the time period.

Bounded interviews have been used successfully in a wide range of applications. Note, however, that the effects of bounding are just the opposite of those for aided recall. Bounding will reduce telescoping and improve information on details but will have no effect on omissions. If omissions are the more serious problem, bounded interviews may even cause larger errors, since bounded interviews eliminate compensating biases. Using both aided recall and bounded recall should result in low actual and net biases.

The major problems with the bounding procedures now in use are that they require multiple interviews and may be too costly and too time-consuming for most researchers. An alternative is to use bounding procedures in a single interview (Sudman, Finn, and Lannom, 1984). That is, you start with questions about an earlier time period and use the data from that period to bound the reports of the current period. Thus, for example, in an interview conducted in the middle of June, a respondent might first be asked about clothing purchases during the month of May. Questions would then be asked about clothing purchases in June, with the May date used for bounding. Although there may be concerns of compounded biasing (suppose the estimate for May is too high), this method provides surprisingly accurate estimates.

Consider the Use of Secondary Records

Another method of reducing telescoping and improving information on details is to use household records, where available (Sudman and Bradburn, 1974). A search for records, as with a household inventory, is best accomplished in a face-to-face interview.

Although such a search is not impossible in a telephone interview, it is unnerving for both respondent and interviewer, since neither can see what the other is doing. If the search takes too long, it could have an adverse effect on the subsequent flow of the interview.

An alternative that has been used with phone surveys is to mail the respondent a questionnaire in advance, indicating the types of records that will be useful to consult. Thus, the search is usually conducted before the interview. Where records are available, the interviewer should note whether or not they were used, since more accurate reporting will come from the respondents who used records. On mail and Web-based surveys, respondents can be asked to use records, but there is no strong motivation for them to do so, nor any way for the researcher to determine whether they did. Of the many kinds of records available, some of the most commonly used include the following:

Bills for goods and services usually have the date of purchase of the product or the date the service was rendered, as well as the name of the supplier and other details. These can be used for studies of medical care, legal care, home repairs, and gasoline purchases, as well as for other expenditures.

Insurance reimbursement forms provide information on medical and other insured costs.

Checkbook records or canceled checks provide similar information to bills, except that the details are not available or are less precise.

Titles and leases provide information on the characteristics of dwelling units and motor vehicles.

Other financial records, such as insurance policies, bankbooks, and stock certificates, provide information about assets and savings.

All records, especially those dealing with financial assets, are likely to be considered somewhat personal by respondents. Although it is good to encourage respondents to use these records, do not insist if they are reluctant or if the records cannot be readily located.

Learn to Use Diaries and Panel Research

An alternative procedure that reduces reliance on recall and thus provides more accurate information about behavior is the use of diaries. The respondent or diary keeper is asked to record events immediately after they occur, or at least on the same day. Diaries have been used for a variety of topics, including consumer expenditures, food preparation, automobile use, television viewing, and health care (see Figure 2.4). These are all examples of frequent, nonsalient events that are difficult to recall accurately.

Diaries have been used primarily in panel studies, where households or individuals report their behavior over time, thus making it possible to measure change at an individual level (Sudman and Wansink, 2002). However, some panel studies, such as most voting studies, use repeated interviews and not diaries; and some menu studies and Bureau of Labor Statistics Consumer Expenditure Surveys only use diaries to obtain reliable information for a single time period.

Diaries are not used more often because they are costly and require survey techniques that are not familiar to many researchers. One reason for the increased costs is that diary keepers are usually compensated for their record-keeping activities, whereas respondents to most other studies are not. Also, to obtain the same level of cooperation as on other careful personal interviews, personal recruiting (face-to-face or by telephone) and extensive personal follow-up activities are required. As a result, the cost of data gathering is greater than for one-time interviews, although the cost per unit of information obtained is lower. Some researchers have used less expensive mail procedures for recruiting and collecting diaries, but cooperation with these procedures is much lower. (See additional discussion in Chapter Ten.) Three findings from Sudman and Wansink (2002) that are relevant to this topic are as follows:

1. Ledger diaries (as in Figure 2.4), where events are entered by category, yield slightly more accurate information and are easier for the diary keeper to fill out and for the researcher to process than are journal diaries, where events are entered in the sequence they occur. The categories are helpful because different types of events require different details. Also, the headings act as reminders to record keepers of what is required.

2. Diaries should be kept relatively short—probably no longer than ten to twenty pages. Longer diaries with more items cause underreporting, particularly on items on the center pages of the diary.

3. Diary studies should ask for reports of several items rather than a single type of behavior or purchases of a single product. Otherwise, the record keeper will focus on this behavior and is likely to change this behavior. A diary study that asks only for reports of purchases of cereal is likely to lead, at least in the short run, to increased purchases and consumption of cereal.

Even though they are costly, diaries should be seriously considered if you are attempting to obtain accurate, detailed information about frequent, low-salience behavior.

Use the Right Words

The general principle is simple: use words that everyone in the sample understands and that have only the meaning you intend. Writing questions that satisfy this principle is a difficult art that requires experience and judgment. You must expect to engage in a good deal of trial and error—as well as pilot testing—before all the words are satisfactory.

The obvious way to start is to use the simplest words that describe the behavior being measured. Often, however, many respondents may not know the single word that best describes the behavior. The classic, widely adopted solution suggested by Payne (1951) is to explain the word first and then provide the word itself. For example, the question "Do you procrastinate?" will confuse respondents who do not know what the word means, and the question "Do you procrastinate—that is, put off until tomorrow what you can do today?" may talk down to others. The best form of the question is to ask "Do you put off until tomorrow what you can do today—that is, procrastinate?" This form uses the technical word at the end and does not appear to talk down to respondents.

Slang and colloquialisms should normally be avoided, not because such words violate good usage but because many respondents will not know what the words mean. If the sample is homogeneous and most respondents would use the same slang, however, the use of slang may be helpful. Thus, a study of delinquent boys from one ethnic group in a community could use the slang of that community. Here the use of slang is similar to the use of technical terms in a study of a professional group. In Figure 2.8, for example, the questions "Do you have a chisel plow?" and "Do you use reduced tillage?" are meaningful to most farmers although not to most college students, inner-city people, or survey researchers. When surveying unfamiliar groups, an initial group interview with a small (nonrandom) sample of that group may be helpful in indicating the types of words to use or avoid. Such group interviews are not definitive but may still be useful when the population studied is heterogeneous.

Yet even more troublesome than an unknown word is a word that has multiple meanings in the context of the question being asked. Since many words have multiple meanings, we often depend on the context in which it is used to help clarify its meaning. Some words, however, are difficult to understand even in context. The following examples are taken from Payne's Rogue's Gallery of Problem Words (1951, chap. 10):

Any, anybody, anyone, anything. May mean "every," "some," or "only one."

Fair. Meanings include "average, pretty good, not bad," "favorable, just, honest," "according to the rules," "plain," "open."

Just. May mean "precisely," "closely," "barely."

Most. A problem if it precedes another adjective, as it is not clear whether it modifies the adjective or the noun, as in "most useful work."

Saw, see, seen. May mean "observe" or may mean "visit a doctor or lawyer."

Other words may have unexpected meanings to some respondents. A careful pilot test conducted by sensitive interviewers is the most direct way to discover these problem words. Since respondents' answers may not always reveal their possible confusion about meanings, it is often useful to ask a respondent at the end of a pilot test "What did you think we meant when we asked [word or phrase]?"

Determine the Appropriate Length of Questions

It has generally been the practice to make questions as short as possible. This practice was based on research on attitude questions, which indicated that response reliability declines as the length of the question increases. Research on behavior questions, however, indicates that the findings for attitude questions do not apply to behavior questions (Cannell, Marquis, and Laurent, 1977; Cannell, Oksenberg, and Converse, 1977; Bradburn, Sudman, and Associates, 1979). For behavior topics, longer questions help reduce the number of omitted events and thus improve recall. There are three main reasons why longer questions improve recall.

First, longer questions provide memory cues and act as a form of aided recall. In an experiment, we compared a short question with a long question dealing with wine drinking. Note that the longer question lists possible uses of wine and reminds the respondents of possible settings and occasions to help with recall.

Did you ever drink, even once, wine or champagne? (If yes): Have you drunk any wine or champagne in the past year?

Wines have become increasingly popular in this country during the last few years. (By wines, we mean liqueurs, cordials, sherries, and similar drinks, as well as table wines, sparkling wines, and champagne.) Have you ever drunk, even once, wine or champagne? (If yes): You might have drunk wine to build your appetite before dinner, to accompany dinner, to celebrate some occasion, to enjoy a party, or for some other reason. Have you drunk any wine or champagne in the last year?

The second reason longer questions can result in better accuracy is that the longer question takes more time for the interviewer to read, and it gives respondents more time to think. All else being equal, the more time respondents spend on the memory task, the more they will recall.

The third reason longer questions are used has to do with the recent finding in psychological experiments that the length of the reply is directly related to the length of the question. If the interviewer talks more, the respondent will also talk more. If a written question is longer, the respondent will write more. Although length of response is not necessarily a direct measure of quality of response (particularly on attitudinal questions), longer responses will often lead to remembering additional events, cued by the respondent's own conversation.

Yet longer questions have the same possible disadvantages as aided recall. Although longer questions reduce omissions, the implicit demand for a positive response may increase telescoping.

Thus, as we shall see in the next chapter, long questions are useful for behavior that may be socially undesirable but may lead to an overreporting of socially desirable behavior.

Using Respondents as Informants

Up to this point we have mostly assumed that respondents are reporting only their personal behavior. For cost and availability reasons, you will often want respondents to report about other members of the household, and you may sometimes even want them to report about friends or organizations. Thus, one household informant, usually the principal shopper, may be asked to report about food purchases of all household members; a mother may be asked about the illnesses and doctor visits of all her children. Or one adult may be asked to report on the voting behavior of all other adults in the household.

You would expect, and research confirms, that reports about others are generally 10 to 20 percent less accurate than reports about the respondent's own behavior, unless that behavior is threatening (Marquis and Cannell, 1971; Menon, Bickart, Sudman, and Blair, 1995). Informants learn about the behavior of others by participating in the activity with them, observing them, or talking with them about it. In some cases, the informant may not know about the behavior. For example, children may purchase snacks away from home or participate in leisure activities that parents don't know about. The behavior may also be unimportant and hence go unnoticed, such as purchasing personal care products or listening to the radio. In still other cases, the behavior, such as a minor illness, may not be salient and may even be forgotten by the person who was not directly involved.

However, if the respondent does know about the salient behavior, such as a hospitalization or voting, information from informants may be highly reliable. The use of informants is especially efficient when you are screening the population for specific qualities, such as for people who golf or who are Gulf War veterans. False positives can be eliminated in the more extensive interview conducted with the subsample of people who are reported to have the given characteristic. False negatives, those with the required attribute who are not reported by informants, are, however, missed by this screening.

Summary

In this chapter we have stressed that respondents may not be able to recall previous behavior. Anything that can be done to make this task easier should lead to improved quality of data as well as increased respondent and researcher satisfaction with the interview. The techniques suggested for helping jog the respondent's memory of an event and for reducing telescoping included the following: (1) include aided recall, (2) make the question specific, (3) select an appropriate time period to ask about, (4) use bounded recall, (5) use secondary records, (6) use diaries and panel research, (7) use the right words, and (8) make questions the appropriate length.

In general, it is critical to select tasks that can be realistically accomplished. Here the use of informants must be considered. With easy tasks and appropriate procedures, highly accurate reports of behavior can be obtained from these informants. When the task is difficult, however, even the best procedures will not produce error-free results. In this situation the best alternative, in our judgment, is neither to reject all results because complete accuracy cannot be obtained nor to ignore the basic problems with the data. Use the data with caution, recognizing their limitations but also recognizing that slightly flawed results can often be better than no results at all.

Additional Reading

The reader interested in the research findings that led to the recommendations in this chapter will find them in *Thinking About Answers* (Sudman, Bradburn, and Schwarz, 1996; see especially chaps. 6–9); *Autobiographical Memory and the Validity of Retrospective Reports* (Schwarz and Sudman, 1994); and our two earlier books, *Response Effects in Surveys* (Sudman and Bradburn, 1974; see especially chap. 3) and *Improving Interview Method and Questionnaire Design* (Bradburn, Sudman, and Associates, 1979, chap. 2).

The research on counting and estimation is found in Blair and Burton (1987). For useful general books on memory, see *Human Memory: Theory and Practice* (Baddeley, 1990); *Organization of Memory* (Tulving and Donaldson, 1972); and *Elements of Episodic Memory* (Tulving, 1983). See also Linton (1975, 1978, 1982); Means and Loftus (1991); and Wagenaar (1986).

For details on how to use diaries and to conduct and analyze research from either continuous or discontinuous consumer panels, see *Consumer Panels*, 2nd ed. (Sudman and Wansink, 2002).

Chapters 9 and 10 in *The Art of Asking Questions* (Payne, 1951) are especially useful as supplementary reading for this chapter. The reader who wishes to become familiar with current research on questionnaire construction should consult the following journals, which frequently feature such research: *Public Opinion Quarterly, Journal of Marketing Research, Journal of the American Statistical Association, Journal of Consumer Research, Journal of Personality and Social Psychology, Sociological Methods and Research*, and *Census Bureau Technical Papers*.

Chapter Three

Asking Threatening Questions About Behavior

Survey researchers have long recognized that threatening questions about a person's behavior need to be carefully worded. Barton (1958, p. 67) amusingly summarized many of the techniques nearly half a century ago. At the time, pollsters devoted time and energy to discovering ways to ask embarrassing questions in nonembarrassing ways. We give here examples of a number of these techniques, as applied to the question "Did you kill your wife?"

a. The Casual Approach:

   "Do you happen to have murdered your wife?"

b. The Numbered Card Approach:

   "Would you please read off the number on this card that corresponds to what became of your wife?" *(Hand card to respondent)*

   (1) Natural death   (2) I killed her   (3) Other (What?)

c. The Everybody Approach:

   "As you know, many people have been killing their wives these days. Do you happen to have killed yours?"

d. The "Other People" Approach:

   (1) "Do you know any people who have murdered their wives?"
   (2) "How about yourself?"

e. The Sealed Ballot Approach:

In this version you explain that the survey respects people's rights to anonymity in respect to their marital relations, and that they themselves are to fill out the answer to the question, seal it in an envelope, and drop it in a box conspicuously labeled "Sealed Ballot Box" carried by the interviewer.

f. The Kinsey Approach:

At the end of the interview, stare firmly into respondent's eyes and ask in simple, clear-cut language, such as that to which the respondent is accustomed, and with an air of assuming that everyone has done everything, "Did you ever kill your wife?"

Some of the basic procedures described by Barton are still used today, but others have been discarded as ineffective. In addition, the development of powerful computer technology has led to new methods that increase respondents' confidence that their answers are confidential. Yet as questions become more threatening, respondents are more likely to overstate or understate behavior, even when the best question wording is used. For example, to this day, one of the most threatening questions still concerns household income. (Chapter Nine discusses how to reduce the threat of this question.)

Checklist of Major Points

1. Self-administered computer-assisted procedures can reduce question threat and improve reporting on sensitive questions.

2. Open questions are generally better than closed questions for obtaining information on the frequencies of socially undesirable behavior. Closed questions, however, may reduce the threat of reporting whether or not one has *ever* engaged in a socially undesirable behavior.

3. Long questions are better than short questions for obtaining information on frequencies of socially undesirable behavior.

4. The use of familiar words may increase the frequency with which socially undesirable behaviors are reported.

5. To reduce overreporting of socially desirable behavior, use data from knowledgeable informants when possible.

6. For socially undesirable behavior, it is better to ask whether the respondent has ever engaged in the behavior before asking whether they currently engage in that behavior. For socially desirable behavior, it is better to ask about current behavior first rather than asking about their usual or typical behavior.

7. To reduce the perceived importance of the threatening topic, embed it in a list of more and less threatening topics.

8. Consider alternatives to standard questions such as randomized response or card sorting.

9. Do not depend on wording such as "Did you happen to" to improve reporting of threatening questions. Such wording may actually increase the perceived threat of the question.

10. To increase both reliability and validity, consider using diaries or asking questions in several waves of a panel.

11. Avoid asking the same question twice in a questionnaire as a reliability check. This will annoy respondents and may increase the perceived importance of the topic to the respondent.

12. Ask questions at the end of the interview to determine how threatening the topics were perceived to be by the respondent.

13. Attempt to validate, even if only on an aggregate level.

Six Examples of Questions on Socially Desirable Behavior

Disease Detection Activities

Health care researchers have usually found that disease prevention activities are seen as desirable behavior and are overreported when compared to medical records. Figure 3.1 gives a series of questions asking about tests used to detect possible cancers in women. This series of questions asks about mammograms, Pap smears, and breast examinations by a physician. All preventive activities tend to be substantially overreported, but mammograms are more distinct events and are reported more accurately than Pap smears and breast examinations. Different study results vary in the degree of over-reporting, but mammograms are roughly overreported by 40 percent, Pap smears and breast examinations by 100 percent or more. The questions attempt to sequence the behavior in a way that improves reporting accuracy.

Library Card Ownership

What is the best way to determine if a person owns a library card? It might seem as though a straightforward question would work best. Consider the question "Do you have a library card for the Denver Public Library in your own name?"

On the surface, this question may appear nonthreatening, but since reading is generally considered a desirable activity, library card ownership is likely to be overstated. In fact, with this particular question, people overstated library ownership by 10 to 20 percent (Parry and Crossley, 1950).

For socially desirable behavior, the extent of overstatement depends not only on the level of desirability and the wording of the question, but also on the proportion of the population who have not behaved in the socially desirable manner. Thus, the potential for overstatement is greater on library card ownership than for seat belt usage, since only a minority of adults have library cards. Figure 3.2 shows another approach that was used when trying to assess library card ownership in the Chicago area.

This version attempted to reduce overreporting by asking additional questions about attitudes toward library facilities and about card ownership of other household members—thereby removing the stress from one specific question. Yet even in this version there was still 10 to 20 percent overreporting by all respondents. There

Figure 3.1. Questions on Cancer Screening.

1. a. A Pap smear is a routine test, often part of a pelvic examination, where the doctor uses a swab to take a sample from the mouth of the womb or cervix. Have you ever *had* a Pap smear test?

   ☐ Yes

   ☐ No

   b. How many Pap smear tests have you had in the *past five years*, since (Month) (Year)?

   _____ Pap smear tests

2. a. A mammogram is an x-ray taken only of the breasts by a machine that presses the breast against a plate. Have you ever *had* a mammogram?

   ☐ Yes

   ☐ No

   b. How many mammograms have you had in the *past five years*, since (Month) (Year)?

   _____ mammograms

3. a. A breast examination is when the breast is felt for lumps by a doctor or medical assistant. Have you ever *had* a breast examination by a doctor or medical assistant?

   ☐ Yes

   ☐ No

   b. How many breast examinations have you had in the *past five years*, since (Month) (Year)?

   _____ breast examinations

Source: Survey Research Laboratory, cited in Sudman and others, 1997.

was no evidence that this version was effective. The same level of overreporting (or possibly a little larger) was found in Chicago as was found earlier in Denver.

Book Reading

Figure 3.3 shows various questions about book reading. As with library card ownership, book reading is a socially desirable activity, and the proportion of persons reading a book in the past six months

Figure 3.2. Questions on Library Card Ownership.

1. Would you say the Chicago Public Library facilities in your neighborhood are good, fair, or poor?
   ☐ Good
   ☐ Fair
   ☐ Poor
   ☐ Don't Know

2. Does anyone in your family have a library card for the Chicago Public Library?
   ☐ Yes
   ☐ No (End Interview)

3. Do you have your own Chicago Public Library Card?
   ☐ Yes
   ☐ No

Source: Bradburn, Sudman, and Associates, 1979.

is probably overstated. The degree of overstatement is unknown, since no outside validating information is available.

As Figure 3.3 indicates, one approach (National Opinion Research Center [NORC], 1965) to inquiring about readership is to ask "Have you read any book, either hard cover or paperback, within the past six months? (If you've started but not finished a book, that counts too.)" A second approach (NORC, 1963) would be to ask first about magazine reading and then about book reading. The idea here is that making book reading just one of several items about reading will reduce the focus on this item and the tendency to overreport. Question 1 is longer and provides the types of memory cues discussed in Chapter Two. The results, however, showed no difference in the proportion of people who read a book in the past six months. In both versions half of all respondents reported themselves to be readers.

The wording in the third approach (Gallup, 1971) does not make the question specific (as we recommended in Chapter Two, since, instead of indicating a set time period it asks "When did you

Figure 3.3. Questions on Reading.

APPROACH 1

Have you read any book, either hard cover or paperback, within the past six months? (If you've started but not finished a book, that counts too.)

☐ Yes

☐ No

APPROACH 2

a. Do you read any magazines regularly?

   ☐ Yes

   ☐ No

b. Have you read a book in the past six months?

   ☐ Yes

   ☐ No

APPROACH 3

When, as nearly as you can recall, did you last read any kind of book all the way through either a hardcover book or a paper bound book? *(If date is given)* What was the title? [The Bible and textbooks were omitted.]

Source: National Opinion Research Center, 1965.

last read . . . ?"). It may, however, avoid the overstatements of socially desirable behavior that occur when a specific time period is indicated. The Gallup published results are based on reading in the past month, excluding Bible reading and textbooks, and thus cannot be directly compared with the National Opinion Research Center (NORC) results.

Seat Belt Usage

The Gallup (1973) wording of this question is "Thinking about the last time you got into a car, did you use a seat belt?" The question is careful not to ask about usual or typical behavior. To have asked about typical behavior would be more threatening and those who do not wear seat belts would be less likely to admit it. Asking only about a single event from among common events, such as getting into a car, might appear to reduce the amount of information obtained, but many respondents will answer this question by accurately reporting what they usually do since it is difficult to remember separate episodes of routine behaviors.

Charitable Giving

The wording of a question in a study in charitable giving in Denver (Parry and Crossley, 1950), used to obtain information on contributions to a local charity (called the Community Chest), combined the specificity suggestions made in the previous chapter with the suggestion to cross-reference secondary sources. One survey question, for example, asks, "Did you, yourself, happen to contribute or pledge any money to the Community Chest during its campaign last fall?"

The results were compared with the actual records of the Denver Community Chest. About one-third of the respondents reported giving and actually gave, and 34 percent did not give but reported that they did. As may be seen, words such as "happen to" evidently have little effect on reducing overreporting. In such a case, using a more direct question does not appear to have much effect on overreporting.

Voting and Voter Registration

Voting studies are among the most frequently conducted in the United States. Studies conducted after elections, however, almost always overstate the fraction of the population voting, as well as the fraction voting for the leading candidate.

Figure 3.4 gives examples of voting and registration questions used by several survey organizations at various times during the course of a year. Despite their attempts to reduce overreporting, most were unsuccessful. A number of different strategies are used to attempt to reduce overreporting. Some of these strategies are as follows:

Figure 3.4. Voting Questions.

1. In 1996 Bill Clinton ran on the Democratic ticket against Bob Dole for the Republicans, and Ross Perot as an independent candidate. Do you remember for sure whether or not you voted in that election?

   ☐ Yes, Voted

   ☐ No, Didn't Vote

   ☐ Don't Know

   (If Yes) Which one did you vote for?

   ☐ Bill Clinton

   ☐ Bob Dole

   ☐ Ross Perot

   ☐ Other *(Specify)* _____

   ☐ Don't Know

2. In talking to people about elections, we often find that a lot of people were not able to vote because they weren't registered, they were sick, or they just didn't have time. Which of the following statements best describes you: One, I did not vote (in the election this November); Two, I thought about voting this time—but didn't; Three, I usually vote, but didn't this time; or Four, I am sure I voted?

   ☐ I did not vote (in the election this November)

   ☐ I thought about voting this time, but didn't

   ☐ I usually vote, but didn't this time

   ☐ I am sure I voted

Source: Burns and others, 2001.

Using words like "for certain" or "for sure" to indicate that not remembering is a possible answer

Indicating that there are good reasons why people cannot always vote

Providing the names of the candidates as a reminder and to help avoid confusion with other elections

Asking the question as one of a series of other questions deal-ing with political attitudes

Interestingly, one method that effectively reduces overreport-ing is to obtain voting information from a household informant for all household members, instead of obtaining individual data. The relationship between household informants and reporting accuracy is an important one that will be discussed later on in this book. Reporting accuracy is also a function of the actual percentage of people voting. Presidential election questions are probably answered most accurately, since more registered voters actually vote in presidential elections. In May 1949, 13 percent of the population claimed to have voted in the 1948 presidential election and did not, according to the voting records. People were also asked if they had voted in the presidential election four years earlier in 1944. Of those claiming to have voted, 23 percent could not be matched with reported voting records.

Of respondents in the NORC survey, 65 percent reported that they had voted in 1976 (General Social Survey, 1977–78). The Current Population Survey based on data from a household informant indicated that 59 percent of the population had voted (U.S. Bureau of the Census, 1976). The actual percentage voting was 57.5 percent. Although some of the differences between NORC and the Current Population Survey may be the result of other factors, these results suggest that for voting and other socially desirable behaviors, more reliable information is obtained from an informant rather than from the individual directly, because informants find questions about others less threatening than questions about themselves.

Substantially higher overreporting of voting is possible in elections where fewer people vote. Primary and most local elections are less salient to respondents and easier to confuse with other elections. It is also difficult for the researcher to provide memory cues, because the list of candidates is long. For these elections, it would be especially desirable to use an informant if possible. Nevertheless, substantial overstatements should still be expected.

Ideas about what technique best alleviates errors in reporting on voting have changed in recent years. In a recent survey regarding November 2000 voting and registration, the U.S. Census Bureau focused on increasing the number of people who truthfully completed the questionnaire. (See Figure 3.5.) The questions therefore

Figure 3.5. Voting Questions that Improved Accuracy.

1. In any election, some people are not able to vote because they are sick or busy or have some other reason, and others do not want to vote. Did you vote in the election held on Tuesday, November 7?
   - ☐ Yes
   - ☐ No

2. What was the main reason you did not vote?
   - ☐ Illness or disability (own or family's)
   - ☐ Out of town or away from home
   - ☐ Forgot to vote (or send in absentee ballot)
   - ☐ Not interested, felt my vote wouldn't make a difference
   - ☐ Too busy, conflicting work or school schedule
   - ☐ Transportation problems
   - ☐ Didn't like candidates or campaign issues
   - ☐ Registration problems (i.e. didn't receive absentee ballot, not registered in current location)
   - ☐ Bad weather conditions
   - ☐ Inconvenient hours, polling place or hours or lines too long
   - ☐ Other _____

Source: U.S. Bureau of the Census, 2001.

centered on making participants feel comfortable reporting on whether or not they voted in the presidential election. They were first asked if they voted. The initial question took great care to make it clear that a person may not be able to vote or may choose not to vote for many reasons. If respondents answered no, they were then asked why they did not vote, and they were given eleven different answer options from which to choose. The next questions then dealt with when and how the person registered to vote.

The intent of this survey was clearly to obtain an accurate estimate of the number of voters in the 2000 election. In contrast to previous U.S. Census Bureau reports, this report based voting and registration rates on the citizen population of voting age—taking into account that not all people of voting age in the United States are citizens and are eligible to vote. This change in criteria also changed the end voter turnout rate a full five percentage points, from 55 percent to 60 percent of voting-age citizens. In the end, though, this is only one attempt in a line of attempts to garner a more accurate response from the survey.

Four Examples of Questions on Socially Undesirable Behavior

Traffic Violations

Traffic violations range in threat from relatively minor violations, such as a parking ticket, to much more serious violations, such as driving under the influence of alcohol. In a methodological study we conducted in Chicago, two separate strategies were used in an attempt to improve reporting. First, a series of questions was asked about various traffic violations so that respondents would not know that driving under the influence of alcohol was the topic of primary research interest. Second, randomized response procedures were used. Figure 3.6 shows how the interviewer presented these procedures. (These procedures were also used on other topics in the questionnaire.) Using randomized response makes it possible to estimate the proportion of the population engaging in certain threatening behaviors, but it does not help determine the isolated behavior of a single, specific respondent. (The procedure is explained in greater detail later in the chapter.)

Randomized response is one method for assuring respondents that the interviewer will not know what answer is given. It gives them a feeling of anonymity. Another method is to use self-administered questionnaires. Although increasing the anonymity of response generally reduces reporting errors, such errors are not eliminated entirely. (See Figure 3.6.) For very threatening socially undesirable behavior such as drunk driving, 35 percent of a sample of respondents chosen from traffic court records denied being charged with drunken driving even with randomized response procedures. Still, this was a lower response error than the 50 percent underreporting that was found using standard procedures.

Figure 3.6. Survey of Traffic Violations.

1. There are some questions that are asked in survey research that are too difficult to ask directly because many people think they are too personal. While it is understandable that people feel this way, there is a real need for information for the population as a whole. We now have a way that makes it possible for people to give information, without telling anyone about their own situation. Let me show you how this works: we will use the next question I have here as an example. *(Hand R. Card F.)* As you see, there are two questions on the card. One deals with the "real" question that the research is concerned with; the other is completely unrelated. Both questions can be answered "yes" or "no." One of the two questions is selected by chance and you answer it. (I'll show you how that works in a minute.) I do not know which questions you are answering. . . .

   (Hand R. box.) It is very simple, as you will see. You use this little plastic box. Notice that the box has red and blue beads in it. By shaking the box, you can get one of those beads to show in the little "window" in the bottom corner of the box. Try it. *(Encourage R. to "play with" the box a little, to get used to it.)* Okay. Now you'll notice that one of the questions on the card has a red circle next to it, and one has a blue circle. The question that you answer is selected by chance. Shake the box again and look at the color of the bead that shows in the window now—don't tell me what color it is. If the bead is blue, you answer the "blue circle" question on the card; if the bead is red, you answer the "red circle" question. I can't see which bead is in the window; and you don't tell me which question you are answering. Just tell me if your answer is "yes" or "no."

   CARD F. (Red) Have you received a ticket for parking in the last twelve months? (Blue) Is your birthday in the month of June?

2. *(Hand R. Card G.)* Please shake the box again and, using this card, answer the question whose color matches the bead in the window. Is your answer "yes" or "no"?

   CARD G. (Red) Have you received a ticket for going through a red light in the past 12 months? (Blue) Is your birthday in the month of July?

3. *(Hand R. Card H.)* Now shake the box again and, using this card, answer the question whose color matches the bead in the window. Is your answer "yes" or "no"?

   CARD H. (Red) During the last 12 months, have you been charged by a policeman for speeding? (Blue) Is your birthday in the month of August?

4. *(Hand R. Card I.)* Now shake the box again. Use this card and answer the question whose color matches the bead in the window. Is your answer "yes" or "no"?

   CARD I. (Red) During the last 12 months, have you been charged by a policeman for driving under the influence of liquor? (Blue) Is your birthday in the month of September?

Source: National Opinion Research Center, 1972, cited in Bradburn, Sudman, and Associates, 1979.

Illegal Drug Use

Illegal drug use is a major health as well as a major legal problem, and measuring trends is critical for policy purposes. It is obvious that illegal drug use is seen as a socially undesirable behavior among most segments of society. In annual studies conducted by the Research Triangle Institute (RTI) for the National Institute on Drug Abuse, self-administered procedures have been developed so that the interviewer does not know what answers were given. Figure 3.7 gives excerpts from the questionnaire that indicate the information requested.

The most direct method for a self-administered questionnaire would be to have respondents read the questions and answer them with no interviewer present. Unfortunately, the drug questionnaire is complex and many respondents would have trouble reading the questions and following the instructions. Initially, RTI attempted to solve this problem by having the interviewer read the questions while the respondent filled out an answer sheet. More recently they have used an audio computer-assisted self interview. With this method, which will be discussed in greater detail later in this chapter, the respondent is given a laptop computer and earphones. The questions are asked by a recorded voice and the respondent enters the answers into the computer. Again it should be stressed that such self-administered methods reduce, but do not eliminate all reporting errors.

It might appear that a question like number 3 in Figure 3.7 asking for number of days of lifetime use would be difficult or impossible for users to answer. One possible value for such a question pointed out by Wentland and Smith (1993) is that such a question may suggest by the answer categories that the use of marijuana is widespread, which would reduce underreporting of marijuana use.

Use of Alcoholic Beverages

Although many people do not find questions about their use of alcoholic beverages to be threatening, some—especially heavy

Figure 3.7. Questions on Illegal Drug Use.

1. The next questions are about marijuana and hashish. Marijuana is also called "pot," "grass," or "dope." Marijuana is usually smoked, either in cigarettes called joints, or in a pipe. It is sometimes cooked in food. Hashish is a form of marijuana that is also called "hash." It is usually smoked in a pipe. Have you ever, even once, used marijuana or hashish?

   ☐ Yes

   ☐ No

2. How old were you the very first time you actually used marijuana or hashish?

   _____ years old

   ☐ I have never used marijuana or hashish

3. Altogether, on how many days in your life have you used marijuana or hashish?

   ☐ I have never used marijuana or hashish

   ☐ 1 to 2 days

   ☐ 3 to 5 days

   ☐ 6 to 10 days

   ☐ 11 to 49 days

   ☐ 50 to 99 days

   ☐ 100 to 199 days

   ☐ 200 to 299 days

   ☐ 300 to 399 days

   ☐ 400 or more days

4. How long has it been since you last used marijuana or hashish?

   ☐ I have never used marijuana or hashish

   ☐ Within the past 30 days

   ☐ More than 30 days but less than 6 months ago

   ☐ 6 months or more but less than 1 year ago

   ☐ 1 year or more but less than 3 years ago

   ☐ 3 years or more ago

5. Think specifically about the past 30 days—that is, from your 30 day reference date up to and including today. During the past 30 days, on how many days did you use marijuana or hashish?

   _____ number of days on which I used marijuana or hashish

   ☐ I have used marijuana or hashish, but not in the past 30 days

   ☐ I have never used marijuana or hashish

(Similar questions asked about cigarettes, alcohol, analgesics, tranquilizers, stimulants, sedatives, inhalants, hallucinogens, cocaine and heroin.)

Source: Research Triangle Institute, 1990, cited in Turner, Lessler, and Gfroerer, 1992.

drinkers—may. Figure 3.8 presents a series of questions, the first asked by Gallup to determine whether respondents use alcohol, how much respondents use alcohol, and how often. The Gallup question is short, simple, and explicit. The NORC questions formed a series in a longer questionnaire and were designed to make it easier for respondents to recall and to admit their use of alcoholic beverages. The progressive nature of the questioning makes it easier for heavy drinkers to answer the questions without avoiding the issue or underreporting their consumption frequency.

Note that respondents are first asked whether they have ever drunk alcoholic beverages or a specific beverage such as beer. At this stage some respondents who have used and are using alcohol will not want to admit it. If they deny alcohol use, they will not be asked any questions about current behavior.

A comparison of the Gallup and NORC versions suggests that the NORC version—which asked if respondents used beer in one question, or wine in another question, or other specific alcoholic beverages in other questions—is perceived as less threatening than the Gallup version, which asked if respondents used any alcoholic beverage. A higher percentage of respondents report using wine and beer in the NORC version than report using *any* alcoholic beverage in the Gallup question. This is probably because some respondents who are willing to report using wine and beer may be unwilling to report using alcoholic beverages because this term is perceived as meaning hard liquor.

After respondents report that they have drunk beer, wine, or liquor, it is effective to use long and open-ended questions to ask respondents how much they drink—such as "When you drank beer, how often did you drink it on average?"—without giving any indication of a possible range of answers. When we compared these open-ended questions with short closed-ended questions where answer categories were given, we found that the quantities reported on the long, open-ended form were more than double those on the

Figure 3.8. Questions on Alcoholic Beverage Use.

1. Do you ever have occasion to use any alcoholic beverages such as liquor, wine, or beer, or are you a total abstainer?

2. Now we have some questions about drinking for relaxation. The most popular alcoholic beverage in the country is beer or ale. People drink beer in taverns, with meals, in pizza parlors, at sporting events, at home while watching television, and many other places. Did you ever drink, even once, beer or ale? *(If no, go to Q. 3) (If yes)* We are especially interested in recent times. Have you drunk any beer or ale in the past year?

   ☐ Yes *(Ask a, b, and c.)*

   ☐ No *(Ask a and b.)*

   a. When you drank beer or ale, on the average how often did you drink it? Include every time you drank it, no matter how little you had.

   b. Most of the times you drank beer, on the average how many bottles, cans, or glasses did you drink at one time?

   c. Thinking about more recent times, have you drunk any beer or ale in the past month?

3. Wines have become increasingly popular in this country over the last few years; by wines, we mean liqueurs, cordials, sherries, and similar drinks, as well as table wines, sparkling wines, and champagne. Did you ever drink, even once, wine or champagne? *(If no, go to Q. 4.) (If yes)* You might have drunk wine to build your appetite before dinner, to accompany dinner, to celebrate some occasion, to enjoy a party, or for some other reason. Have you drunk any wine or champagne in the past year?

   ☐ Yes *(Ask a, b, and c.)*

   ☐ No *(Ask a and b.)*

   a. When you drank wine or champagne, on the average how often did you drink it? Include every time you drank it, no matter how little you had.

   b. Most of the times you drank wine or champagne, on the average about how many glasses did you drink at one time?

   c. Thinking about more recent times than the past year, have you drunk any wine or champagne in the past month?

4. Part of our research is to try to find out the best way to ask questions. Sometimes, as we go through the questionnaire, I'll ask you to suggest terms that we might use, so that you will feel comfortable and understand what we mean. For instance, my next few questions are about all the drinks like whiskey, vodka, and gin. What do you think would be the best things to call all the beverages of that kind when we ask questions about them?

   (If no response, or awkward phrase, use "liquor" in following questions. Otherwise, use respondent's word(s).)

Figure 3.8. Questions on Alcoholic Beverage Use, *continued.*

People drink _____ by itself or with mixers such as water, soft drinks, juices, and liqueurs. Did you ever drink, even once, _____? *(If no, go to Q. 5.) (If yes)* You might have drunk _____ as a cocktail, appetizer, to relax in a bar, to celebrate some occasion, to enjoy a party, or for some other reason. Have you drunk any _____ in the past year?

☐ Yes *(Ask a, b, and c.)*

☐ No *(Ask a and b.)*

a. When you drank _____, on the average how often did you drink it? Include every time you drank it, no matter how little you had.

b. Most of the times you drank _____, on the average about how many drinks did you have at one time?

c. Thinking about more recent times than the past year, have you drunk any _____ in the past month?

5. Sometimes people drink a little too much beer, wine, or whiskey so that they act different from usual. What word do you think we should use to describe people when they get that way, so that you will know what we mean and feel comfortable talking about it?

   (If no response, or awkward phrase, use "intoxicated" in following questions. Otherwise use respondent's word(s).)

   (If R. has answered yes for drinking any alcohol in the past year) Occasionally, people drink a little too much and become _____. In the past year, how often did you become _____ while drinking any kind of alcoholic beverage?

6. Next, think of your three closest friends. Don't mention their names, just get them in mind. As far as you know, how many of them have been _____ during the past year?

Source: Q.1, Gallup, 1977; Q.2–Q.6, National Opinion Research Center, 1972, cited in Bradburn, Sudman, and Associates, 1979.

short, closed-ended form. In Questions 4 and 5, an additional effort was made to reduce the threat by asking respondents to use their own words when discussing liquor and drunkenness. This procedure also appeared to improve reporting, but not so much as the use of long, open-ended questions.

Sexual Activity

Figure 3.9 presents a series of self-administered questions from the NORC study on sexuality (Laumann, Gagnon, Michael, and Michaels, 1994). The researchers examined responses controlling for interviewer evaluations of respondents' frankness and comprehension of the questions and saw no differences. Of course, this does not mean that all sexual activities were accurately reported. It has frequently been noted that interviewers cannot really tell when respondents are not answering truthfully. Nevertheless, the use of self-administered forms for these really threatening questions almost certainly reduced threat.

Note that the frequency questions give answer categories rather than simply asking for an open answer on how many times or with how many partners. Respondents who found the question sensitive or had trouble remembering might have used a middle answer to indicate what researchers thought was the most likely possibility. Nevertheless, by far the most common answer given for the number of sexual partners was one.

Again, it can be seen that the careful sequencing of these questions provides two advantages in improving reporting accuracy. First, it differentiates and clarifies the activities being investigated, so as to not cause confusion over the "definition" of sex. Second, it also leads up to the more uncomfortable questions by asking the more general questions to begin with.

Figure 3.9. Questions on Sexual Activity.

1. There is a great deal of concern today about the AIDS epidemic and how to deal with it. Because of the grave nature of the problem, we are going to ask you some personal questions and we need your frank and honest responses. Your answers are confidential and will be used only for statistical reports. How many sex partners have you had in the last 12 months?

   ☐ No partners
   ☐ 1 partner
   ☐ 2 partners
   ☐ 3 partners
   ☐ 4 partners
   ☐ 5-10 partners
   ☐ 11-20 partners
   ☐ 21-100 partners
   ☐ More than 100 partners

2. Have your sex partners in the last 12 months been . . .

   ☐ Exclusively male?
   ☐ Both male and female?
   ☐ Exclusively female?

3. About how often did you have sex in the past 12 months?

   ☐ Not at all
   ☐ Once or twice
   ☐ About once a month
   ☐ Two or three times a month
   ☐ About once a week
   ☐ Two or three times a week
   ☐ Four or more times a week

4. Masturbation is a very common practice. In order to understand the full range of sexual behavior, we need to know the answers to a few questions about your experiences with masturbation. By masturbation we mean self-sex or self-stimulation, that is, stimulating your genitals (sex organs) to the point of arousal, but not necessarily to orgasm or climax. The following questions are not about activity with a sexual partner, but about times when you were alone or when other people were not aware of what you were doing. On average, in the past 12 months how often did you masturbate?

   ☐ More than once a day
   ☐ Every day
   ☐ Several times a week
   ☐ Once a week

☐ 2-3 times a month
☐ Once a month
☐ Every other month
☐ 3-5 times a year
☐ 1-2 times a year
☐ 0 times this year

FEMALES ONLY (A comparable set was asked of males)

5. Have you ever performed oral sex on a man?
☐ Yes
☐ No

6. Has a man ever performed oral sex on you?
☐ Yes
☐ No

7. Have you ever had anal sex?
☐ Yes
☐ No

8. Have you ever been paid by a man to have sex?
☐ Yes
☐ No

Source: Laumann, Gagnon, Michael, and Michaels, 1994.

Nine Techniques to Make Threatening Questions More Accurate

Use Self-Administered Methods

Probably the most widely used method for reducing question threat is to make the question self-administered. This works for both socially desirable and socially undesirable behaviors. Respondents are less likely to overreport desirable behaviors such as voting or giving to charity when responding on a computer or piece of paper rather than answering an interviewer. They are also less likely to underreport socially undesirable behavior and even attitudes that are perceived as socially undesirable.

It must be recognized, however, that self-administered methods do not yield perfect information. Some behaviors are so threatening to respondents that they would not report the behavior even if assured of perfect anonymity. More often, however, respondents do not *completely* trust the assurances of anonymity. They recognize that someone, if not the interviewer, will be looking at their answers and that there is some possibility they might be personally identified. The more threatening the question, the less effective anonymity will be.

Before the days of computer-assisted interviewing, the methods usually involved respondents reading the questions, circling the answer, and then putting the completed form in a sealed envelope that was returned to the interviewer. Alternatively, they would sometimes put completed forms into a sealed ballot box with a lock to simulate the box found at polling places. One especially effective form of self-administration involves group administration, whereby groups of people each complete individual questionnaires that are then collected into a common box or envelope. Since the forms contain no identifying information, group members have a strong feeling of anonymity. This is a likely explanation for why drug studies conducted in classrooms generally yield higher reports of usage than individual drug interviews.

Currently, when the interview is conducted with a computer, the respondent is given a computer and enters the answers directly into it. If the respondent has difficulty reading, the interviewer may read the question and the respondent may enter the answer. Even in this scenario, having the interviewer read the question appears to reduce the respondent's sense of anonymity. Audio computer methods that eliminate the interviewer entirely are now increasingly used. The questions are read by a recorded voice and the respondent hears them on a set of earphones and enters the answer. No one else in the room can hear the questions. Almost all the other features of computer-assisted interviewing discussed in detail in Chapter Ten (such as branching and skipping questions) are also available.

Use Card Sorting and Randomized Response

Card sorting is a procedure that has been used in Great Britain in face-to-face interviews to measure crime and juvenile delinquency (Belson, Millerson, and Didcott, 1968). Here the interviewer hands respondents a set of cards that list various behaviors, including threatening ones. Respondents are asked to place each card into a "yes" or "no" box. During later points in the interview, the interviewer can ask the respondent to reconsider the cards in the "no" box and to resort the cards if necessary. The thought behind card sorts is that it might be easier for some respondents to admit a socially undesirable behavior (or not to claim a socially desirable behavior) when performing a nonverbal task. As far as we know, however, card sorting has not been empirically validated or compared with alternative procedures.

The randomized response technique is really a randomized questioning technique. It is a method that ensures respondents' anonymity by making it impossible for either the interviewer or researcher to know what question the respondent was answering (Greenberg and others, 1969; Horvitz, Shaw, and Simmons, 1967; Warner, 1965). Specifically, the interviewer asks two questions, one threatening and the other completely innocuous. For example, Question A contains a very threatening question, such as "During the last 12 months have you been charged by a policeman for driving under the influence of liquor?" Question B is a nonthreatening question, such as "Is your birthday in the month of September?" Both of these questions have the same possible answers, "yes" and "no." Which question the respondent answers is determined by a probability mechanism. We and others have used a plastic box containing fifty beads, 70 percent red and 30 percent blue. The box was designed so that, when it was shaken by the respondent, a red or blue bead seen only by the respondent would appear in the window of the box. If the bead is red, the threatening question is answered; if blue, the innocuous question is answered.

To illustrate how the procedure works, suppose that out of a sample of 1,000 respondents, 200 answered "yes" to the pair of questions given above and 800 answered "no." The expected number of persons answering "yes" to the question about the month of their birthday is approximately 25 ($1,000 \times .3 \div 12$). This assumes that birth dates are equally distributed over the twelve months and that .3 of the respondents saw a blue bead. Thus, the net number of people answering "yes" to the question on drunken driving is $200 - 25$, or 175. The number of people who answered Question A is approximately $.7 \times 1,000$, or 700. The percentage of people who admit being arrested for drunken driving is $175 \div 700$, or 25 percent.

By using this procedure, you can estimate the undesirable behavior of a group while fully protecting the anonymity of the respondent. With this method, however, you cannot relate individual characteristics of respondents to individual behavior. That is, standard regression procedures are not possible at an individual level. If you have a very large sample, group characteristics can be related to the estimates obtained from randomized response. For example, you could look at all the answers of young women and compare them to the answers of men and older age groups. On the whole, much information is lost when randomized response is used. Even if the information obtained from randomized response were error-free (and it is not), the loss of information has made this procedure much less popular than it was when first introduced.

The accuracy of information obtained by randomized response depends on the respondent's willingness to follow instructions, understand the procedure, and tell the truth in exchange for anonymity. Unfortunately, for very threatening questions, such as our example of drunken driving given earlier, there is still substantial underreporting of socially undesirable behavior.

Randomized response is also not an appropriate procedure for asking questions about socially desirable behavior, where it may lead to even higher levels of overreporting than standard methods. Randomized and anonymous response procedures are appropriate to use when researching behavior such as abortion and bankruptcies, where the respondent may not personally be ashamed of the action but may not know how the behavior is viewed by the interviewer.

Aside from the issue of reporting quality, some readers may wonder whether procedures such as randomized response and card sorting have any negative effects on respondent cooperation by disrupting the flow of the interview. All evidence indicates that quite the contrary is the case. Both respondents and interviewers enjoy card sorting exercises or shaking a box of beads. Interviewers report that respondent cooperation improves when there is some variety in the tasks.

Use Open-Ended Questions

As a general rule survey researchers prefer closed questions because they are easier to process and they reduce coder variability. (See Chapter Five.) In attempting to obtain frequencies of threatening behavior, however, there is no difficulty in coding, since the answer is numeric. For example, Question 2A in Figure 3.8 asks how often the respondent drank beer and allows for such answers as "Daily," "Several times a week," "Weekly," "Monthly," and so on. All these answers can be converted to number of days per month or year.

It may not be obvious why the open-ended question here is superior to a closed-ended question that puts possible alternatives on a card and asks the respondent to select one. One reason is that the closed question must arrange the alternatives in a logical sequence, from most frequent to least frequent, or the reverse. In either case, the most extreme answer, "Daily," would be either at the extreme top or bottom of a list provided on a card. Heavy drinkers who drank beer daily would need to select the extreme response if they reported correctly. There is, however, a general tendency for respondents to avoid extreme answers and to prefer an answer in the middle of a list because it is thought to indicate those values that the researcher thinks are most likely in the population.

This applies to attitude and knowledge questions as well as behavior. Thus, some of the daily drinkers would choose a response more in the middle, thereby causing a substantial understatement.

An alternative explanation is that the open-ended questions allow the really heavy drinkers to state numbers that exceed the highest precodes. When researchers set precodes, they tend to set the highest value at a level that will still have fairly high frequencies. If the tail of a distribution is long, the highest precode category does not capture the really heavy drinkers. For more discussion of open questions, see Bradburn, Sudman, and Associates, 1979, Chapter Two.

There is one occasion when asking a closed-ended question may be desirable. This is when one is interested in learning whether the respondent has *ever* done what some might consider a socially undesirable act, such as masturbation, in the past month. Asking a closed frequency question such as Question 4 in Figure 3.9 may suggest to respondents that masturbation is widely practiced and that an answer at the lower end of the scale would not shock anyone.

Use Long Questions with Familiar Words

The advantages and possible disadvantages of longer questions about nonthreatening behavior were discussed in Chapter Two, and that discussion need not be repeated. When questions are asked about the frequency of socially undesirable behavior, overreporting is not a problem with most segments, and longer questions help relieve the tendency to underreport. It is important to use these longer questions to try to provide additional cues to memory. Thus, Question 3 in Figure 3.8 begins by pointing out the popularity of beer and wine and listing examples of their uses.

Longer questions increased the reported activities of socially undesirable behavior by about 25 to 30 percent, as compared with the standard short questions. Longer questions, however, had no effect on respondents' willingness to report *ever* engaging in socially undesirable activity, such as drinking liquor or getting drunk (Bradburn, Sudman, and Associates, 1979).

Some critics of survey research procedures claim that using standardized wordings makes the interview situation artificial. They claim that such stilted wording makes it more difficult for some respondents to understand the question and provide truthful responses and that slang would be easier for most respondents to understand. Furthermore, these people contend that slang and colloquialisms are often used in normal conversation when the behavior being discussed is socially undesirable and thus are appropriate for questions regarding such behavior.

In contrast to this position, other researchers are concerned that using slang and varying the question wording from respondent to respondent introduces uncontrolled method variability. This problem is greatest with attitude questions where answers clearly depend on how the question is asked, but less critical for behavior questions where understanding the question is most important. Still, how the behavior question is asked may significantly affect how threatening it is perceived to be.

One approach that reduces the threat is to have the respondent (not the interviewer) make the decision on the word to use, when the standard words such as "liquor" or "sexual intercourse" may be too formal. In our research, we learned that most respondents preferred the term "love making" to "sexual intercourse," and some used even more direct colloquialisms. For liquor, many respondents used words such as "booze." The interviewer would then use the respondents' words. This is easy to do in computer-assisted interviewing where once the word is typed into the computer by the interviewer it can be programmed to appear in subsequent questions. For example, Question 4A in Figure 3.8 would ask "When you drank booze, on the average how often did you drink it?" The use of familiar words increased the reported frequencies of socially undesirable behavior about 15 percent, as compared to the use of standard wording (Bradburn, Sudman, and Associates, 1979).

When some respondents are asked to give the word they would prefer to use, they either do not know or they give an inappropriate response. Thus, on the pretest one respondent used the word "poison" to describe liquor. In this situation the interviewer must always have a fallback word that he or she could type in. Typically, this is the standard word, such as "liquor" or "sexual intercourse."

Use Informants

In the previous chapter, we pointed out the cost efficiencies of using household informants, but indicated that this might be at the cost of some loss in quality of information. For threatening questions, however, especially those dealing with socially desirable behavior, informants may provide *more* reliable information than respondents. It is, of course, necessary to ask about behavior that the informant might know about others, either from observation or through conversations. This could include topics such as voting, book reading, or use of alcohol and drugs (Bradburn, Sudman, and Associates, 1979).

The question may be asked about identifiable members in the same household or about unidentified friends or relatives. In either situation, respondents will not be so threatened answering questions about the behavior of others as they would be answering questions about their own behavior. An exception to this rule is asking parents to report about children. Parents may be more threatened and thus report lower levels of socially undesirable behavior than their children, or they may just not know.

Use Diaries and Panels

In Chapter Two we discussed using diaries that provide repeated written records for improving memory about nonsalient events. Diaries and consumer panels also reduce the respondent's level of threat. First, any event becomes less threatening if it is repeated over time and becomes routine. Respondents who might initially hesitate to report purchasing beer or contraceptives become less inhibited as time goes by.

Second, with repeated exposure, respondents gradually gain confidence in the organization or researcher gathering the data. Over time, respondents get a better understanding that the data are gathered to be used in aggregate form and that there are no personal consequences of reporting any kinds of behavior. The evidence suggests that confidence in the research and the perceived threat of the questions both level off fairly rapidly after two or three diaries or interviews. This is fortunate, since otherwise substantive data on trends would be confounded with response effects (Ferber, 1966).

Finally, diaries embed some threatening topics into a more general framework to avoid conditioning. Such embedding also appears to be effective for reducing threat. For example, respondents who reported health expenditures in a diary (Sudman and Lannom, 1980) reported higher levels of expenditures for contraceptives than did respondents who were interviewed several times. The diaries here seem to be having the same effect as anonymous forms.

Embed the Question

The threat of a question is partially determined by the context in which it is asked. If more threatening topics have been asked about earlier, a particular question may appear less threatening than if it had been asked first. Yet there are limitations to the use of this procedure. As we shall see in Chapter Ten, you would not want to start with very threatening questions since this could reduce respondent cooperation during the rest of the questionnaire. Also, putting the most threatening behavior question first will probably make the underreporting on that question even worse. Suppose, however, you were interested only in beer drinking. Then you would ask an early question about liquor drinking to reduce the threat of the beer drinking question. If you were particularly interested in shoplifting, you might use the following order (adapted from Clark and Tifft, 1966).

Did you ever, even once, do any of the following:

Commit armed robbery?   ☐ Yes   ☐ No

Break into a home, store, or building?   ☐ Yes   ☐ No

Take a car for a ride without the owner's knowledge?
   ☐ Yes   ☐ No

Take something from a store without paying for it?
   ☐ Yes   ☐ No

In a more general sense, the threat of individual questions is also determined by the general context of the questionnaire. Thus, a questionnaire that deals with attitudes toward alcoholism is more threatening than a questionnaire that deals with consumer expenditures. Consequently, respondents may be more willing to admit that they use alcohol when the question is one of a series of questions about consumer expenditures or leisure-time activities or lifestyles.

It can sometimes be difficult for a researcher to decide whether to use questions that are not directly related to the threatening topics being studied but are included only to embed the threatening questions. These added questions increase the length of the questionnaire and the cost of the study. We suggest, however, that judicious use of such questions can increase respondent cooperation and data quality with only small increases in cost. An artful investigator, when faced with the need to embed threatening questions, can choose additional questions that contribute to the richness of the research, even if these questions are not of primary interest. In other words, you can use other questions to take some of the emphasis off of your primary interest in a given survey.

Choose the Appropriate Time Frame

All else equal, questions about events that have occurred in the past should be less salient and less threatening than questions about current behavior. Thus, for socially undesirable behavior, it is better to start with a question that asks "Did you ever, even once . . . ," rather than to ask immediately about current behavior. Refer to Questions 2, 3, and 4 (about drinking beer, wine, and liquor) in Figure 3.8. Other examples might be the following questions about delinquent behavior. "Did you ever, even once, stay away from school without your parents knowing about it?" "Did you ever, even once, take something from a store without paying for it?"

After asking "Did you ever . . . ," the interviewer then asks about behavior in some defined period, such as the past year. As was pointed out in the previous chapter, it is difficult for respondents to remember accurately details on events in the distant past unless the events are highly salient.

For socially desirable behavior, however, just the reverse strategy should be adopted. It would be very threatening for respondents to admit that they never did something like wearing a seat belt or reading a book. Thus, the Gallup question on seat belt usage—"Thinking about the last time you got into a car, did you use a seat belt?"—is superior to the question "Do you ever wear seat belts?" Such wording works only for fairly common behavior. For less common behavior, an interviewer can obtain the same effect by asking about the behavior over a relatively short time period. Thus, instead of asking "Do you ever attend concerts or plays?" the interviewer would ask "Did you attend a concert or play in the past month?"

Make the Questions Less Threatening

As amusingly illustrated by Barton at the beginning of this chapter, researchers have often attempted to load questions in order to make them less threatening. There have been, however, few controlled experiments to test the effectiveness of these loading procedures, so we are unable to confidently attest to their effectiveness. Nevertheless, we discuss them here since they have some intuitive appeal. For undesirable behavior, the following loading techniques have been used:

1. *Use the "everybody does it" approach.* The introduction to the question indicates that the behavior is very common, so as to reduce the threat of reporting it. For example, "Even the calmest parents get angry at their children some of the time. Did your child(ren) do anything in the past seven days, since (*date*), to make you, yourself, angry?" Another version is given in the introduction to Question 2 in Figure 3.8: "The most popular alcoholic beverage in the country is beer." Of course, the "everybody does it" statement must appear to be reasonable to the respondent. If not, such as in the Barton example—"As you know, many people have been killing their wives these days"—the statement will be ineffective and may actually backfire and increase threat.

2. *Assume the behavior, and ask about frequencies or other details.* It is usually undesirable to assume that a person is doing something, since a question making that assumption leads to overreporting of behavior. For behavior that is underreported, however, this may be what is needed. For example, a closed question, "How many cigarettes do you smoke each day?" with "None" as a category at the top and with answers ranging from one to forty or more, may reduce the threat of reporting smoking.

For financial questions, assuming the presence of assets and asking about details improves reporting. Thus, instead of asking "Do you or members of this household have any savings accounts?" the question is phrased as follows: "Turning to savings accounts—that is, accounts in banks, savings and loan associations, and credit unions—are there separate accounts for different family members or do you have different accounts in various places under the same names, or what? Since I have several questions on each account, let's take each one in turn. First, in whose name is this account? Where is it?" (Ferber, 1966, p. 331). Note that this question also provides memory cues to the respondent.

3. *Use an authority to justify behavior.* Respondents may react more favorably to a statement if it is attributed to someone they like or respect. An example might be the following introduction to a question about drinking liquor: "Many doctors now believe that moderate drinking of liquor helps to reduce the likelihood of heart attacks or strokes. Have you drunk any liquor in the past year?" It is probably better to use group designations such as doctors or scientists or researchers and not the names of particular persons, since some respondents will not know of the person or may not consider the person an expert.

Note that these suggestions to load the question toward reporting socially undesirable behavior would have the undesirable effect of increasing overreporting if the behavior were either socially desirable or nonthreatening. Similarly, the following suggestion for reducing overreporting of socially desirable behavior should not be used with socially undesirable topics.

4. *Provide reasons why not.* If respondents are given good reasons for not doing socially desirable things such as voting or wearing seat belts, they should be less likely to overreport such behavior. These reasons may be in the form of questions or statements. Thus, on a seat belt usage question the introduction might be "Many drivers report that wearing seat belts is uncomfortable and makes it difficult to reach switches, such as lights and windshield wipers. Thinking about the last time you got into a car, did you use a seat belt?" Another way to ask the question is as follows: "Do you ever find wearing a seat belt uncomfortable? Do you ever have trouble reaching switches such as lights and windshield wipers when wearing a seat belt? Thinking about the last time you got into a car, did you use a seat belt?"

Determining the Perceived Threat of Questions

It is often very useful to determine at the end of an interview which questions were considered threatening or hard to understand. An example of a series of questions we have used for this purpose is given in Figure 3.10. The most useful of these is Question 4, which asks respondents to indicate whether they thought the questions "would make most people very uneasy, moderately uneasy, slightly uneasy, or not at all uneasy." Note that this is a projective question about most people and is less threatening than the direct questions asking respondents to report about their own uneasiness.

. Such questions can be used not only to determine general levels of threat but also as an indicator of respondent veracity. Respondents who report that the question would make most people uneasy are more likely to underreport than are other respondents.

Use Additional Sources to Validate Accuracy

Although validation from outside sources is always valuable in surveys of behavior, it is particularly important to validate the level of threat associated with a given behavior. As we have seen in this chapter, overreporting and underreporting can be dealt with in various ways, but there is still not enough research to predict in specific cases how big an effect these procedures will have. Moreover, some behaviors such as sexual activity, by their very nature, are private, and no outside validation is possible. Where it is possible, however, validation provides a procedure for evaluating results obtained from alternative methods and ultimately leads to better questionnaires.

Validation at an individual level is most powerful but also most difficult. It is possible, for example, to compare individual reports of doctor and hospital visits to records of medical care providers or insurers, but that requires permission from the individual and cooperation from the provider. It must be remembered that record information is also incomplete and variable in quality. Such methods as chemical analysis of hair, saliva, and urine samples have been devel-

Figure 3.10. Post-Interview Evaluation of Threat.

1. Now that we are almost through this interview, I would like your feelings about it. Overall, how enjoyable was the interview?

2. Which questions, if any, were unclear or too hard to understand?

3. Which of the questions, if any, were too personal?

4. *(Hand R. Card W.)* Questions sometimes have different kinds of effects on people. We'd like your opinions about some of the questions in this interview. As I mention groups of questions, please tell me whether you think those questions would make most people very uneasy, moderately uneasy, slightly uneasy, or not at all uneasy.

   How about the questions on:

   a. Leisure time and general leisure activities?
   b. Sports activities?
   c. Happiness and well-being?
   d. Gambling with friends?
   e. Social activities?
   f. Drinking beer, wine, or liquor?
   g. Getting drunk?
   h. Using marijuana or hashish?
   i. Using stimulants or depressants?
   j. Petting or kissing?
   k. Intercourse?
   l. Masturbation?
   m. Occupation?
   n. Education?
   o. Income?
   p. How about the use of the tape recorder?

Source: National Opinion Research Center, 1974.

oped to validate reported use of certain drugs. Obviously chemical analysis requires cooperation from respondents, but, perhaps surprisingly, a majority of respondents are willing to provide such samples. Public behavior such as registering to vote and voting can be checked against voting records, and it is sometimes possible to match expenditure data against bills or company records.

Validation at an aggregate level is easier if appropriate outside measures can be located. At the very least, it is worth searching carefully for such measures before concluding that no validation is possible. If the behavior involves a product or service, you can compare consumer reports with those of manufacturers, retailers, or suppliers of the service, as with purchases of beer, wine, and liquor. For socially desirable behavior such as giving to charity, you can compare the amounts reported with the total amounts received; reported play and concert attendance can be compared with figures on total tickets sold. But be careful to avoid comparing apples and oranges. In many cases there will be a nonhousehold component in the validation data. Thus, business firms also contribute to charity and purchase goods from retailers. On the other hand, validation data may be useful, even if the comparisons are not perfect.

Summary

Threatening behavior questions are intrinsically more difficult to ask than are nonthreatening questions. As the questions become very threatening, substantial response biases should be expected, regardless of the survey techniques or question wordings used. For less threatening questions, carefully designed question formats and wording can substantially improve response accuracy.

The procedures suggested in this chapter for obtaining more accurate reports of threatening topics include: (1) using self-administered methods to increase perceptions of confidentiality, (2) using card sorting and randomized response, (3) using open-ended questions, (4) using long questions with familiar words, (5) using informants, (6) using diaries and panels, (7) embedding the question, (8) choosing the appropriate time frame, (9) making the questions less threatening. For socially desirable behavior, ask respondents about their most recent behavior rather than about their usual behavior. For socially undesirable behavior, ask respondents whether they have ever engaged in a particular behavior before asking about their current behavior.

Additional questions are useful at the end of the interview to determine the respondent's level of perceived threat. Validation, at either an individual or aggregate level, is helpful.

Additional Reading

Much of the work in this chapter is based on research reported in *Improving Interview Method and Questionnaire Design* (Bradburn, Sudman, and Associates, 1979; see especially chaps. 1, 2, 5, 9, and 11). Research on the effects of anonymity on responses to threatening drug questions is presented in Turner, Lessler, and Gfroerer (1992). Additional information on the use of audio-CASIC methods can be obtained from the Research Triangle Institute or the National Institute on Drug Abuse. A description of the procedures for validating drug reports is given in Mieczkowski (1999). Wentland and Smith (1993, chap. 4) summarize a broad range of studies on sensitive topics, including alcohol-related behavior, deviant behavior, and sexual behavior.

Earlier research on anonymity has been done by Ash and Abramson (1952), Colombotos (1969), Fischer (1946), Fuller (1974), Hochstim (1967), and King (1970). For studies of randomized response see Greenberg and others (1969); Horvitz, Shaw, and Simmons (1967); and Reinmuth and Geurts (1975). The initial paper on this topic was by Warner (1965).

Consult also the journals referred to in Chapter Two for other examples of treatment of sensitive topics. In addition, in nearly any given inquiry, specific questioning methods are continuously being investigated. Advances in these areas may be specific to health reporting, alcohol or drug use, financial behaviors, and risk-related activities.

Chapter Four

Asking Questions About Attitudes and Behavioral Intentions

Setting out rules for formulating questions about attitudes is more difficult than for behavioral questions because questions about attitudes have no "true" answer. By this we mean that attitudes are subjective states that cannot, even in principle, be observed externally. Attitudes exist only in a person's mind. They can be consistent or inconsistent, clear or unclear, but they cannot be said to be true or false. Thus, in studying the effects of different wordings and different contexts on answers to attitude questions, we have no external standard with which to validate different forms of questions. We must rely on observing how answers may be affected by different factors. Researchers must decide for themselves which form of question is best for their purpose.

In this chapter we introduce the principal factors that challenge question writers, and we suggest reasonable solutions. The best advice we can offer those starting out is to borrow (with credit) questions that have already been used successfully. By borrowing questions, you can spare yourself much agony over the formulation of the questions and extensive pretesting. If the questions have been used frequently before, most of the bugs will have been ironed out of them. Also, if the questions have been used on population samples similar to the one in which you are interested, you get the advantage of comparative data. Replication is greatly encouraged, but make sure that the attitude question you borrow is about the attitude you want to study and not about something different.

Checklist of Major Points

1. Make sure the attitudes you are measuring are clearly specified.

2. Decide on the critical aspects of the attitude to be measured, such as cognitive, evaluative, and behavioral components. Do not assume that these components must be consistent.

3. Measure the strength of the attitude by building a strength dimension into the question itself. Either ask separate questions about attitude strength or ask a series of independent questions, each of which reflects the general attitude.

4. Measure behavioral intentions either directly or by asking about the likelihood a respondent will engage in a behavior. For infrequent behaviors, likelihood measures are best; for frequent behaviors, direct measures are better.

5. Avoid double-barreled and one-and-a-half-barreled questions that introduce multiple concepts and do not have a single answer.

6. Whenever possible, separate the issues from the individuals or from the sources connected with the issues.

7. Consider using separate unipolar items if bipolar items might miss independent dimensions.

8. Recognize that the presence or absence of an explicitly stated alternative can have dramatic effects on response.

9. Specify alternatives to help standardize the question.

10. Pretest new attitude questions to determine how respondents are interpreting them. Using split ballots in pretests is highly desirable.

11. Ask the general question first if general and specific attitude questions are related.

12. Ask the least popular item last when asking questions of differing degrees of popularity involving the same underlying value.

13. Ask exactly the same questions in all time periods, if at all possible, when attempting to measure changes in attitude over time.

Identifying the Object of the Attitude

Attitudes do not exist in the abstract. They are about or toward something. That something is often called the attitude object. The object of attitudes can be practically anything. It can range from being quite specific (such as the President or cornflakes) to quite abstract and general (such as civil liberties or the right to privacy). As with all questions, the cardinal rule is to ask what you want to know, not something else.

With attitudes, however, it is more difficult to know what you want to know because the attitude object is often ambiguous or ill-defined. The context in which questions are asked has a greater impact on attitude measurement than on behavior questions because the meaning of the questions may be strongly influenced by the context in which they appear. Even preserving the exact wording of an individual question may not be enough to guarantee that two questionnaires are comparable; other questions in the questionnaires may alter the perceived meaning of the questions.

The first step in formulating attitude questions is to make sure you know and clearly specify the attitude object. In other words, be clear about what your research question is and what you are trying to find out. In many instances, that requires considerable thought and articulation. For example, consider the following question: "Do you think the government is spending too much, about enough, or too little on homeland defense?" What is the attitude object to which this question refers? One might say at first glance that it refers to government policy toward homeland defense, but which government—federal government, state government, or local government? What is meant by "homeland defense"? Does it include only defense against attack by terrorists?

Does it include civil disturbances or rebellions? Does it include defense against natural disasters such as earthquakes, tornadoes, or against electrical grid failures or nuclear power plant explosions? Since many questions contain such ambiguities, extensive pretesting is necessary if you are to develop good standardized questions that eliminate misleading, noisy ambiguities.

Unfortunately, because of budget limitations and a belief that question wording is a simple matter that does not require great skill or experience, many researchers do not devote the needed time and effort to pretesting questions.

For the pretest phase, Belson (1968) has suggested a technique now known as cognitive interviewing, whereby respondents are asked to restate, in their own words, what they think the meaning of a question to be. This technique is analogous to back translating when questions are translated into another language. Another technique of cognitive interviewing is to ask respondents to verbalize the thought processes they go through when they are answering questions. After using cognitive interviewing, Belson pessimistically concluded that even with well-developed, simplified questionnaires, many respondents do not understand a question in the way it is intended by the researcher.

Lack of clarity is particularly common among attitude objects that are frequently discussed in the media, such as "welfare," "big business," "civil rights," and "profits." For example, in one study discussed by Payne (1951), more than one-third of the population did not know what "profits" meant. Of the remainder, a substantial number had an idea of profits that was quite different from that used by companies who reported them. Fee (1979) investigated the meanings of some common political terms used in public opinion studies. Adopting a variant of Belson's method, she asked respondents to elaborate on their understanding of particular terms, such as "energy crisis." She found that at least nine different meanings were attached to the term "energy crisis." Similarly, the term "big government" elicited four distinct connotations or images: (1) "welfare," "socialism," and "overspending"; (2) "big business" and "government for the wealthy"; (3) "federal control" and "diminished states' rights"; and (4) "bureaucracy" and "a lack of democratic process." The images tended to be held by people with differing political orientations or levels of education and were related to different attitudes. Without knowing which of the images respondents held, a researcher might not be able to interpret responses to questions about "big government." There is no reason to believe that the situation has changed dramatically since then.

In short, ambiguity pervades questionnaires. Pretesting and experiments with question wording can resolve some of the ambiguity with regard to respondents' understanding of questions; but they can do so only if you have a clear notion of what you are trying to find out. If you do not know what you want to know, respondents are unable to help.

The Three Components of Attitudes

The terms *opinion* and *attitude* are not clearly differentiated from one another. In general, opinion is most often used to refer to views about a particular object such as a person or a policy, and attitude is more often used to refer to a bundle of opinions that are more or less coherent and are about some complex object. One might have an opinion about a particular proposal to change a Medicare provision and a more general attitude about Medicare. Opinions are more often measured by single questions; attitudes tend to be measured by a set of questions that are combined on the basis of some measurement model.

Attitudes are thought of as having three components: cognitive, evaluative, and behavioral components. The cognitive component consists of a set of beliefs about the attitude object (such as "How healthy is pizza on the following dimensions?"). The evaluative component consists of evaluation of the object; for example, do respondents think it is good or bad or do they like it or not ("Do you like pizza as a food?"). The behavioral component is related to respondents' attitudes in relation to their actions ("How many times will you eat pizza in the next month?"). In practice, attitude questions are mostly about beliefs and evaluations. Questions that try to measure the action component are discussed later in this chapter.

Different Attitude Components Require Different Questions

It is generally believed and empirically supported that there is a strain toward consistency among these attitudinal components. People are less likely to believe something derogatory about something they like and are in favor of, and they do not usually act in support of things they disapprove of. The belief that these three components are consistent is sometimes so strong as to lead researchers to neglect assessing the components independently. They assume they can infer other components of the attitude by measuring only one component. For example, respondents who believe a particular product has positive attributes will be favorably disposed to the product and will buy it. Similarly, someone who votes for a particular candidate knows something about the candidate and generally has a favorable view of that candidate. Unfortunately, attitudes are often much more complex and differentiated. Even though components of the attitude correlate in general ways, the components are still different. It is particularly difficult to make inferences about action from simple measurements of the cognitive and evaluative components of the attitude because factors other than the attitude affect action.

Even when you are measuring a single component, such as the evaluative component, using different evaluative words may produce different results. Similar (if not synonymous) terms that indicate a positive orientation toward an attitude object may have somewhat different connotations and yield different responses. For example, the terms "approve and disapprove" and "like and dislike" are frequently used in attitude questions, but little attention is paid to possible differences in implication between them. An empirical test of the similarities of these terms was obtained in a context of questions about year-round daylight savings time (Murray and others, 1974). The following two questions were asked of the same respondents in a national probability sample in March and April of 1974:

> As you know, we recently switched from standard time to [year-round] daylight savings time. That means that it now gets light an hour later in the morning than before we switched over. It also means that it now gets dark an hour later in the evening than before we switched over. How do you feel about being on [year-round] daylight savings time now? Would you say you like it very much, like it somewhat, dislike it somewhat, or dislike it very much?

> As you know, the United States Congress put our country back on daylight savings time this winter as part of a two-year experiment to try to save energy. Some people think that we should continue to have daylight savings time all year round— that is, not turn the clocks back at the end of next October. Would you approve or disapprove of remaining on daylight savings time all year round next year, or don't you care one way or the other?

Although a cross-tabulation of the responses indicated a positive correlation between the two items, 14 percent of those who liked year-round daylight savings time "very much" "disapproved" of it, and 10 percent of those who disliked it "very much" "approved" of it. The correspondence between the two evaluations was highest for those who felt strongly about the issue. The correspondence between the two evaluations was considerably less for those with more moderate likes or dislikes. These findings support the belief that strongly held attitudes are generally more resistant to effects of question wording than are weakly held attitudes.

Assessing the Strength of Attitudes

Strength is a concept that can be applied to each of the three components of attitudes. Evaluations may be strongly or weakly held, beliefs may be certain or uncertain, and actions may be definitely committed to or only vaguely contemplated. Three general strategies for measuring attitude strength are as follows: (1) build a strength dimension into the question itself by measuring evaluations and strength at the same time; (2) use a separate question to assess the strength; (3) assess strength by asking a series of independent questions, each one reflecting the same general underlying attitude. In this third case, the measure of attitudinal strength is determined by the total number of items a person agrees with. This third method of asking multiple items can be applied to each of the components, although in practice attitude strength is more usually assessed in the general or overall evaluative dimension.

Perhaps the most frequent method of measuring intensity of attitudes is to build an intensity scale into the response categories. People's responses indicate not only the direction of their evaluation but also their intensity or certainty. A common method is to ask respondents a question that measures both the direction and the intensity of an evaluation, as in the first question on daylight savings time quoted in the previous section. This question could have been asked as two separate questions. For example, "Do you like or dislike [year-round] daylight savings time?" and "Do you like or dislike it [year-round daylight savings time] somewhat or very much?" In this case, the simplicity of the like-dislike dimension and the simplicity of the two intensity modifiers suggested that they could be combined into a single question that respondents could easily comprehend. Note that respondents who said they did not care either way were not urged to say which direction they were leaning in. In this case, however, respondents were discouraged from indicating indifference, since a "Don't care" response category was not included. (This point will be discussed more fully in the next chapter.)

Using separate questions to evaluate attitude strength is illustrated in another daylight savings time survey. Here the researchers believed that attitude strength was not evenly divided between those who preferred daylight savings time and those who did not prefer it. Therefore, researchers decided to measure separately the general orientation pros and cons and the strength of those feelings. The form of the NORC question is given in Figure 4.1. In this case it was found that those who did not approve of daylight savings time in fact felt more strongly about it than those who did approve of it. Again, those who said they had no preference or did not know were not prodded to see whether they might lean one way or the other.

Aggregate Measures of Attitude

Another strategy for measuring the strength of attitudes is to combine answers to several separate questions, each one of which is thought to be a measure of the attitude. This method is most often

Figure 4.1. Questions on Daylight Savings Time.

As you know, the time that we set our clocks to can be changed if we wish. For example, in most parts of the country, we set our clocks ahead one hour in the summer, so that it gets dark at around 9 o'clock instead of 8 o'clock. This is known as daylight savings time.

Some people think that we should go onto daylight savings time all year around, that is, turning the clocks ahead one hour and leaving them there. Would you approve or disapprove of going onto daylight savings time all year round, or don't you care one way or the other?

☐ Approve *(Ask a.)*
☐ Don't care
☐ Disapprove *(Ask a.)*
☐ Don't know

    a. How strongly do you feel about it? Do you (dis)approve very strongly, pretty strongly, or not too strongly?
       ☐ Very strongly
       ☐ Pretty strongly
       ☐ Not too strongly

Source: National Opinion Research Center, 1977.

employed to measure general attitudes about abstract objects such as "liberalism" or "freedom of speech." The general attitude is thought of as a single dimension, usually running from pro to con, or from low to high, or as being anchored at two ends with conflicting orientations. The general attitude is conceptualized as giving rise to many specific opinions about more specific cases. This form of measuring attitude strength often rests on an implicit or explicit mathematical measurement model relating the responses to particular questions to positions on an attitude scale.

Public opinion polls typically use single questions to measure either beliefs or more often evaluative aspects of attitudes about objects. An example of this is the classic Gallup presidential rating question, "Do you approve or disapprove of the way [name of president] is handling his job as president?"

In contrast to the single question approach, scientific and many commercial surveys often use several questions to measure the different aspects of an attitude, and they then combine the questions in a scale that allows for greater differentiation. If these multi-item scales are carefully constructed, they can produce a more reliable measure of attitudes because they filter out a lot of random "noise" that contributes to measurement error.

Likert Scales and Guttman Scales

A number of scaling techniques have been developed based on somewhat different underlying models of attitude measurement. The most popular is the Likert scale, named after Rensis Likert, a pioneer in the field of attitude measurement. The fundamental idea behind Likert scales is that an attitude can be thought of as a set of propositions about beliefs, evaluations, and actions held by individuals. If you ask respondents to agree or disagree with a sample of propositions about the attitude object, you can combine the answers to get a better measure of the attitude. A number of different statistical techniques are used to determine whether a particular set of questions actually forms a scale (see Additional Reading), but they all rely on the idea that a good scale has a high intercorrelation of the items.

Another commonly used scale type is the Guttman scale, named after Louis Guttman, another pioneer in attitude measurement. Guttman's approach was to devise questions that measured increasing agreement (or disagreement) with attributes of the attitude object. In contrast to the Likert model where the total number of items agreed to without regard to their order is the measure of the attitude, items in a Guttman scale are ordered such that some items should be agreed to only by those who are low on the attitude and others should be agreed to only by those who are high on the attitude scale.

An example of the difference in approach applied to attitudes about free speech is presented in abbreviated form in Figure 4.2. The first format is that of the Likert scale. Several items are stated in propositional form and respondents are asked to indicate the degree of their agreement or disagreement with the statement. The scale score is then determined by giving numerical values to the response categories and adding up the values given to respondents' responses.

The second format in Figure 4.2 is that of a Guttman scale. Here the items are presented in an order of increasing commitment (or opposition) to free speech. Various methods for combining responses can be used. The simplest is to count the number of "yes" and "no" answers as appropriate. Some decision would have to be made about the "don't knows." One alternative is to leave them out or to treat them as lying somewhere between the "yes" and "no" responses. More complex treatments include giving more weight to the less frequent responses or weighting the less frequent responses according to some a priori view of the relationship between the content of the hypothetical speech and the strength of a belief in freedom of expression. Again we stress that you must make such decisions on the basis of your research question and your conception of the measurement model. Guttman scales are somewhat harder to develop and thus are not so commonly used as Likert scales.

Figure 4.2. Two Formats for Measuring Attitude Toward Free Speech (Abbreviated Questions).

LIKERT FORMAT

Please tell me how strongly you agree or disagree with the following statements. Do you agree strongly, agree somewhat, disagree somewhat, or disagree strongly that . . .

1. Communists should be allowed to teach in school.

2. People should be allowed to make speeches supporting the view that whites are genetically superior to other races.

3. Books advocating the violent overthrow of the government should be banned from public libraries.

GUTTMAN FORMAT

Consider a person who believes that whites are genetically superior to all other races. If such a person wanted to make a speech in your community claiming that whites are genetically superior to blacks, should he be allowed to speak or not?

☐ Yes, allowed

☐ Not allowed

☐ Don't know

Should such a person be allowed to teach in a college or university or not?

☐ Yes allowed

☐ Not allowed

☐ Don't know

If some people in your community suggested that a book he wrote which said that whites were genetically superior should be taken out of your public library, would you favor removing this book or not?

☐ Favor

☐ Not favor

☐ Don't know

It is beyond the scope of this book to deal in detail with these models, but it is important to know that explicit measurement models often provide criteria to help measure attitude. Working back and forth between pretesting questions and testing responses against an explicit measurement model can greatly aid in the development of valid attitude scales. Consult one of the references listed at the end of the chapter for more information about measurement models.

Many researchers create scales without properly testing whether the scales meet statistical criteria for a good scale. Researchers are well advised to explicitly articulate the measurement model they are using and to get appropriate statistical consulting advice when they are in doubt about how to refine and test their scaling procedures.

Asking Behavioral Intention Questions

There is often an assumed relationship between attitudes and behaviors. That is, people are asked attitude questions about products because their attitudes might reflect what they buy, and people are asked their opinions about political candidates because their answers might reflect how they will vote. When behavior is impossible to measure, such as when it relates to an unreleased new product or an upcoming presidential campaign, we often use attitude measures as a surrogate for behavior.

- A basic and frequently useful conceptualization of the attitude-behavior connection uses the intermediate step of behavioral intentions. This view basically contends that attitudes are related (to some extent) to behavioral intentions, and these intentions are, in turn, related to actual behavior (see Figure 4.3). Certainly there are a lot of other factors in the equation. In the final analysis, however, a good predictor of behavior is the consistency of behavioral intentions and attitudes toward the object.

For instance, respondents' attitudes toward a soft drink might be related to their intentions to buy that soft drink within the next week, and these intentions might be related to actual purchase.

Figure 4.3. Behavioral Intentions Can Link Attitudes and Behaviors.

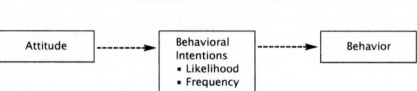

Similarly, one's attitude toward exercising and eating less might be related to the intention to "lose ten pounds before my high school reunion," and this intention is likely to be related to actual weight loss. Although a number of other factors make these relationships imperfect, it is often believed there is a general mapping from one's attitude to behavioral intentions.

One important reason for measuring behavioral intentions (instead of just attitudes) is that behavioral intentions can help differentiate between people who choose an endpoint on a scale. For instance, if two people really like a product and rate it as a 9 on a 9-point scale, there is no way to determine whether one plans to consume the product three times or thirty times within the next year.

Behavioral intention questions can be used to estimate how likely one is to perform a behavior (buy a car in the next year, or donate money to a presidential candidate's campaign). They can also be used to estimate how frequently one is likely to perform a behavior (exercise in the next year, call long distance in the next month), and so forth. Both are of interest in a number of cases. In this section we will discuss how and when it is important to ask one type of question versus the other.

Asking Likelihood Questions Regarding Incidence

"Do you plan on buying a new car in the next year?" This is an incidence question that does not focus on how many cars that person will purchase in the next year, but instead focuses on how likely the respondent is to buy a car. The two most common types of behavioral intention questions are yes-no questions and likelihood questions. Consider the following two examples.

1. **Will you buy a new car within the next 12 months?**
   ☐ Yes   ☐ No

2. **How likely are you to buy a new car within the next 12 months?**
   Not Very Likely 1— 2 — 3 — 4 — 5 — 6 — 7 — 8 — 9 *Very Likely*

In telephone and electronic surveys, yes-no questions are frequently asked. This type of question is primarily useful as a screening question. These yes-no behavioral intention questions provide very specific answers that can be translated into hard data estimates ("21% will buy a car within the next year"). Unfortunately, these percentages are likely to be in error. Because yes-no questions force all undecided people to choose either yes or no, the data are noisy and often inaccurate.

Likelihood questions avoid this problem. With likelihood questions, respondents who are somewhere in the middle can answer somewhere in the middle. For academic researchers, likelihood questions have the advantage of providing reasonably high levels of discrimination. For practitioners, they have the disadvantage of not being able to readily transform the responses into percentages or projections. That is, it is much more satisfying (and seemingly more definite) to say "21% of the respondents will buy new cars in the next twelve months" than to say "on a likelihood scale of 1 to 9, the average reported likelihood of buying a new car within the next twelve months is 4.1."

One solution to this dilemma is to ask respondents the yes-no question and then ask them a likelihood question. The yes-no question can be used in summary measures and the likelihood question can be used to weight the estimates or statistically adjust the data to improve the estimates. For instance, people can be asked (yes or no) if they think they will eat at a fast-food (quick service) restaurant in the next week. They can then be asked to estimate how likely they think they are to eat there. Two people can answer "yes" to the question, but the person who answers the likelihood question as being "extremely likely" or as "100% likely" is different from the person who answers "somewhat likely" or as "60% likely."

A second solution is to ask two different types of likelihood questions that provide a range of responses. One can be a more general question that represents the baseline condition. ("How likely are you to buy a car within the next twelve months?") The second can provide a realistic or more favorable "upper bound" scenario. ("How likely are you to buy a car within the next twelve months if car prices drop by 10%?") The use of two (or more) likelihood questions provides some measure of sensitivity and also provides a comparison point when reported in conjunction with their answers to the first question.

Consider the questions that the Girl Scouts used to anticipate demand for their annual cookie sales. Questions were asked in two different ways.

1. **How likely are you going to be to buy Girl Scout Cookies this year?**

   Not Very Likely 1— 2 — 3 — 4 — 5 — 6 — 7 — 8 — 9 *Very Likely*

2. **If approached, how likely are you to buy Girl Scout Cookies from a friend's daughter?**

   Not Very Likely 1— 2 — 3 — 4 — 5 — 6 — 7 — 8 — 9 *Very Likely*

The first question is general and runs the risk of having a person overlook extenuating circumstances. The second question is specific and runs the risk of overestimating demand when sales efforts do not involve a friend's daughter. Together, however, they enabled the organization to bracket a response range. These results can then be used either to estimate a range of expectations or to do scenario-based planning (such as calculating possible sales if parents asked their friends to buy cookies).

Not surprisingly, reports of the likelihood of buying cookies increases dramatically when a person is specifically asked about being approached by a friend's daughter (Question 2) than when the person doing the selling is not specified in the question. The significant difference between these two answers was used to underscore how important face-to-face sales were to the success of cookie sale efforts.

Asking Frequency-Related Questions Regarding Future Behavior

A second way to ask questions of behavioral intentions is to ask people to estimate how many times they will engage in the behavior within a specified period of time. This approach is particularly useful when investigating frequent behaviors. Typically questions are asked as either a fill-in-the-blank question or as a frequency question with fixed intervals. Consider these two questions asked after the BSE crisis with beef in Europe.

1. How many times will you eat beef for your evening meal in the next month?

   _____ times in the next month

2. How many times will you eat beef for your evening meal in the next month?

   ☐ 0   ☐ 1–2   ☐ 3–5   ☐ 6–10   ☐ 11–20   ☐ 21–30

The first type of question, the fill-in-the-blank question, offers a response mode that is free of range biases, interval biases, or anchoring effects. Despite these advantages, it is often less frequently used than the interval question (Question 2) because it provides more possibility for data entry error than does a checked box. It is also a favorite in electronic surveys. Although the fill-in-the-blank version is generally preferable, if the interval question is to be used, appropriate intervals must be carefully considered. Although Question 2 above used six categories (0, 1–2, 3–5, 6–10, 11–20, 21–30), there are a wide variety of other numerical intervals that could have been used (for instance, 0, 1–5, 6–10, 11–15, 16–20, 21–30).

When deciding what intervals to use in a frequency question, the first important notion is that zero should be its own separate category. Once this is established, one important consideration is that the response categories provide wide discrimination across the entire range of responses. For example, if a pilot test showed that most people will eat beef four or fewer times in the next month, the categories might be 0, 1, 2, 3–4, 5–15, 16–30. If the mean is more around ten, then the categories should be more spread out.

Another issue is how many categories should be offered. Despite a number of theoretical considerations, this is generally determined by assessing how much space one wants to use in conjunction with what categories can provide the greatest differentiation. If the intervals are spaced out to maximize variation (through use of pilot tests), fewer boxes will be needed. If precision is a concern, use fill-in-the-blank questions.

When You Should Ask Likelihood Questions Instead of Frequency Questions

As noted, measures of behavioral intentions (for a particular time period, such as "within the next month") can be obtained either through likelihood measures or through frequency estimates. Likelihood measures can be directly obtained by asking respondents how likely ("Highly Unlikely" = 1 to "Highly Likely" = 9) they are to perform that behavior within a given time period. Behavioral intentions can also be measured by asking respondents to estimate the number of times they might perform that behavior within a similar time period.

These two different measures of behavioral intent have different relative strengths. With infrequent behaviors, frequency estimates will be skewed toward 0 (especially over a relatively short period of time). This is partially a drawback of numerical estimates that provide no gradation between 0 and 1 unit. In such cases, frequency estimates would provide less variance and less information than an estimate of likelihood. As a result, likelihood estimates would allow a greater gradation in response and would be more sensitive.

In contrast, with frequent behaviors, a frequency estimate will be more accurate than a likelihood estimate. The reason is that frequency estimates are more likely to be normally distributed. As a result, a frequency estimate is likely to provide more variance and more information than is a likelihood measure, which would undoubtedly be at or near 1.0 (100 percent probable). Under these circumstances, frequency estimates would more accurately correspond with actual behavior.

One study (Wansink and Ray, 1992) examined situations when likelihood questions were preferable to frequency questions by asking people to estimate their upcoming three-month consumption of a number of different products. Three months later, respondents were contacted again and asked for their actual (recalled) consumption. For products they frequently consumed (frequent behaviors), numerical estimates were much more accurate than likelihood estimates. For products they infrequently consumed (infrequent behaviors), likelihood estimates were more accurate than numerical estimates.

· What happens when there is high variation in the frequency of behavior? One solution is to use both likelihood and a frequency estimation measure and use them to triangulate on the behavior. Instead of taking one measure, take both measures along with a measure of how frequently respondents report this behavior for a prior time period (week, month, year, etc.). The measure of respondents' prior behavior can be used to divide the population into frequent or infrequent exhibitors of that behavior. If one is trying to compare multiple behaviors (mall walking vs. golfing vs. going to the gym), or behavior toward certain stimuli (like various ads), analyzing the frequent users separately from the infrequent users can be useful. It is also important when analyzing these data to drop nonusers from the analysis. Be sure, however, to report that those not using the product were eliminated.

Important Issues When Writing Questions

There is no one correct way to formulate questions. In this section we briefly discuss several different dimensions for formulating questions. Each is useful in some situations, and no one formulation is clearly better than others in all situations. The choice of question formulation is largely determined by the research question and, to some extent, by the taste of the researcher.

Should You Use Unipolar or Bipolar Questions?

Unipolar questions are those that ask respondents' opinion about one attitude object in isolation from other objects; for example, "Do you favor or oppose a flat rate income tax?" Bipolar questions are those that ask respondents to choose between two contrasting objects; for example, "Do you favor a graduated income tax rate as we have now or do you favor changing to a flat rate income tax?"

Unipolar questions have the advantage of focusing respondents' attention on the particular attitude object and obtaining an evaluative rating on it that is minimally influenced by other considerations. It is an appropriate type of question to use if you think the attitude toward the particular object is itself unidimensional. (A unidimensional attitude would be one where attitudes toward the object range from high to low without being strongly influenced by alternatives.) Attitudes about free speech might be such a case. We think of people in favor of free speech as having intensity levels that range from being strongly in favor to being strongly opposed. Variations in attitude are along a single dimension of support or opposition and people can be arrayed along this dimension.

Even if an attitude is thought to be unidimensional, you can ask about two (or more) views about the same object. In fact, in many instances it is precisely the posing of two opinions at opposite ends of a dimension that constitutes the question. You might be interested in a response at only one end of the dimension; that is, you might want to know whether respondents are in favor of something or not, but not whether they are opposed to it. In these instances you would ask a simple, straightforward question, such as "Do you favor the flat tax?" Although there is nothing wrong in principle with asking a question like this with the implied alternative that the respondent does not support a flat tax, the answer "no" is not so informative as it might appear on the surface. A "yes" appears to mean unambiguously that the respondent supports the tax, but a "no" might mean that the respondent opposes it, or has no opinion about it, or does not care one way or the other, or has mixed feelings about it. (When the question is worded "Do you favor the flat or not?" the level of support may change by a few percentage points.)

Unipolar items, when rephrased into what appear to be their opposites, often produce surprising results. A famous study by Rugg (1941) showed that even such apparently opposite words as "allow" and "forbid" can produce dissimilar results. Rugg asked matched samples of respondents the questions "Do you think the United States should allow public speeches against democracy?" and "Do you think the United States should forbid public speeches against democracy?" When the question was one of allowing public speeches, 21 percent of the respondents supported free speech; when the question was phrased that the United States should forbid free speech, 39 percent denied that proposition and supported free speech.

With this and other studies as a basis, it has become a generally accepted practice to use both ends of the implied dimension to phrase simple unipolar questions; for example, "Do you favor or oppose the flat tax?" Respondents then choose either pro or con positions or something in between. If an intensity dimension is added to the question, respondents are asked to choose one or the other end of the dimension with some gradations in between; for example, "Do you strongly support, support somewhat, oppose somewhat, or strongly oppose the flat tax?"

Accounting for Multidimensional Attitudes

Some attitudes are about objects that are multidimensional, and it is difficult to understand the attitude without taking other alternatives into consideration. Tax policy might be such a case. By focusing on a single aspect of tax policy, such as a flat rate, the question might in fact bias the measurement because opinions about the flat rate might depend on what it is compared to. Research indicates that you can get quite different readings on opinion about many subjects when the questions pose different comparisons. In such cases you need to ask the question in such a way that respondents must choose between two alternatives. A good example of this is in the bipolar example above in which respondents were asked whether they favor the graduated income tax or a flat tax.

Given the extreme sensitivity of opinion questions to the formulation of alternatives, you must give careful consideration to the wording of the alternatives that are offered. Which alternatives are chosen, of course, depends entirely on the research question being investigated. Alternatives provide the frame of reference that the respondents use in expressing their opinions. You will want to be sure that respondents use the same frame of reference you are using. To ensure that the frame of reference is the same, you should do a considerable amount of pretesting and examine different ways to phrase alternatives. Pretest respondents should be asked to indicate what they understood the alternatives to mean in order to provide evidence that they are indeed interpreting the questions in the way you intended. If at all possible, a sufficiently large pretest should be done with split ballots, so that the effects of the stated alternatives can be empirically investigated. If large effects are found between different alternatives, you should continue investigations until you understand what is producing the effect.

Sometimes what looks like a clear unidimensional concept turns out to be multidimensional. A dramatic effect of using unipolar items was found when developing a scale to measure psychological well-being (Bradburn, 1969). Instead of a series of bipolar items in which respondents reported themselves as either "excited" or "bored," "cheerful" or "depressed," "happy" or "unhappy," and so on, questions were phrased in a unipolar manner. Respondents were asked in separate questions whether they had felt, for example, "on top of the world" or "depressed" during the past few weeks. Respondents answered each question "yes" or "no." A surprising finding was that, although responses to the positively worded questions correlated with one another, and the negatively worded items correlated with one another, responses to the positive items had a zero relationship to responses to the negative items. Thus the concept of psychological well-being turned out to be multidimensional. Although unipolar items will often produce results similar to those found with bipolar items, bipolar items make it difficult to discover interesting independence of dimensions.

Using Question Filters

Questions about complex attitudes sometimes need to be broken down into a series of simpler unipolar questions. The particular questions to be asked may be contingent on answers to previous questions. This technique is called filtering or branching. It is a useful technique to decompose complex attitudes so that you do not have to use difficult multidimensional questions that require a number of qualifying clauses.

A good example of the use of filters come from an adaptation of a question about the first Gulf War, shown in Figure 4.4. The question was designed to be asked about three months before the start of the war to measure public opinion about support of a war with Iraq. Note that there is a question that is asked of respondents who gave a response to the previous question that needed elaboration in order to get at the various conditions and dates that were being discussed as policy options at the time.

Sometimes the use of filters produces some surprising results. For instance, the use of filters with this question gives a different view of public opinion than would be obtained if you only used the first

Figure 4.4. Example of Use of Filters.

1. As you may know, the U.N. Security Council has authorized the use of force against Iraq if it doesn't withdraw from Kuwait by Jan. 15. If Iraq does not withdraw from Kuwait, should the United States go to war against Iraq to force it out of Kuwait at some point after Jan. 15 or not?

   ☐ Yes (Ask A.)

   ☐ No

   ☐ Don't know

   A. (If Yes) How long after Jan. 15 should the U.S. wait for Iraq to withdraw from Kuwait before going to war?

      ☐ Go to war immediately

      ☐ Wait up to 3 months

      ☐ Wait longer than 3 months

      ☐ Never go to war

Source: Gallup Organization, 2002.

question. On the basis of the first question, it appeared that a majority of the public supported a war beginning in January. If one considers the answers to the subsequent question posed to those who said "no" to the first question, you would conclude that a much larger majority actually supported a war within three months of the interview.

Not using follow-up questions when respondents answer "no" to a question can also cause a problem. For example, in the 1973 and 1975 General Social Surveys (GSS), respondents were first asked, "Are there any situations that you can imagine in which you would approve of a man punching an adult male stranger?" Many respondents answered "no" to this question. Fortunately, respondents were then asked a series of questions about specific conditions under which they might approve of such an action, such as "The stranger had hit the man's child after the child accidentally damaged the stranger's car" or "The stranger was beating up a woman and the man saw it." Respondents were asked about the qualified situations regardless of whether they had answered "yes" or "no" to the general questions. This was done even though the qualifications should have only been logical subsets or specific conditions of a "yes" response to the general question (approve of hitting an adult stranger). In fact, 84 percent of those who disapproved of hitting an adult stranger in any situation they could imagine went on to indicate approval in one or more of the five situations presented. The "disapprovers in general" averaged about 1.82 approvals for hitting when specific situations were described. Smith (1981) suggests that many respondents are not interpreting the general question literally as asked. Instead they are responding to the absolute phrase "Are there any situations you can imagine" as if it meant "In general."

If the attitude object is complex and you start off with a question to which respondents can answer "yes" or "no," it is best to consider following up with the respondents who answer "no" by asking additional questions that might reveal aspects of the attitude not revealed by the initial response.

Using Questions that Include a Middle Point

We discussed earlier how dichotomous responses can be expanded by using modifiers (such as "very," "somewhat," "a little") to also provide a measure of intensity. A question of considerable concern to opinion researchers is whether one should include a middle alternative in unipolar questions. That is, should a 4-point scale be used or a 5-point scale. Including a middle alternative would offer an indifference point between being for or against a particular view.

The common practice in survey research has often been to omit middle categories explicitly and try to "push" respondents toward one end or the other of a dimension. The reasoning behind this practice is that very few people are genuinely indifferent or in the middle. Most who think of themselves as being in the middle are in fact leaning a little bit toward one or the other end of a continuum of wholehearted support to wholehearted opposition. It is clear from empirical work that an explicit middle alternative will often be taken by respondents in a forced-choice situation if it is offered explicitly. This suggests that removing the category might be artificially forcing a person to take a leaning they do not have.

◉ Research shows that including a middle alternative does in fact increase the size of that category but does not affect the ratio of "pro" to "con" responses or the size of the "don't know" category. As has generally been believed, those who do not feel very strongly about the issues are most susceptible to the effect of a middle alternative. On the whole, the inclusion of the middle category does not change the relationship between responses to the items and background characteristics such as the respondent's educational level. In some instances, however, the wording changes affect the intercorrelation among different opinion items that were supposed to measure the same underlying attitude.

Although it is impossible to make any hard and fast rule, our advice is contrary to contemporary general practice. We recommend including a middle category unless there are persuasive reasons not to. The addition of the middle category does not usually change the ratio of support to opposition, and the inclusion of the middle category will give as much information about the ratio of general favorableness to unfavorableness as will a question that omits the middle category. The size of the response to the middle category can give extra information about the intensity of attitudes—information that might be absent in a forced-choice situation. In general, we feel that middle-of-the-road or indifferent respondents should not be forced to express opinions.

Avoiding Double-Barreled and One-and-a-Half-Barreled Questions

One of the first things a researcher learns in questionnaire construction is to avoid double-barreled questions, that is, questions in which opinions about two objects are joined together so that respondents must answer two questions with one answer. Even a novice survey researcher would wince at a question like "In the coming presidential election, do you support Senator Pace and peace, or do you support Governor Guerra and war?"

Less blatant examples may slip by the inexperienced question formulator. Consider the following question. "Are you in favor of building more nuclear power plants so that we can have enough electricity to meet the country's needs, or are you opposed to more nuclear power plants even though this would mean less electricity?"

Combined in this one sentence are two questions about two different attitude objects: nuclear power plants and the supply of electricity. The sentence contains an assumption that nuclear power plants are the only way to increase the supply of electricity. Making such an assumption could load a question in favor of one particular kind of response. For example, if the first part of the question (about nuclear power plants) had a 50-50 opinion split in the population and the second part of the question (about having enough electricity) had a 90-10 opinion split, the conjoining of the two would suggest greater support for nuclear power plants than actually exists.

The size of the effect would depend on the relative strength of the opinion regarding the first issue. For issues about which opinions are very strongly held, the effect of the second barrel of the question might be reduced. Respondents with strongly held opinions might not pay any attention to the second part of the question. Correspondingly, the effect probably would be stronger for issues that are less strongly held or for respondents who hold less strong opinions on every issue. Questions need not be double-barreled in order to contain bias. Even with highly correlated opinions, many respondents will not respond the same way to both barrels of a question.

A less obvious version of a double-barreled question is one that attributes an attitude or a behavior to a well-known person or organization, such as the President of the United States or the United States Supreme Court. Even careful professional pollsters occasionally use such questions in an effort to make the question more specific. Some might argue that certain issues are so closely related to individuals or organizations that it is unrealistic to separate them. We believe, however, that it is usually better to separate issues from sources, if at all possible. This is especially true for issues that are not very salient to respondents. For such issues, respondents may react primarily on the basis of their attitude for or against the source and not on the issue.

A more subtle form of combining questions might be called the one-and-a-half-barreled question. In this form the question is posed about a single attitude object, and respondents are asked to respond along a scale showing favor or disfavor. The responses start quite straightforwardly along a single dimension, but somewhere along the line a second opinion object is introduced as part of the response continuum. A one-and-a-half-barreled question is illustrated in Figure 4.5.

Here the response categories begin with strong support and appear to be moving steadily toward strong opposition. All of a sudden, in the third statement, the mention of national defense (really another implicit question) brings to bear opinions about another attitude object, namely, defense policy. Then in the fourth response category, respondents are reminded that the agreement is with Russia. As a result, opinion was pulled toward less support for the treaty, whereas respondents reported stronger support for the SALT treaty in other surveys without such references.

Double-barreled questions and even one-and-a-half-barreled questions can be avoided if the question writer is alert to the problem. At times, however, even experienced question writers will fail

Figure 4.5. One-and-a-Half-Barreled-Questions Related to the SALT II Treaty.

The United States is now negotiating a strategic-arms agreement with the Soviet Union in what is known as SALT II. Which one of the following statements is closest to your opinion on these negotiations?

☐ I strongly support SALT II

☐ SALT II is somewhat disappointing, but on balance I have to support it.

☐ I would like to see more protection for the United States before I would be ready to support SALT II.

☐ I strongly oppose the SALT II arms agreement with the Russians.

☐ I don't know enough about the SALT II to have an opinion yet.

to notice that they have added an extra consideration somewhere along the line and that, as a result, two attitude objects have become joined in one question. Whenever—as in the SALT II question— the reasons for holding opinions appear as qualifications in the question itself or in a response category, a red flag should go up.

Bias Related to the Context and Meaning of Adjacent Questions

Interviews are forms of conversations. Whenever they take place in person or on the telephone, they flow as conversations (albeit sometimes rather peculiar conversations that are dominated by the question-and-answer sequence). Survey participants are responding not only to the actual questions but also to the context in which the questions are being asked. This includes such things as the stated purpose of the interview, the sponsor of the survey, the topics being asked, the norms of ordinary conversation between strangers, and other factors. Because questions are asked sequentially, answers to questions trigger thoughts in respondents' minds that may spill over and influence the answers to later questions.

The potential biasing effect of the positioning of questions in a questionnaire has long been recognized as a problem in survey and market research. Since the earliest days of survey research, studies of question order have produced both positive and negative results. Although we still do not understand many of the processes involved in order effects, research on cognitive aspects of surveys have enabled us to better understand the effect of order and gives us guidance about where to expect such effects. We can describe situations that should alert the investigator to the possibility of order effects. (The order problem is also discussed in Chapter Ten in the discussion of funneling and reverse funneling. For more detailed explanation of the cognitive mechanisms that create context and order effects, see Sudman, Bradburn, and Schwarz, 1996.)

Why should order matter? Stating explicit alternatives provides a context or framework within which the respondent answers questions. So, too, the order of questions provides a context within which questions are answered. Questions that are quite closely related tend to increase the saliency of particular aspects of the object. For example, in an early study by the American Marketing Association (1937), the placement of questions seemed to influence women's attitudes toward advertising. When questions about advertising followed questions about dress advertising, women's attitudes toward advertising were more positive than when general advertising questions preceded the dress questions. The explanation for this finding was that women tended to think about all types of advertising when the questions were not preceded by a more narrowly defining set of questions about dress advertising. Since women's attitudes toward dress advertising were more favorable than toward other types of advertising, they responded more favorably to advertising questions when earlier questions directed their attention toward dress advertising.

General and Specific Questions

Frequently we are interested in asking about attitudes toward some general object and then following up with questions about more specific aspects of that object. For instance, we might be interested in respondents' attitude toward abortion in general, and also about abortion in particular circumstances.

When a general question and a more specific-related question are asked together, the general question is affected by its position, whereas the more specific question is not. An example is two questions of this sort that appeared in the 1975 General Social Survey:

"Taking things all together, how would you describe your marriage? Would you say that your marriage is very happy, pretty happy, or not too happy?"

"Taken all together, how would you say things are these days? Would you say that you are very happy, pretty happy, or not too happy?"

The results of a split-ballot experiment (where the order of such questions was rotated) indicated that responses to the more general question relating to overall happiness was affected by the order of the questions, but the specific question on marriage happiness was not. (Of course, only respondents who were currently married were asked both questions.) One explanation for these findings is that when the general question comes first, it is answered in terms of one's whole life, including marriage. In contrast, when the more specific question about marriage happiness comes first, the overall happiness question is interpreted as referring to all other aspects of life except marriage. It is as if respondents, already having been asked the question about marriage happiness, were excluding this part of their lives from further consideration. Schuman, Presser, and Ludwig (1981) have reported similar findings for general and specific attitude items relating to abortion.

Although it is consistently found that only the general question is influenced by placement, the direction of the effect is not consistent and varies from question to question. In general, the direction of the effect appears to depend on the relation of the thoughts that are triggered by the specific question and how respondents interpret these as they answer the subsequent general question. If the specific question triggers positive associations, it appears to increase positive responses to the general question. If the thoughts aroused by the specific question are negative, the effect appears to be negative. The specific question may narrow the interpretation to the meaning of the general question and have a corresponding effect on answers to the general question. Although you may be able to predict the direction of the change by knowing whether the answers to the specific question tended to be positive or negative, split-ballot experiments are necessary to answer the question definitively.

Because you may be interested in comparing the answers of general questions to data from other surveys (for instance, to compare effects across time), it is usually best to put a general question first so that responses are not influenced by the more specific questions.

Putting the general question first also makes it easier for others to compare their data with yours.

Unintentionally Activating Norms and Values that Cause Biases

Many questions ask about attitudes that are grounded in values or norms. Posing questions that engage the same or similar values may activate thoughts about those values that then influence responses to subsequent questions.

We mentioned earlier that there is a general tendency for respondents to be consistent in their attitudes. This is particularly true with value-based questions. The placement of questions relative to one another may increase or decrease the cues for such value consistency. A well-known study by Cantril (1944) showed that questions about respondents' willingness to allow Americans to enlist in the British and German armies before 1941 was affected by the order in which the questions were asked. A higher proportion of respondents were willing to allow Americans to enlist in the German army when this question followed a similar question about enlisting in the British army than when it occurred in a reverse position.

Similar order effects were reported by Hyman and Sheatsley (1950) regarding reciprocity between the Soviet Union and the United States in the free exchange of news. Recent studies have shown similar effects in questions about trade deficits and import quotas. In these situations, questions involving the same underlying value (reciprocity) are asked about objects with differing degrees of popularity. When the more popular item comes first, it appears to have the effect of heightening the value, so that it applies in the second and less powerful instance. There is no reciprocal effect when reversed, however.

In this case, the rule is the opposite from that with general and specific items. It is best to ask the question that has the highest level of support first since it will not be affected by the order, but will activate consideration of the underlying value and make respondents think more about the implications of their answers for their value consistency.

Cautionary Note

At the beginning of this chapter we advised the writer of attitude questions to borrow questions (with credit) that have been used in other questionnaires. We end the chapter on a note of caution. Because many questions are susceptible to order effects, you must pay considerable attention to the order in which the borrowed questions were originally used, particularly if you are interested in trend data. The use of identically worded questions in different orders may have the effect of nullifying the advantage of using the same question. Identically worded questions may not have the same meaning to respondents when they appear in different contexts.

Summary

Attitude questions are highly susceptible to the wording that is used, especially if the questions are not very salient to respondents. ✳
In this chapter we discussed the basic preparation that should precede the writing of new questions. Using existing questions and scales is usually desirable, although you should be alert to possible context effects when comparing results.

There are two important points about measuring behavioral intentions. First, attitude measures will not always be sensitive enough to measure behavioral intentions, particularly when all attitudes are highly favorable. Second, usage intentions can be measured through likelihood estimates or through frequency estimates, and each measure is effective under different circumstances. Frequent behaviors are most accurately measured using frequency estimates. Infrequent behaviors are most accurately measured using likelihood estimates

We stressed that both you and the respondent must understand the attitude object and that you should avoid multiple concepts in

• Must be Clear to respondents

a single question. Alternative components of attitudes and measures of attitude strength were discussed, with a warning that these are not always consistent. The wording of explicit alternatives in closed questions can have a major impact on the distribution of attitude responses. The chapter concludes with a discussion of the effects of context and order of questions on responses.

Additional Reading

For a general discussion of attitudes and measurement issues, see the article "Attitude Measurement" by Schwarz (2001) in the *International Encyclopedia of the Social and Behavioral Sciences*; *Attitude Strength* (Petty and Krosnick, 1995); and *Attitudes and Persuasion* (Petty and Cacioppo, 1996). Schuman and Presser (1981) give excellent summaries of much of the empirical work on attitude question wording. Chapters 6–8 of *The Psychology of Survey Response* (Tourangeau, Rips, and Rasinski, 2000) and Chapters 3–6 in *Thinking About Answers* (Sudman, Bradburn, and Schwarz, 1996) review the cognitive psychological theory on which much of our discussion rests.

Chapter Five

Asking and Recording Open-Ended and Closed-Ended Questions

Previously we discussed a number of issues pertaining to the formulation of questions about attitude or opinions. This chapter is concerned with techniques for recording answers to questions. To some extent, the distinction between question formulation and techniques for recording answers is an artificial one, because the form of the question often dictates the most appropriate technique for recording the answer—that is, some questions take on their meaning by their response categories. For example, the question used for many years in the Current Population Survey to measure employment status was "What were you doing most of last week?" The question only became meaningful when the response categories were incorporated into the question: "What were you doing most of last week—working, keeping house, going to school, or something else?"

Of course, many of the examples given in the previous chapter also specified the answer categories. However, a number of additional critical issues and options regarding response formats exist, and we believe they justify their own chapter. Although we cannot hope to cover every possible form of response format that has been used in survey research, we shall mention the principal variations and highlight a few valuable response formats we believe are underutilized in current practice.

Checklist of Major Points

1. Use open-ended questions sparingly; they are primarily useful for developmental work, to explore a topic in depth, and to obtain quotable material. Closed-ended questions are more difficult to construct, but they are easier to analyze and generate less unwanted interviewer and coder variance.

2. Avoid interviewer field coding if at all possible. If necessary, it is better to have field coding done by the respondent.

3. Start with the end of a scale that is the *least* socially desirable. Otherwise, the respondent may choose a socially desirable answer without hearing or reading the entire set of responses.

4. Do not use verbal rating scales with more than four or five verbal points. For more detailed scales, use numerical scales.

5. Consider using analogies such as thermometers, ladders, telephone dials, and clocks for numerical scales with many points.

6. Respondents can rank their preferences for alternatives only when they can see or remember all alternatives. In telephone interviews, ranking should be limited to two or three alternatives at a time. In self-administered and face-to-face interviews where cards are used, respondents can rank no more than four or five alternatives. If many alternatives are present, respondents can rank the three most desirable and the three least desirable.

7. Rankings can be obtained by a series of paired-comparison questions. Respondent fatigue, however, limits the number of alternatives that can be ranked.

8. Rather than having people respond to a list simply by telling them to "Check as many as apply," the information will be much more complete and valuable if each item is individually responded to with a "yes" or "no," "applies" or "does not apply," "true for me" or "not true for me," and the like.

9. In face-to-face interviewing, even very complex ratings can be accomplished by means of card-sorting procedures.

Using Open-Answer Formats

A potentially valuable part of any survey questionnaire consists of open-ended questions. Respondents answer open-ended questions in their own words, rather than just tick one of the limited list of alternatives provided by the surveyor. The interviewer simply records verbatim the respondent's answer to the question. Blank spaces or fields are left in the questionnaire after the question, and the respondent or the interviewer writes or types in a response. Interviewers are expected to indicate by probe marks (usually an X placed after a respondent's answer) where they intervened to ask a question or to seek clarification. An example of a respondent and interviewer dialogue in the open-answer format might be as follows:

Interviewer: What are the most important problems facing the nation today?

Respondent: I don't know. There are so many.

Interviewer: That's right; I'd just like to know what you think are the most important problems.

Respondent: Well, there's certainly government spending.

Interviewer: Government spending. How do you mean? Could you explain that a little? What do you have in mind when you say "government spending"?

Respondent: There's no end to it. We have to cut down federal spending somehow.

Interviewer: Any others?

Respondent: No, I think those are the most important ones.

The first response indicates that the respondent may need more time or more license to think about the question. The interviewer's probe gives the respondent encouragement and time to think. The next response, "government spending," is ambiguous, since it does not specify what level of government is meant or what aspect of spending. Again the interviewer must probe. The interviewer then asks the final follow-up question.

Advantages and Disadvantages of Open-Ended Questions

The advantages of the open-ended format are considerable, but so are its disadvantages. In the hands of a good interviewer, the open format allows and encourages respondents to fully give their opinions with as much nuance as they are capable of. It also allows respondents to make distinctions that are not usually possible with precoded (or closed-ended) formats (see next section), and it allows them to express themselves in language that is comfortable for them and congenial to their views. In many instances an open-ended format can also produce vignettes of considerable richness and quotable material that will enliven research reports. It is an invaluable tool when you want to go deeply into a particular topic, and it is an absolutely essential tool when you are beginning work in an area and need to explore all aspects of an opinion area.

Yet the richness of the material can also be disadvantageous if you need to summarize the data in concise form. For example, to reduce the complexity of the data to fewer or simpler categories and in order to treat the data statistically, you must code responses into categories that can be counted. Coding free-response material (sometimes called cognitive responses or verbal protocols) is not only time-consuming and costly but it also introduces a degree of coding error. If the material is very elaborate, you must develop coding manuals, train coders to use the categories, and do periodic reliability checks in order to estimate the amount of coding error. All of this costs time and money, and—as with any addition to a surveying process—allows for even more error.

But it isn't only the results that are affected by open-ended questioning. Open-ended questions also take more time, thought, patience, and concentration to answer than closed questions. If the question comes more or less out of the blue, the respondents' thoughts will not be organized and may emerge somewhat haphazardly and in a confused fashion.

What is reported first is sometimes taken by investigators to indicate the saliency of issues or the importance of things to the respondents. We would caution against such interpretations, however. Many aspects of the questioning process, including especially the preceding questions, affect what is easily accessible cognitively and likely to be reported first. The order in which things are reported may be more a function of the interview situation than a characteristic of the respondent. See the discussion of context effects in Chapter Four for a fuller discussion.

Uncovering Key Insights from Open-Ended Questions

Often valuable information is overlooked in answers to open-ended questions. In some cases, researchers may dismiss any comments that conflict with their own analysis of the issues.

In other cases, researchers may pay attention only to the most commonly mentioned open-ended answers and not to the unique ones. One advantage of open-ended questions is that they can uncover uncommon but intelligent opinions of which the surveyor would otherwise have remained unaware. If surveyors focus only on frequent responses, they will continue to be unaware of these ideas.

Of course, the most frequent responses to open-ended questions are also valuable. When evaluating service satisfaction, for instance, open-ended questions often point to the service issues that are most important to customers. Although customers might rate a number of service aspects as low or as high, it will be the vehement comments or the effusive ones that will show what's really important to them.

Improving the Quality of Open-Ended Questions

For respondents to provide meaningful answers of the sort that justify the expense of using open-ended questions, they must be given time to get their thoughts in order and then express them fully on a topic. They can be rushed along only at the cost of losing considerable amounts of information.

Using open-ended questions requires greater interviewer skill in recognizing ambiguities of response and in probing and drawing respondents out, particularly those who are reticent or not highly verbal. This aspect of the open-ended format has made some investigators wary of its use except in situations when they have the time and money to provide well-trained and well-supervised interviewers and coders. Open-ended response formats may work better with telephone interviews, where close supervision of interviewer quality can be maintained, although there is evidence that shorter answers to open-ended questions are given on the telephone (Groves and Kahn, 1979). No matter how well controlled the interviewers may be, however, factors such as carelessness and verbal facility will generate greater individual variance among respondents than would be the case with precoded questions.

Questions concerning age, state of residence, or credit-hours earned may be more easily answered by filling in blanks than by selecting among categories. If the answers are numerical, an open-answer response mode can enhance the power of inferential statistical procedures. Even if these handwritten answers are eventually assigned to categories for analysis, there is more flexibility in determining what categories can be used. If estimates are being taken (such as distance to work or weight), however, it is usually better to offer response categories.

Using Closed-Answer Formats

A closed-answer response is recorded in predetermined categories selected by respondents or the interviewer as appropriate. These involve a wide range of questions, including those that ask respondents to check the box or circle the response that is most appropriate. For closed questions, a distinction is made between "field-coded" (interviewer-selected) response categories and "pre-coded" (respondent-selected) categories.

The Dangers of Field Coding

In a field-coded question, the question itself might be identical to that of an open-answer format, but instead of a blank space for the interviewer to write in the respondent's exact words, a set of codes are printed or appear on the screen. The interviewer simply checks each topic that is mentioned. For example, for the question "What are the most important problems facing the nation today?" the topics might include such things as terrorism, deficit spending, unemployment, the Middle East situation, health care costs, and the environment. Such categories are typically formulated from pretests or from results of the same question used in an open-ended fashion.

In order to preserve the information about the order in which answers were given, the questionnaire might include precoded responses in separate columns for first-mentioned topic, second-mentioned topic, and so on. With such field coding, provision can be made for an "Other" category, so that responses that have not been anticipated or are not frequent enough to warrant a separate coding category can also be recorded.

Field coding is a technique applied by those who wish to retain the advantages of the open format, but without its cost disadvantages. It allows respondents to answer in their own words and it reduces costs and coding time, since the interviewer codes the respondents' answers into predetermined response categories at the time of interview. Interviewers are often instructed to write the respondents' verbatim answers and to then do the coding after the response is completely recorded in order not to prejudge the meaning. In practice, however, when precodes are available, interviewers typically do not fully record answers, particularly if the precodes would make the verbatim comments redundant. However, if the interviewer does not record the respondent's answers

verbatim, there is no way to check the accuracy of the interviewer's field coding.

Unfortunately, the field-coding technique looks better in theory than in practice. Since coding problems occur even when independent coders have the answers written in front of them and
have a manual to explain coding categories, the problems are
multiplied when a less trained interviewer tries to fit real-time
responses into a set of succinct codes. Although interviewers can
ask respondents to elaborate further if there is doubt about an answer's category, the pressure of the interview situation makes it
likely that greater coding error will be introduced in a field-coding
situation than in office coding.

We recommend that field coding be avoided if at all possible. If
it seems necessary in some cases, we recommend that, at least in
face-to-face interviews, respondents be allowed to answer in their
own words and then a printed card with coding categories be
shown. The coding categories should be printed on a card, so that
they may be shown to the respondents. The interviewer and the
respondent can then agree which category the response should fit
into. This method of involving the respondent in the coding helps
convert the question into a precoded question without it unnatu-
rally constraining the response categories.

Making Precoded Questions More Effective

In the precoded questions, response alternatives are either explicitly
stated in the question, such as with telephone interviewing, or they
may be printed on a card the respondent is given in a face-to-face (or
computer–screen-to-face) situation. For example, respondents may
be asked, "In general, do you find life exciting, pretty routine, or dull?"
They are then asked to choose one of the response categories. If
respondents choose to say something else, interviewers are instructed
to probe, to get respondents to choose one of the categories, or to
match respondents' answers to one of the answer categories.

When precoded questions are used, much of the cognitive work has already been done through pretesting and other developmental work. Respondents are given both the topic and the dimensions on which answers are wanted. Precoding makes the task easier and more passive for respondents because they can sit back and respond to fairly complex questions without having to search their own memories and organize their own thoughts. However, this may lead to more superficial responses, and, if the questions are not well formulated, it may also lead to biases in the answers.

Precodes appear to guarantee comparability of responses across individuals because they use the same terms. That appearance may be illusory if different respondents interpret questions differently, or if the categories are not interpreted by respondents as you intend. In experiments where both free-response formats and precoded formats have been used (such as in questions about personal worries or aspects of jobs that are important to individuals), the distribution of responses from open-ended questions is different from the distribution one gets from the precoded questions. Why these differences appear or which form is more valid is not known.

In the fully precoded question, the response categories can be printed in the questionnaire or appear on the screen, and the interviewer selects the answer given by the respondents. Precodes serve two purposes. First, they give the response dimensions (and scale) along which the investigator wishes the respondents to respond. Second, they provide the numerical codes that will then be used for the machine processing of the data. If a printed questionnaire is set up properly, an operator can key the data directly from the questionnaire without having to transcribe data from the questionnaire to a coding or keying sheet.

For very large surveys (with five thousand or more respondents), optical-scanning technology is sufficiently well developed that questionnaires may be designed so that they are easy for interviewers to use and can also be optically scanned to transfer the data directly from the questionnaire to machine-readable form. For computer-assisted interviewing or Web surveys, the answers are recorded electronically when the interviewer or respondent selects them.

Constructing Response Categories

The wording and number of response categories can influence responses. Consider these two examples:

> Compared with American families in general, would you say your family income is far below average, below average, average, above average, or far above average? (Probe) Just your best guess.

> Compared with American families in general, would you say your family income is poor, fair, good, or excellent?

There are three points about these examples that have general application to the construction of response categories. The first is that the five categories in the first question are about the maximum number that respondents can understand without the help of visual aids. Even five categories stretch the respondents' abilities to keep the whole scale in mind at once. In this instance, however, respondents are able to anchor the scale with two categories above and two below "average," and thus they do not have to pay too much attention to the actual words. When you are using a simple verbal rating scale in which each term is different, as in the second question, the scale should include no more than four items unless the items appear on a printed list given to respondents.

Second, note that the two questions are quite different. The first invokes the notion of average income, which is a number that may or may not be known to respondents. Although the question is clearly intended to ask about the respondents' perceptions of their relative incomes rather than actual calculations, still, to an unknown degree, respondents will have more or less accurate information about the "average" against which they are asked to compare their incomes. If you are really interested in finding out where respondents' income is compared to the average, you can compute it from the reported family income and published figures about average family income.

⸰ Questions using the concept of "average" will get different responses from those that use an absolute rating scale based on such terms as "excellent," "good," "fair," and "poor." A scale based on absolute terms is clearly subjective and has no objective middle point. It may well be a better type of scale to use if you are interested in people's views about how well off they are in particular dimensions of their lives.

When concepts like "average" are used, there must be an odd number of points (such as 5, 7, or 9) on the rating scale symmetrical around the middle or average point. In some cases, using an odd number of points on the rating scale will produce a pileup in the middle category. With use of the term "average," however, the pileup tends to occur either in the first category above average or the first category below average, depending on the content of the question. Few people like to be average (with income being one notable exception). The use of absolute rating points tends to give a somewhat more symmetrical distribution of response, although this is not invariably the case.

⸰ The third consideration in these types of scales is whether to start with the lowest (or worst) category and proceed to the highest (or best) category or vice versa. Although we know of no good evidence that one form is universally better than another, it is our view that if numbers are used, they should increase from left to right (or top to bottom) and this should correspond with the lowest (or worst) category and proceed to the highest (or best). Some questions seem to lend themselves more naturally to starting with the best end of the scale and proceeding to the worst, and others seem to lend themselves better to a reverse ordering. We think a good general rule to follow is to start with the end of the scale that is the least desirable. If the more desirable categories come first, the respondent might choose one of those categories without waiting to hear the entire set of response categories.

Using Numerical Rating Scales

If you wish to go to a rating scale with more than seven points, it can sometimes be helpful to use a visual aid or device that employs something beyond the use of words. Most of the examples we will present here are variations on a fairly simple theme. The basic strategy is to use a numerical scale running from 0 or 1 to some number and give English value equivalents to the lowest and the highest categories as anchoring points for the ends of the scales. Figure 5.2 gives one example of this method. The figure shows the question as it appears in the questionnaire seen only by the interviewer and as it appears on the card seen by the respondent. If a series of substantive opinion questions is to be asked, and if the same scale can be used for all questions, the interviewer can read the anchoring points to the respondent for each separate question.

Odd or Even?

A much-debated point is whether to give respondents an odd or even number of response categories. We believe you must always provide for an odd number of categories, in order to reserve a middle or indifferent point for respondents who insist on taking middle positions or who are undecided or indifferent about the two ends of the continuum. The difference lies in whether you explicitly give respondents the middle option or whether you give them an even number of categories and conceal the middle position from them.

If presented with an even number of response categories, respondents who feel in the middle must "lean" toward one end or the other of the distribution unless they are firm about their middle position. The arguments for using even or odd numbers of categories are similar to those described in Chapter Four in the section

"Using Questions That Include a Middle Point." There is no right or wrong number of categories. It depends entirely on the research topic being investigated and how important it is to you to have some indication of the direction in which people in the middle are leaning. With a very large number of points on the scale, the question is probably moot, since respondents would be responding more to the approximate position than they would be to the actual numbers.

Few or Many?

Another issue is how many categories should be offered and on what scale (5 points, 7 points, 9 points?). Some think that offering a scale with a larger number of points will help increase the variance in responses and better help distinguish extreme opinions.

Although a number of theoretical considerations exist, how to number categories is generally determined by weighing how much space one wants to use against what can provide the greatest differentiation. If the intervals are spaced out to maximize variation (through the use of pilot tests), fewer boxes will be needed. If precision is a concern, use fill-in-the-blank questions.

A method that obtains readings by use of a 100-point scale is shown in Figure 5.1. Here the scale is analogous to a thermometer, containing many numbers with which respondents will be familiar. Another common image used in rating scales is that of a ladder. The image, introduced by Cantril (1965), seems particularly well adapted to ratings that involve vertical or hierarchical dimensions, such as occupational prestige ratings or questions about the degree to which one has fulfilled one's aspirations. Other graphic images, limited only by the imagination of the investigator and the necessity that respondents understand them, might be used for these types of scales. The difficulty with these scales is they often become idiosyncratic to the topic, and care must be taken to ensure that they will be accepted by the parties to whom the research will be presented (policymakers, sponsors, editors, or reviewers).

Figure 5.1. A Rating Thermometer.

I'd like to get your feelings toward some of our political leaders and other people who are in the news these days. I'll read the name of a person and I'd like you to rate that person using something we call the feeling thermometer. It is on Page 2 of your booklet. The feeling thermometer can rate people from 0 to 100 degrees. Ratings between 50 degrees and 100 degrees mean that you feel favorable and warm toward the person. Ratings between 0 degree and 50 degrees mean that you don't feel favorable toward the person. Rating the person at the midpoint, the 50-degree mark, means you don't feel particularly warm or cold toward the person. If we come to a person whose name you don't recognize, you don't need to rate that person. Just tell me and we'll move on to the next one. The first person is Bill Clinton. Where on that feeling thermometer would you rate Bill Clinton?

a. Bill Clinton   _____

b. Al Gore   _____

c. George W. Bush   _____

d. Pat Buchanan   _____

e. Ralph Nader   _____

f. John McCain   _____

g. Bill Bradley   _____

h. Joseph Lieberman   _____

i. Dick Cheney   _____

j. Hillary Clinton   _____

100°	Very Warm or Favorable Feeling
85°	Quite Warm or Favorable Feeling
70°	Fairly Warm or Favorable Feeling
60°	A Bit More Warm or Favorable Than Cold Feeling
50°	No Feeling at All
40°	A Bit More Cold or Unfavorable Feeling
30°	Fairly Cold or Unfavorable Feeling
15°	Quite Cold or Unfavorable Feeling
0°	Very Cold or Unfavorable Feeling

Source: Burns and others, 2001.

Visual aids are difficult for telephone interviewing, but it is possible to ask respondents to look at their telephone keypads and use the numbers on the keypad as a rating scale. They can be told that 1 represents the low point on the scale and 8 or 9 the other end of the scale. A nondigital clock or watch face might be another familiar graphic form that could be used.

Blanks or Intervals?

Researchers must decide what format of questionnaire they will use. Although the fill-in-the-blank version is generally preferable, if interval questions are used, appropriate intervals must be carefully established. Whereas frequency-related questions might use six categories (0, 1–2, 3–5, 6–10, 10–20, 20–30), a number of different intervals could be used (for instance, 0, 1–5, 6–10, 11–15, 16–20, 20–30). As pointed out in Chapter 4 (p.134) it is important to remember that zero must be its own separate category. It is also important to have some idea from pretests or other data what the distribution of frequencies is likely to be. Respondents use the range of frequencies presented in the response categories to form ideas about what the researcher believes the distribution to be. There is abundant evidence that the categories presented to respondents influence their responses and can alter substantially the frequency estimates based on the data.

Using Rankings

Sometimes you may be interested in the relative ranking of attributes or the rank ordering of preferences among different policy positions rather than in a respondent's agreement or disagreement with particular opinions. Rankings are most easily done in written questionnaires, where respondents can see all the alternatives to be ranked and can fill in the rankings themselves. It is possible, however, to rank a small number of items in personal interviews. It is

Figure 5.2. Numerical Rating Scale.

Consider this question from the General Social Survey from NORC (1980):

> Some people think that the government in Washington ought to reduce the income differences between the rich and the poor, perhaps by raising the taxes of wealthy families or by giving income assistance to the poor. Others think that the government should not concern itself with reducing this income difference between the rich and the poor. *(Hand respondent card.)*

Here is a card with a scale from 1 to 7. Think of a score of 1 as meaning that the government ought to reduce the income differences between rich and poor, and a score of 7 as meaning that the government should not concern itself with reducing income differences. What score between 1 and 7 comes closest to the way you feel? *(Circle one.)*

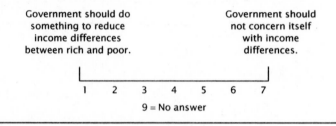

| Government should do something to reduce income differences between rich and poor. | | | | | | Government should not concern itself with income differences. |

1   2   3   4   5   6   7

9 = No answer

Source: National Opinion Research Center, 1980.

much more difficult to do complete ranking on the telephone, although partial rankings may be possible.

Ranking Complete Preferences

Figure 5.3 shows a method of ranking five aspects of a job in order of preference. The respondent has a card that lists all aspects of the job to be ranked. That way all the rank categories are visible at once. Also note that the respondent need rank only four items explicitly; by elimination, the remaining item is ranked fifth.

We know of no studies on the number of items that can be ranked by this method before the respondent becomes confused, although we think that five to seven may be the upper limit. When there are larger numbers of items that cannot be conveniently ranked, other methods must be employed. These methods generally take the form of asking the respondent to rank only those items at

Figure 5.3. Ranking Complete Preferences of Job Qualities.

Would you please look at this card and tell me which one thing on this list you would *most* prefer in a job? *(Circle one code in Column A.)*

Which comes *next*? *(Circle one code in Column B.)*

Which is the *third* most important? *(Circle one code in Column C.)*

Which is the *fourth* most important? *(Circle one code in Column D.)*

	A *Most*	*B* *Next*	*C* *Third*	*D* *Fourth*
1. High income	1	2	3	4
2. No danger of being fired	1	2	3	4
3. Working hours are short, lots of free time	1	2	3	4
4. Chances for advancement	1	2	3	4
5. Work important and gives a feeling of accomplishment	1	2	3	4

Source: National Opinion Research Center, 1980.

each end of the distribution (the best and the worst). The respondent ranks the most important and the least important only, allowing the middle part to be left unranked. This seems to be a sensible procedure, since most people have fairly clear ideas of what they would rank high and what they would rank low but are rather uncertain about the rankings in the middle. Indeed, with ranking tasks of more than four or five items, respondents often complain of the difficulty of the task and the uncertainty of their preferences for the middle rankings.

Ranking Extreme Preferences

Another method for obtaining ranks of a rather large number of attributes is shown in Figure 5.4, which contains thirteen qualities thought to be desirable in children. The respondents are not asked to rank all thirteen. Instead, they are asked to select the three qualities they think are the most desirable. From these three, they are asked to pick the one that would be most desirable, thus establishing rank one. If it is important to establish second- and third-place rankings, respondents may pick among the remaining two what they think is the next desirable. The third-ranked quality would thereby be established by elimination. Respondents are also asked to pick the three least desirable qualities and, among those three, the one they consider the least important. In this manner fairly clear differentiations can be built up at each end of the scale, but no differentiation in the middle.

Sometimes respondents find ranking difficult to do and will select no more than a first choice. Rankings are particularly difficult for respondents when the items to be ranked are quite different from one another (such as policy preferences) or are all either very desirable or very undesirable.

Ranking Through Paired Comparison

Another method for obtaining rankings, which is not often used in surveys but which we think could be more widely used, is paired comparisons. Each pair of alternatives is compared and ranked according to preference. Several examples involving paired comparison are given in Figure 5.5. Questions 5 through 7, for example, involve three response alternatives. The paired-comparison method has the advantage that the respondent considers each alternative in comparison with each other alternative, one at a time. Respondents can consider preferences in a more discrete fashion. It is a particularly good method when the choices are among objects that are all desirable or undesirable.

If there is a consistent preference structure, the method should obtain a transitive ordering of the alternatives; that is, if A is preferred to B and B is preferred to C, then A should be preferred to C. Sometimes, however, it turns out that the ordering is not transitive: A is preferred to B, B is preferred to C, but C is preferred to A. The straight ranking method forces transitivity on the rankings. If you use that method, you might fail to discover that people's preferences

Figure 5.4. Ranking Extreme Preferences of Children's Qualities.

Now to a different subject. *(Hand R. Card I.)*

A. Which *three* qualities listed on this card would you say are the *most desirable* for a child to have? *(Circle THREE CODES ONLY in Column A.)*

B. Which *one of these three* is the *most* desirable of all? *(Read the three R. chose. Circle ONE CODE ONLY in Column B.)*

C. All of the qualities listed on this card may be desirable, but could you tell me which *three* you consider *least important*? *(Circle THREE CODES ONLY in Column C.)*

D. And which *one* of these three is *least important* of all? *(Read the three R. chose. Circle ONE CODE ONLY in Column D.)*

	Most Desirable		Least Important	
	A Three Most	B One Most	C Three Least	D One Least
1. that a child has good manners.	2	1	4	5
2. that a child tries hard to succeed.	2	1	4	5
3. that a child is honest.	2	1	4	5
4. that a child is neat and clean.	2	1	4	5
5. that a child has good sense and sound judgment.	2	1	4	5
6. that a child has self-control.	2	1	4	5
7. that he acts like a boy or she acts like a girl.	2	1	4	5
8. that a child gets along well with other children.	2	1	4	5
9. that a child obeys his or her parents well.	2	1	4	5
10. that a child is responsible.	2	1	4	5
11. that a child is considerate of others.	2	1	4	5
12. that a child is interested in how and why things happen.	2	1	4	5
13. that a child is a good student.	2	1	4	5

Source: National Opinion Research Center, 1980.

Figure 5.5. Paired-Comparison Method of Ranking.

1. On balance which of these two groups do you think is making more effort to look after the environment?
   - ☐ Business and industry
   - ☐ People in general

2. And which of these two groups do you think is making more effort to look after the environment?
   - ☐ Government
   - ☐ Business and Industry

3. And which of these two groups is making more effort to look after the environment?
   - ☐ People in general
   - ☐ Government

4. And which of these two groups is making more efforts to look after the environment?
   - ☐ Scientists
   - ☐ People in general

5. And which of these two groups is making more efforts to look after the environment?
   - ☐ Government
   - ☐ Scientists

6. And which of these two groups is making more effort to look after the environment?
   - ☐ Scientists
   - ☐ Business and industry?

Source: Adapted from GSS, 2000.

are not so consistent as they appear to be. If inconsistencies in ranking appear through the use of the paired-comparison method, you can then follow up with questions about why the apparent inconsistency appears and thereby learn more about respondents' attitudes. If the question concerns policy, further investigation may reveal subtleties of policy preferences that when taken together are not seen but that become apparent when judged two at a time.

The paired-comparison method becomes unwieldy when a large number of items need to be compared. The number of comparisons increases geometrically with the number of alternatives. We suspect that four alternatives are about the maximum that can be used with the paired-comparison method in the normal survey situation. It is a method, however, that might be easier to use on the telephone than some of the straight ranking methods, since respondents have to keep only two things in mind at once.

Using Lists

Certain series of questions lend themselves to a list format. For example, respondents may be given a list of adjectives and asked to list the ones that they might use to describe themselves. Such a question is shown in Figure 5.6. In format A, a list of adjectives is given, and respondents are asked to circle as many as apply to themselves. In format B, respondents are asked to go through the list one by one and check whether each adjective describes them or does not describe them. Format A is adapted from a self-administered questionnaire given to college students. It is economical in format and allows the investigator to obtain a great deal of data in a small space. Although such a large number of adjectives is feasible in a self-administered questionnaire, it would be problematic in a personal interview. An interview situation would certainly require a card for respondents to look at while answering.

Although format B appears to be somewhat more cluttered and less appealing on a self-administered questionnaire, it will produce better and more useful responses. With format A ("[Circle] as many

Figure 5.6. Two Formats for Listing Adjectives in Self-Descriptions.

FORMAT A

Listed below are some adjectives, some of which are "favorable," some of which are "unfavorable," and some of which are neither.

Please circle the ones that best describe you. Consider as ideal only those that are most characteristic of you as a person. Most people choose five or six, but you may choose more or fewer if you want to.

Ambitious	1	Happy	5	Obliging	9
Calm	2	High Strung	6	Outgoing	10
Cooperative	3	Impetuous	7	Quiet	11
Dominant	4	Moody	8	Talkative	12

FORMAT B

Listed below are some adjectives, some of which are "favorable," some of which are "unfavorable," some of which are neither.

Please indicate for each adjective whether the adjective describes you or does not describe you.

	Describes me	Does not describe me	Don't know
Ambitious	1	2	3
Calm	1	2	3
Cooperative	1	2	3
Dominant	1	2	3
Happy	1	2	3
High Strung	1	2	3
Impetuous	1	2	3
Moody	1	2	3
Obliging	1	2	3
Outgoing	1	2	3
Quiet	1	2	3
Talkative	1	2	3

Source: Adapted from National Opinion Research Center; format A, 1961; format B, 1982.

as apply"), it is difficult to interpret what the absence of a check mark means. Although the presence of a check mark indicates a positive instance, its omission might indicate that in fact the adjective does not apply, or that respondents did not notice that adjective because they were hurrying over the list, or that they were not sure whether it would apply. There also are individual differences in the disposition to use large or small numbers of adjectives to describe oneself, which further complicates the interpretation of data based on the instruction "Check as many as apply."

In format B, respondents have to consider each adjective and decide whether it applies or does not apply to them. If they do not check an adjective, the investigator may infer that respondents hurried over it without seeing it or that they could not decide whether it applied to them. Even though it is somewhat more cumbersome to administer, we strongly recommend that when lists are used, each item be responded to with a "yes" or a "no," an "applies" or "does not apply," or a "true for me" or "not true for me," rather than with the instruction "Check as many as apply." Research indicates that the "Check as many as apply" format gets fewer responses than format B.

Visual and Manual Aids

We have discussed a number of ways to provide response formats. All of these depend on verbal cues or a written card that the respondents and interviewer can read. These cards typically provide text (or some portion of text) that the interviewer reads to the respondent. Even though the respondents are holding the cards, it is important that the interviewers actually read the questions aloud to avoid language problems or sight difficulties. In all these strategies, the respondent is basically passive, and the interview should flow in a question-and-answer format, with the respondent being called on to do nothing but speak. In this section we consider a few response formats that provide respondents with visual material or materials that require them to do something other than talk.

Pictures

The advent of Web-based surveys greatly increases the opportunity to use pictures in a questionnaire. Complex opinions, particularly those respondents might have difficulty keeping in mind through simply hearing them, can be presented pictorially. This method enables you to present two or more opinions simultaneously, and the format allows respondents to consider their own opinions in relation to the questions. In this way, respondents can imagine questions as being concretely expressed by individuals, rather than in the abstract.

If you wished to consider the effect of the characteristics of the person expressing the opinion as well as the opinion itself, you could use the pictorial form to indicate the opinion, the sex, or the ethnic identity of the person holding the opinion. Of course, pictorial stimuli would be necessary if attitudes about a product's appearance, style, or packaging were being investigated.

Card Sorting

When you want to rate a large number of items or make very difficult ratings in a face-to-face interview, card sorting is a useful device. Here the respondents sort cards into piles according to some set of instructions, as in Figure 5.7. Although using cards increases the amount of material interviewers must carry with them, most interviewers are generally enthusiastic about using such materials because card tasks give respondents something active to do during the course of the interview. Researchers report that a card task breaks up the routine of the interview and effectively motivates respondents to answer questions further on in the interview.

The card-sorting task can be extended beyond sorting on one dimension. NORC successfully used this method in a study where respondents' opinions about possible political events were rated on two dimensions: (1) the respondents' beliefs about the probability

Figure 5.7. Card Sorting.

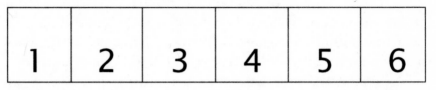

Least Serious   Most Serious

Here is a ruler with six spaces on it *(Hand ruler to respondent.)* and several cards with kinds of crimes on them. *(Hand crime cards to respondent.)* The space at the right end of the ruler, number six, is for crimes that you think are most serious. If you think the crime listed on the card is most serious, put it in the space at the right-hand end of the ruler. The space at the left-hand end of the ruler is for crimes that you think are least serious. If you think the crime listed on the card is least serious, put the card in the space at the left-hand end of the ruler. If you think the offense falls somewhere in between, just put it in the space that matches how serious you think that offense is. If you change your mind, just put the card where you think it goes.

(Observe the respondent's placement of the cards. If he seems unsure of how to perform the task, explain it again, remaining close to the above wording. After he has placed all eight cards, continue below.)

Are you sure that you have all the cards where you want them? You may go back and change them if you want.

(When the respondent is sure he's through, pick up the cards from one space at a time and record below the number of the space in which the respondent placed the card. Code 7 if the respondent could not place a card on the ruler.)

	Placed in Space Number
Stealing $500 in cash from an employer	_____
Passing bad checks for $500	_____
Cheating a relative out of $500	_____
Cheating a business partner out of $500	
Stealing $500 worth of goods from a giant corporation	_____
Cheating the government out of $500 in taxes	_____
Cheating a stranger out of $500 in a business scheme	_____
Stealing $500 worth of supplies, materials, or goods from an employer	_____

Source: National Opinion Research Center, 1966.

that the events would occur and (2) their opinions of the desirability or undesirability of the particular event. In order to secure these ratings, the interviewer needed more than a single measuring device, such as that shown in Figure 5.8. The device designed for this purpose was a matrix that looked somewhat like a checkerboard.

Down the side of the matrix, on a scale from 10 to 0, was a measure of the probability that the event would occur. Across the top of the matrix was the positive or negative value the respondent would place on the event if it did occur. In this way the investigator was able to calculate the subjective expected utility of respondents for a particular set of events, such as the labeling of genetically altered foods or a peace treaty between North and South Korea. Respondents were given a large foldout board with seventy-seven pockets in a matrix form, as shown schematically in Figure 5.8. For each event being rated, respondents placed a card with the name of the event in the pocket that represented both the probability that the event would occur (the rows) and the desirability of the event (the columns).

Figure 5.8. Card Sorting in Two Dimensions.

	Want Very Much Not to Happen			Don't Care One Way or Another			Want Very Much to Happen
10 Certain or							
Nearly Certain	−3	−2	−1	0	+ 1	+2	+3
9	−3	−2	−1	0	+ 1	+2	+3
8	−3	−2	−1	0	+ 1	+2	+3
7	−3	−2	−1	0	+ 1	+2	+3
6	−3	−2	−1	0	+ 1	+2	+3
5 As Likely as							
Not Likely	−3	−2	−1	0	+ 1	+2	+3
4	−3	−2	−1	0	+ 1	+2	+3
3	−3	−2	−1	0	+ 1	+2	+3
2	−3	−2	−1	0	+ 1	+2	+3
1	−3	−2	−1	0	+ 1	+2	+3
0 Impossible or							
Nearly Impossible	−3	−2	−1	0	+ 1	+2	+3

Source: National Opinion Research Center, 1963.

Card sorting techniques could be used effectively in Web-based surveys employing the programming technology that is used in computer games.

Summary

This chapter started with a discussion of the uses of open-answer formats and closed-answer formats (with precoded or field-coded response categories). Although there are some important uses of open answers, most questions you write should probably be precoded. Field coding by the interviewer should be avoided as much as possible, since it introduces another possible source of error.

Respondents can generally only remember a maximum of five responses unless visual cues are used. Using graphic images such as thermometers and ladders and using card sorting for complex ratings has been effective, even in two dimensions.

In discussing procedures for obtaining rankings, we pointed out that respondents have great difficulty ranking many items and that, in this case, you might be willing to settle for the three most and the three least desirable items. Paired comparisons are also possible, but the number that can be ranked is limited by respondent fatigue. Even at the risk of boring the respondent, however, we argue that it is better to obtain an answer to each item on a list, rather than to tell respondents to indicate only those that apply.

Additional Reading

There are not many easily available discussions of response options for questions. One of the best is Don Dilman's *Mail and Internet Surveys: The Tailored Design Method, 2nd edition* (2000).

Much more is available on methods of combining the data from separate questions into scales for analytic purposes. A good general discussion of attitude scaling is in Kidder (1981, chap. 9) and Bailey (1978). A somewhat more technical treatment of scaling is found in McIver and Carmines (1981).

Chapter Six

Asking Questions that Measure Knowledge

Although not so common as behavioral questions, knowledge-related questions have many uses in surveys. They can be used to help explain political behavior, which is strongly impacted by one's level of knowledge. They can be used by agencies such as the U.S. Department of Education to determine the literacy and educational achievement of adults as an indication of the effectiveness of the educational process.

They can be used for designing and implementing information programs or advertising campaigns on public health issues such as cancer or family planning. Information on the current public level of knowledge about a subject such as cancer or a product such as a new electric car is needed before an effective information campaign can be mounted. After benchmarking a general level of knowledge, the effectiveness of an information campaign can then be tracked with additional surveys after the campaign has begun or been completed.

Finally, knowledge-based questions are used to obtain community or organizational information from community leaders, leaders or members of organizations, residents, or those who observed or participated in a particular event.

Checklist of Major Points

1. Before asking attitude questions about issues or persons, ask knowledge questions to screen out respondents who lack sufficient information or to classify respondents by level of knowledge.

2. Consider whether the level of difficulty of the knowledge question is appropriate for the purposes of the study. For new issues simple questions may be necessary.

3. When possible, reduce the threat of knowledge questions by asking them as opinions or by using such phrases as "Do you happen to know," or "As far as you know," or "Can you recall, offhand."

4. When identifying persons or organizations, avoid over-estimates of knowledge by asking for additional information or including fictitious names on the list.

5. If yes-no questions are appropriate, ask several on the same topic to reduce the likelihood of successful guessing.

6. For knowledge questions requiring numerical answers, use open-ended questions to avoid either giving away the answer or misleading the respondent.

7. To increase reliability when obtaining information about an organization or geographical area, use multiple key informants or individual respondents.

8. Consider using pictures and other nonverbal procedures for determining knowledge.

9. When attempting to determine level of knowledge, do not use mail or other procedures that allow respondents to look things up or to consult with others.

Examples of Knowledge Questions

The following sections describe different examples of how knowledge questions have been asked of respondents and informants. Each example illustrates some of the techniques used to ask knowledge questions and where opportunities lie for improvement.

Knowledge of Historical Events

Gallup asked the two questions shown in Figure 6.1 on July 4, 1999. About 12 percent of respondents gave a wrong answer to the first question or said they did not know; 24 percent gave a wrong answer to Question 2 or said they did not know.

Figure 6.2 presents the results from a series of questions asked during the period 1988–1994 about events in World War II and specifically about the Holocaust. The results are taken from an article by Smith (1995). The questions are arranged in order of decreasing knowledge, and they are from the following sources: (1) Roper, 1992, 1994; (2) Gallup, 1991; (3) *Minneapolis Star Tribune*, 1988; (4) Survey Research Center, 1992; (5) Gallup, 1991; (6 and 7) Roper, 1992, 1994; (8) CBS, 1994. It may be noted that when given a choice among world leaders, almost 90 percent of respondents knew who the leader of Nazi Germany was. This is a clear illustration that knowledge questions requiring recognition (choosing the correct answer from a series of possible answers) are much easier than knowledge questions that used unaided recall.

Question 7, which asks about how many Jews were killed in the Holocaust, gives the respondent six choices. The tendency for respondents who are uncertain about an answer is to assume that something near the middle category is correct. To neither coach nor mislead respondents, it is better to make such a question open-ended.

Knowledge of a Public Issue

The issue of biotechnology and genetically modified foods has reached a critical point, as it now concerns countries and firms globally. The ongoing debate in European countries has been translated into consumers' concerns in opinion surveys on several occasions. At the current time, opinion surveys indicate a good deal of

Figure 6.1. Questions About U.S. History.

1. As far as you know, what specific historical event is celebrated on July 4th?

2. As far as you know, from what country did America gain its independence following the Revolutionary War?

Source: Crabtree, 1999.

Figure 6.2. Questions About World War II.

	% Correct
1. Who was the leader of Nazi Germany? Was it Joseph Stalin, Adolph Hitler, Hirohito, Winston Churchill, or someone else?	88
2. Would you know specifically what happened 50 years ago relating to Pearl Harbor? (Japan bombed Pearl Harbor)	84
3. I'm going to read you a list of countries. Based on what you know or have learned about World War II, please tell me if each country was an ally of the United States, an enemy, or if it was not really involved in the war.	
Germany (enemy)	84
Great Britain (ally)	83
Japan (enemy)	82
Switzerland (uninvolved)	69
Soviet Union (ally)	67
Sweden (uninvolved)	56
4. Would you tell me what you think the Holocaust was?	84
5. This coming December the 7th marks the 50th anniversary of a significant event in American history which occurred on December 7, 1941. Would you happen to remember what that event was? (Bombing of Pearl Harbor)	75
6. From what you know or have heard, what were Auschwitz, Dachau, and Treblinka? (Concentration camps)	65
7. Approximately, how many Jews were killed in the Holocaust? 25,000, 100,000, 1 million, 2 million, 6 million, 20 million?	40
8. As far as you know, what does the term D-Day refer to? (Normandy invasion by allies)	27

Source: Smith, 1995.

general awareness of the issue, but much less specific knowledge. The first question in Figure 6.3 asks whether respondents have heard or read about the issue. Gallup has used the same wording for almost every important public issue, so comparisons are possible across issues.

In this instance, 81 percent of respondents reported that they had heard or read about the issue, which is slightly higher than what is typically found for similar types of events. Similar results were obtained from Question 3, asked by the Pew Research Center for the People and the Press. Instead of the Gallup format, Pew asked, "How much, if anything, have you heard or read . . . ?" There did not appear to be any clear advantage of either format over the other.

Figure 6.3. Questions About Biotechnology and Genetic Engineering.

1. As you may know, some food products and medicines are being developed using new scientific techniques. The general area is called "biotechnology" and includes tools such as genetic engineering and genetic modification of food. How much have you heard or read about this issue?

   ☐ A great deal
   ☐ Some
   ☐ Not much
   ☐ Nothing at all

2. As far as you know, do the stores where you shop for food sell fruits, vegetables, or other foods that have been genetically altered, or not?

   ☐ Yes (for sale)
   ☐ No (not for sale)
   ☐ Don't know/refused

3. As you may know, some fruits and vegetables are being genetically altered to make them taste better, last longer, or to increase crop yields. How much, if anything, have you heard about this?

   ☐ A lot
   ☐ Some
   ☐ Only a little
   ☐ Nothing at all

Source: Q.1, Gallup, Mar. 2000; Q.2 and Q.3, Pew Research Center for the People and the Press, Dec. 1999, cited in Shanahan, Scheufele, and Lee, 2001.

Specific knowledge, however, as measured in Question 2 was much lower; 40 percent of respondents did not know if any foods sold at the supermarket were produced through biotechnology. This illustrates that there is a much larger gap between one's general knowledge or awareness of an issue and specific content-level knowledge. We can very easily and wrongly assume that someone is knowledgeable about something they are only vaguely aware of. If it is critical to distinguish between the two, more specific questions need to be asked.

Knowledge of Authors

Figure 6.4 asks respondents about their knowledge of authors. This question followed questions dealing with book reading in general (Gallup, 1999). Although general statistics like this have some value in certain contexts, what is potentially of more interest is to see how author recognition differed across different population segments. We might think that books toward the end of the list (such as Dickens, Hemingway, Fitzgerald, and Melville) would be more

Figure 6.4. Questions About Authors.

1. Now, if you can, please tell me the name of the author for the following books.

	% Correct
The Cat in the Hat (Dr. Seuss)	72
Huckleberry Finn (Twain/Clemens)	48
The Shining (King)	42
The Old Man and the Sea (Hemingway)	29
The Firm (Grisham)	26
A Tale of Two Cities (Dickens)	18
A Farewell to Arms (Hemingway)	18
The Great Gatsby (Fitzgerald)	15
Moby Dick (Melville)	12
Crossings (Steel)	5

Source: Gallup, 1999.

widely recognized by those who had graduated from college than by those who did not. We might also see if there are age-related effects. (It's almost certain there would be age-related differences in knowledge for the World War II questions noted in Figure 6.2.)

In general, such statistics show there can sometimes be a strong causal link between education and knowledge. When you want to clearly distinguish knowledge from education, it is important to get accurate measures of both, so that the effects of education on knowledge can be controlled for in subsequent data analysis.

Name Recognition and Knowledge of Notable People

Name recognition is critical for political candidates during election campaigns. Also, as with public issues, opinion surveys that deal with attitudes toward public figures must first determine level of awareness. Figure 6.5 gives three examples of Gallup questions asking respondents about their knowledge of persons. The questions are in increasing order of difficulty. The first merely asks whether the respondent has heard anything about each of a number of different people. In this format, respondents tend to overstate their knowledge of these persons, either because of name confusion or because of social desirability effects.

One way to reduce this overstatement is shown in the second question. The respondent is asked, "Will you tell me who each one is or what he does?" This requires more information than the first

Figure 6.5. Questions Concerning Name Recognition.

1. Would you please look over this list and tell me which of these persons, if any, you have heard something about? (List follows)

2. Will you tell me who each one is or what he does? (List follows)

3. Here are some photographs of important people. Will you please look at the photographs and tell me their names?

Source: Gallup, 1999.

question. Another procedure for obtaining knowledge of public figures is to show their photographs and ask respondents for their names, as in Question 3. This question is even more difficult than asking who the respondent is or what he does.

This illustration is important in that it shows how different levels of knowledge and relationships can be tapped through these different efforts. If name recognition were higher than face recognition, it might indicate that candidate issues were more salient and associated with his or her name than with a photo. If only the photo were salient, it might mean the opposite—that the face is familiar but the issues are not. As with the authors example in Figure 6.4, it might be important to break these statistics out by education, age, or past voting participation before commenting on or determining campaign strategies.

Health Knowledge

For health policy purposes and health information campaigns, it is important to know what the public knows about various health issues. Figure 6.6 gives a series of health knowledge questions. Questions 1 through 4 are from a study conducted by the University of Illinois Survey Research Laboratory to provide guidance for a cancer information campaign. The remaining questions are from various Gallup surveys (1985, 1987). Note that although these are all knowledge questions, several are couched as opinion questions to reduce threat.

As was underscored in Chapter Three, care must be taken when asking threatening questions about behavior. This instance shows that techniques used to reduce the threat of behavior-related questions can also be used to ask about potentially threatening knowledge-related questions. This can particularly be the issue when appearing to know too much about a topic (such as drugs or promiscuous sexual behavior) might imply a suspiciously high level of familiarity.

Figure 6.6. Questions About Health Knowledge.

1. a. In your opinion, what are the symptoms of breast cancer? *(Do not read categories. Circle all that apply.)*
   - ☐ A lump
   - ☐ Dimpling of the breast
   - ☐ Pain or soreness in breast
   - ☐ Change in shape or color of nipple or breast
   - ☐ Bleeding or discharge from nipple
   - ☐ Other *(Specify)* _____
   - ☐ Don't know

   b. Although breast cancer can occur at different ages, *after* what age do you think it is most likely to occur?

   (Age) _____
   - ☐ Don't know

2. If breast cancer is found early and treated right away, how likely do you think it is that a woman will be able to do most of the things she could do before? Do you think it is . . .
   - ☐ Very likely,
   - ☐ Likely, or
   - ☐ Not very likely?
   - ☐ Don't know

3. What kind of examinations do you know of that can be done to find breast cancer in its early stages? *(Do not read categories. Circle all that apply.)*
   - ☐ Breast self-examination (Skip to Q. 5)
   - ☐ Breast examination by doctor
   - ☐ Mammography (X-ray examination)
   - ☐ Other *(Specify)* _____

4. Have you ever heard of an examination a woman can do by herself to see if there are any signs that something may be wrong with her breasts?
   - ☐ Yes
   - ☐ No

5. Do you think that cigarette smoking is or is not one of the causes of lung cancer?
   - ☐ Yes, is
   - ☐ No, is not
   - ☐ No opinion

(continued)

Figure 6.6. Questions About Health Knowledge, *continued.*

6. Do you think cancer is curable?
   - ☐ Yes, is
   - ☐ No, is not
   - ☐ No opinion

7. Do you think cancer is contagious (catching)?
   - ☐ Yes, is
   - ☐ No, is not
   - ☐ No opinion

8. Do you happen to know any symptoms of cancer? What?

9. In your opinion, are there substantial risks with using the birth control pill?

10. As I read some statements, please tell me whether you agree strongly, agree somewhat, disagree somewhat, or disagree strongly with each one:
    a. A person who drinks only wine and beer cannot become an alcoholic.
    b. The use of alcohol by pregnant women can cause birth defects.
    c. Alcoholism is a disease.
    d. A recovered alcoholic can safely return to moderate drinking.
    e. No one who drinks is immune from alcoholism.
    f. Alcoholism may be hereditary.

Source: Q.1–Q.4, Survey Research Laboratory, 1977; Q.5–Q.10, Gallup, 1985, 1987.

Information on Products and Manufacturers

Figure 6.7 shows two questions (taken from Payne, 1951) about products and companies. The first provides the respondent with the name of the company and asks for the names of products that company makes. The other provides the name of the brand and asks for the name of the company. These questions might be asked in studies of attitudes toward a company or brand. These attitudes, as with attitudes on public issues, would depend on knowledge about the company.

Although there is nothing specifically unique about the way these questions are asked, they represent a sizeable percentage of the types of questions asked in company-sponsored survey research. Answers to these questions are typically linked to behavior to determine how knowledge about a brand or product category is linked with usage frequency or price sensitivity. This is examined in detail in *Consumer Panels* (Sudman and Wansink, 2002).

Community Informants

In a study of integrated neighborhoods and their characteristics, it was important to obtain information about major neighborhood institutions, such as schools and churches, as well as information on community history. Figure 6.8 gives examples of the kinds of questions asked of community representatives, or community informants. In this study, four community representatives—a school leader, a church leader, a community organization leader, and a leading real estate broker—were asked the same set of questions.

As might be expected, not all four informants gave identical answers, but the mean or modal response was used to characterize the neighborhood for further analysis. Most of the information obtained from community informants could not have been obtained in any other way. Published sources were not available or were out of date. Not all community informants were equally knowledgeable. As one might expect, the school leaders knew more about the schools, the church leaders more about churches, and so on. Nevertheless the consensus data were very useful.

Figure 6.7. Questions About Products and Companies.

1. What are the brand or trade names of some of the products the *(Name)* company makes?

2. Will you tell me what company you think makes Frigidaire refrigerators?

Source: Payne, 1951.

Figure 6.8. Questions Asked of Community Informants.

1. What are the names of the public, Catholic, and private schools that children in this area attend? *(Ask a-c for each school before proceeding.)*

    a. Who is principal there?

      (Name) _____

      ☐ Don't know

    b. What would you say is the enrollment?

      (Enrollment) _____

      ☐ Don't know

    c. Is *(Name)* below capacity, just at capacity, slightly overcrowded, or very overcrowded?

      ☐ Below capacity

      ☐ At capacity

      ☐ Slightly overcrowded

      ☐ Very overcrowded

      ☐ Don't know

2. Do both blacks and whites attend this school?

    ☐ Yes *(Ask a.)*

    ☐ No

    ☐ Don't know

    a. Do you happen to know the percentage of blacks in the school?

      (Percent) _____

      ☐ Don't know

3. Could you tell me the names of the churches and temples in the area, or nearby, which people attend? (Probe) Any other denominations? *(Ask a-e for each church/temple before proceeding to the next one.)*

    a. Do you happen to know the name of the minister (priest, rabbi) there?

      (Name) _____

      ☐ Don't know

    b. Do both blacks and whites belong to (Name), or is this an all-white or all-black church?

      ☐ Both *(Ask c and d.)*

      ☐ Whites only *(Ask e.)*

      ☐ Blacks only

      ☐ Don't know

   c. *(Hand Respondent Card 2.)* What were the reactions to the members when the first black family joined?

     ☐ Majority in favor

     ☐ Split

     ☐ Majority opposed

     ☐ Majority strongly opposed

     ☐ Don't know

   d. Approximately what is the percentage of blacks in (*Name*)?

     (Percent) _____

     ☐ Don't know

   e. *(Hand Respondent Card 2.)* What would be the reaction of the members if a black family were interested in joining?

     ☐ Majority in favor

     ☐ Split

     ☐ Majority opposed

     ☐ Majority strongly opposed

     ☐ Don't know

4. Generally, when were the first houses (apartments) built in this neighborhood?

   (Year) _____

   ☐ Don't know

5. Were the first houses (apartments) all built and sold by the same builder, or were they built by many different people?

   ☐ Same builder

   ☐ Many builders *(Ask a.)*

   ☐ Don't know

Source: Bradburn, Sudman, and Gockel, 1971.

Resident Information About Neighborhoods

In the same study described above, information was also obtained from a sample of neighborhood residents, not only about their personal behavior and attitudes but also about the characteristics of the neighborhood in which they lived. Two of these questions are shown in Figure 6.9. Although residents would be expected to be generally less knowledgeable than community leaders, they are better able to report whether or not the family living next door is of the same or a different race.

The last three questions in Figure 6.9 are taken from another NORC study. They ask respondents to report about the physical condition of the surrounding neighborhood with respect to litter, vandalism, and road conditions. In a face-to-face interview, the interviewer can obtain some of this information by observing and recording the condition of the area. Observations, of course, are not possible with telephone interviewing. Even with face-to-face interviewing, the residents will have better knowledge of the area than the interviewer, especially if the questions require more than brief observation.

Figure 6.9. Neighborhood Information from Residents.

1. As far as you know, do both white and black families live in this neighborhood?

   ☐ Yes *(If R. is black, ask a; if R. is white, go to Q. 2.)*
   ☐ No *(Go to Q. 3.)*
   ☐ Don't know *(Go to Q. 3.)*

   a. Would you say that almost all of the families living in this neighborhood are black?

      ☐ Yes
      ☐ No
      ☐ Don't know *(Go to Q. 3.)*

2. Are there any black families living right around here?

☐ Yes *(Ask a-c.)*

☐ No

☐ Don't know

a. About how many black families live right around here?

(Number) _____

b. Do you know any of their names?

☐ Yes

☐ No

c. Is there a black family living next door?

☐ Yes

☐ No

☐ Don't know

3. Are there any vacant lots in this block or on either side of the street?

☐ Yes *(Ask a.)*

☐ No

a. Do any of the vacant lots have one or more of these items on them?

	Yes	No
1. Abandoned household goods	☐	☐
2. Broken bottles	☐	☐
3. Trash or litter	☐	☐
4. Remains of a partially demolished structure	☐	☐

4. On your block, are there any vandalized or abandoned buildings with boarded-up windows or doors, on either side of the street?

☐ Yes

☐ No

5. Is the public street or road nearest your house or building paved?

☐ Yes

☐ No

Source: National Opinion Research Center; Q.1 and Q.2, 1968; Q.3–Q.5, 1973.

It must be recognized, however, that residents, including community leaders, are not merely disinterested observers. They have large emotional stakes in their communities. Answers to factual questions may be affected by attitudes as well as level of knowledge. Thus, single responses about a neighborhood may not be correct. Averaging or otherwise weighting the responses from the same neighborhood increases both reliability and usefulness.

Knowledge of Occupations

Figure 6.10 presents a series of questions used to determine how much people know about various jobs. The principal reason for these questions is to help explain how different people rate the prestige of different occupations. Obviously, one factor involved in rating is knowledge. Note that there are five dichotomous (yes-no) questions for each job. A respondent should be able to get about half the answers right simply by guessing. Thus, it is the total right answers to all ten jobs that discriminates between respondents, and not the right answers to a single question or about a selected job. It is also possible to compare public familiarity with individual jobs, although this was not a primary purpose of these questions.

This nature of knowledge question—the aggregate knowledge question—is often useful when trying to determine one's general level of knowledge in an area. It is particularly useful when the basic knowledge question that would be asked is generally a binary one (yes or no, Republican or Democrat, and so on) that would lend itself well to guesswork.

National Assessment of Educational Progress

The most ambitious program to measure the effects of public education in the United States has been the National Assessment of Educational Progress, a multimillion-dollar project of the U.S. Department of Education. Figure 6.11 presents a series of exercises

Figure 6.10. Questions About Various Occupations.

1. Which of the following tools would a metal caster foundry be likely to use?
   - ☐ A file.
   - ☐ A cold chisel.
   - ☐ A pair of tongs.
   - ☐ A casting rod.
   - ☐ A blowtorch.

2. Which of the following things would a quality checker in a manufacturing plant be likely to do? Would he be likely to:
   - ☐ Wear a business suit?
   - ☐ Operate a cash register?
   - ☐ Write reports?
   - ☐ Supervise production line workers?
   - ☐ Examine products for defects?

3. Which of the following does a newspaper proofreader do?
   - ☐ Corrects the grammar of reporters' stories.
   - ☐ Meets the public on his job.
   - ☐ Checks the work of typesetters.
   - ☐ Rewrites newspaper stories.
   - ☐ Investigates the accuracy of rumors.

4. How many of the following things does a personnel director do?
   - ☐ Administer psychological tests.
   - ☐ Write production specifications.
   - ☐ Hire people.
   - ☐ Tell workers how to do their job.
   - ☐ Sometimes handle the complaints of workers.

5. Which of the following tools would a boilermaker be likely to use? Would he use a:
   - ☐ Jackhammer?
   - ☐ Ladder?
   - ☐ Rivet gun?
   - ☐ Crowbar?
   - ☐ Welding torch?

(continued)

Figure 6.10. Questions About Various Occupations, *continued.*

6. How about an optician? Does he?
    ☐ Prescribe eyeglasses?
    ☐ Grind lenses?
    ☐ Test your vision?
    ☐ Use an optical scanner?
    ☐ Take up stock options?

7. Which of the following would a dairy scientist be likely to use?
    ☐ A centrifuge.
    ☐ A Klein bottle.
    ☐ An oscilloscope.
    ☐ A microscope.
    ☐ A milking stool.

8. What does a dietician do? Does he:
    ☐ Invent new recipes?
    ☐ Draw up menus?
    ☐ Demonstrate cooking utensils?
    ☐ Inspect food products?
    ☐ Sometimes work in a hospital?

9. Which of the following things would a metal engraver be likely to need?
    ☐ A pantograph.
    ☐ A file.
    ☐ A hacksaw.
    ☐ A cold chisel.
    ☐ Acid.

10. What about a geologist? What would he be likely to use?
    ☐ A soldering iron.
    ☐ A rock hammer.
    ☐ A Geiger counter.
    ☐ A library.
    ☐ A geodesic dome.

Source: National Opinion Research Center, 1965.

used with adults to measure knowledge in the social sciences and writing. The standard procedure has been to pay adult participants to attempt the exercises. Standard classroom testing procedures are used, and adults are tested in their homes.

The types of questions used have varied. Although multiple choice questions have mainly been used (see Questions 2 through 11), open questions have also been asked. (See Question 1, which asks for reasons why a decision was made.) An especially interesting example is Question 14, which asks respondents to write a letter giving specific reasons to support their opinion in favor or against lengthening the school year. This question is used to provide an assessment of practical writing skills.

The science questions involve not only knowledge, but also the use of knowledge in problem solving. In Question 12, respondents are given a ruler, a graduated cylinder, scales, water in a jar, string, and a small nonporous rock and are asked to find the volume of the rock. Other physical apparatus are used to determine knowledge. In Question 13, respondents are handed two foam rubber blocks and are told the blocks represent a layer of rock on the earth's crust. They are then asked to use one or both of the blocks to demonstrate a fault in the earth's crust.

These examples are included to remind the reader that, in addition to standard verbal questions and responses, other methods are available for determining level of knowledge. Both respondents and interviewers usually enjoy the variety of asking and answering questions in different ways. Another illustration of the use of graphic procedures are geography questions where respondents are handed outline maps of Europe, South America, or the United States and asked to identify the countries or states.

Measuring Ability

The final example, shown in Figure 6.11, is taken from a study at NORC to determine the qualities that make some people better

Figure 6.11. Selected Questions from
National Assessment of Educational Progress.

1. A major American manufacturing corporation seeks to establish a branch plant in a country that has rich natural resources but very little industry. The leaders of the nation turn down the American corporation's request.

   What reasons can you give for the decision made by the leaders of the foreign nation?

2. Which of the following is a MAJOR goal of the United Nations?
   - ☐ To fight disease
   - ☐ To maintain peace
   - ☐ To spread democracy
   - ☐ To fight the Communists
   - ☐ I don't know.

3. The term "monopoly" describes the situation in which the market price of goods and services is established by which one of the following?
   - ☐ Many sellers
   - ☐ A single buyer
   - ☐ Many buyers and sellers
   - ☐ A single seller or a small group of sellers
   - ☐ I don't know.

4. Which of the following has the power to declare an act of Congress unconstitutional?
   - ☐ The Congress
   - ☐ The President
   - ☐ The United States Supreme Court
   - ☐ The United States Department of Justice
   - ☐ I don't know.

5. The Supreme Court ruled that it is unconstitutional to require prayer and formal religious instructions in public schools. Which of the following was the basis for its decision?
   - ☐ The requirements violated the right to freedom of speech.
   - ☐ There was strong pressure put on the Supreme Court by certain religious minorities.
   - ☐ Religious exercises violated the principle of the separation of church and state.
   - ☐ Every moment of valuable school time was needed to prepare students to earn a living.
   - ☐ I don't know.

6. What is needed to move cars, heat hamburgers, and light rooms?
   - ☐ Conservation
   - ☐ Efficiency
   - ☐ Energy
   - ☐ Friction
   - ☐ Magnetism
   - ☐ I don't know.

7. In hot climates, the advantage of buildings with white surfaces is that white surfaces effectively
   - ☐ absorb light.
   - ☐ diffract light.
   - ☐ reflect light.
   - ☐ refract light.
   - ☐ transmit light.
   - ☐ I don't know.

8. On the average, in human females the egg is released how many days after menstruation begins?
   - ☐ 2 days
   - ☐ 9 days
   - ☐ 14 days
   - ☐ 20 days
   - ☐ 24 days
   - ☐ I don't know.

9. A fossil of an ocean fish was found in a rock outcrop on a mountain. That probably means that
   - ☐ fish once lived on the mountain.
   - ☐ the relative humidity was once very high.
   - ☐ the mountain was raised up after the fish died.
   - ☐ fish used to be amphibians like toads and frogs.
   - ☐ the fossil fish was probably carried up to the mountain by a great flood.
   - ☐ I don't know.

10. An artificial pacemaker is an electronic device used by some patients with heart disease. What does this device simulate or replace?
   - ☐ The auricles
   - ☐ The ventricles
   - ☐ The node in the right auricle
   - ☐ The heart valves between the auricles and ventricles
   - ☐ The valves that control the flow of blood into the aorta
   - ☐ I don't know.

(continued)

Figure 6.11. Selected Questions from
National Assessment of Educational Progress, *continued.*

11. An object starts from rest and moves with constant acceleration. If the object has a speed of 10 meters per second after 5 seconds, the acceleration of the object is
    - ☐ 1m/sec^2
    - ☐ 2m/sec^2
    - ☐ 5m/sec^2
    - ☐ 10m/sec^2
    - ☐ 50m/sec^2
    - ☐ I don't know.

12. *(Place 12" ruler, graduated cylinder, nonporous rock, spring scales, water in jar, and string in front of respondent. Give respondent the workbook.)* In front of you are a small rock and several pieces of apparatus. You are to use whatever apparatus you find necessary to find the VOLUME of the small rock. List all procedures and record all measurements you make in the Workbook in part A. I will be making the same measurements in the same way that you do. When you have determined the volume of the rock, record your answer in part B.

    (If respondent does not proceed, say "Think of some measurements you could make that would give you the volume of the rock.")

    (Indicate the equipment respondent uses.)
    - ☐ Graduated cylinder and water
    - ☐ Graduated cylinder and no water
    - ☐ Ruler
    - ☐ Spring scales
    - ☐ String

13. Geology is the science which studies the Earth, the rocks of which it is made up, and the changes which take place at and beneath the surface.

    (Take out Handout, 2 foam rubber blocks. Pick up one of the foam rubber blocks and twist it to show respondent that it is resilient and can be deformed without harm. Place foam blocks side by side, touching each other and lined up evenly, in front of respondent.)

    The foam blocks represent a layer of rock in the Earth's crust. Use one or both of the foam blocks to demonstrate faulting of the earth's crust; that is, show me a fault.

    (Refer to page 3 to judge respondent's demonstration.)
    - ☐ Correct demonstration
    - ☐ Incorrect demonstration
    - ☐ I don't know.
    - ☐ Did not attempt demonstration

14. Many people think that students are not learning enough in school. They want to shorten most school vacations and make students spend more of the year in school. Other people think that lengthening the school year and shortening vacations is a bad idea because students use their vacations to learn important things outside of school. What is your opinion?

  Write a letter to your school board either in favor of or against lengthening the school year. Give specific reasons to support your opinion that will convince the school board to agree with you.

Source: U.S. Department of Education, 1972–2003.

---

survey research interviewers than others. Since survey interviewing is a complex task, it is reasonable to expect that success would be related to such factors as general ability, reading ability, personal skills, or patience. In attempting to assess the relationship between survey interviewing success and ability, we could simply have asked the interviewers to state their IQs. However, some interviewers might not wish to do so or might not know. Therefore, we measured ability indirectly by asking about grades received in school or the academic subjects they most preferred. In addition to these indirect measures, we used a short intelligence test, adapted from the Wechsler Adult Intelligence Scale (WAIS) Similarities Test (see the following made-up example).

> Different people see different kinds of similarities between things. In what way do you think that these pairs of things are alike?
>
> Saw — Hammer
>
> Lion — Tiger
>
> Hour — Week
>
> Circle — Triangle

The full complement of actual items and the answer scoring can be found by consulting the WAIS Similarities Test. This scale correlated highly with the other measures used and increased the reliability of the overall measure. Note that the introduction to the question indicates different answers are possible. As is usually the procedure in surveys, we did not mention that the test was intended to measure general intelligence, since this could make the respondents nervous. The scoring of the results, however, is based on norms established in standard intelligence testing. This question was included in a mail survey that the respondents filled out in their homes and mailed back. In the usual situation, knowledge questions would not be asked on a mail survey, since respondents could look up the answer or ask for help. For this question, however, there would be nothing to look up; and it is unlikely, although possible, that respondents consulted with others.

Techniques and Strategies for Asking Knowledge Questions

Sometimes researchers think they should do whatever they can to increase the percentage of people who answer a knowledge question correctly. Such efforts can instead only increase the amount of correct guessing. The key is to ask knowledge-related questions in a way that one gets the most accurate assessment of knowledge, not the highest assessment of knowledge. The following techniques can help you in this regard.

Determining Level of Knowledge

The examples suggest that knowledge questions help qualify respondent opinions and should be asked before attitude questions are asked. This order is essential if the knowledge questions are to screen out respondents who do not have sufficient information to answer detailed attitude questions. Even if all respondents answer the attitude questions, respondents will be less likely to overclaim knowledge and more likely to state that they do not know or are undecided in their attitudes if knowledge questions come first.

If the attitude questions are asked first, respondents may feel they are expected to know about the issue and have an opinion. On many public issues it is more important to know that opinion has not yet crystallized than to force an answer. On many issues high or low levels of knowledge can be obtained, depending on the difficulty of the questions.

The easiest type of question is one that asks "Have you heard or read about . . . ?" For example, a question asking "Have you heard or read about the trouble between Israel and the Arab nations in the Middle East?" received 97 percent "yes" answers in a 1973 Gallup Poll. When this same type of question was made more specific, however, asking "Have you heard or read about the recent Sinai Disengagement Pact between Egypt and Israel?" only 59 percent of respondents answered "yes."

Dichotomous and multiple choice questions can be somewhat more difficult for people to answer. The questions in Figures 6.9, which can be answered "yes" or "no," illustrate the most common kinds of dichotomous questions. Other examples from Gallup are "Do you happen to know if the federal budget is balanced, that is, does the federal government take in as much as it spends?" and "From what you have heard or read, do you think we produce enough oil in this country to meet our present needs, or do we have to import some oil from other countries?" These questions are not strictly dichotomous since a "don't know" answer is also possible. The "don't know" answer is more likely to be given if a phrase such as "Do you happen to know . . ." or "As far as you know . . ." is included at the start of the question. Questions 2 through 11 in Figure 6.11 illustrate uses of multiple choice questions, in which the alternatives are given to the respondents. These are, of course, more difficult than dichotomous questions, since the possibility of guessing the right answer is reduced. In all these questions, the answer "I don't know" is explicitly included to reduce guessing and to indicate that "don't know" answers are expected and acceptable.

More difficult still are questions that ask for details. Question 2 in Figure 6.5 and the questions in Figure 6.7 ask respondents for minimal identification about a person or company they have heard about. This information can include titles, reason for fame, and the state or country or product that the person or company is identified with. Answering such questions correctly indicates a higher level of knowledge about that particular person or company than does simple name recognition.

Question 3 in Figure 6.5, which uses pictures, can be used to determine knowledge of personalities and other entertainers. Companies sometimes use this type of question to determine public familiarity with various product package designs when the brand name is removed.

At the next level of difficulty are open qualitative questions, as shown in Figure 6.6, Questions 1 and 3; Figure 6.11, Question 1; and in the WAIS Similarities Test (see "Measuring Ability" section). Although these questions vary in difficulty among themselves, they are, on the average, more difficult than the other types of questions discussed so far. These questions do not usually offer an explicit choice or a "don't know" answer, since successful guessing is unlikely. Indeed, most respondents who do not know say so rather than try to guess, since a bad guess may be more embarrassing than a "don't know" answer.

Most difficult of all—except for those directed to special informants such as community informants—are numerical questions or those dealing with percentages. As we shall note below, efforts to make numerical questions easier by providing multiple choices introduce additional problems. The decision on the type of knowledge questions to use will depend on the researcher's needs. However, questions that are either too easy or too difficult will not discriminate between respondents with different levels of knowledge. As a general rule, easier knowledge questions are most appropriate for public issues in their early stages of development; more difficult questions can be asked about long-standing issues. For example, knowledge questions about the Arab-Israeli conflict in the Middle East can be at a higher level of difficulty than questions about a new national or international crisis.

Similarly, in market research, knowledge questions about long-established products can be made more difficult than questions about new products. Some advocates of particular public policies have attempted to discredit public opinions that oppose their policies by demonstrating that public knowledge of the issues is limited. Although this can sometimes be legitimate, the difficulty level of the questions must also be taken into account. It is always possible to find questions so difficult that virtually no respondents can answer them correctly—especially in a survey where an instant response is required and no advance warning has been given.

Reducing the Threat of Knowledge Questions

As with the threatening behavior questions discussed in the previous chapter, knowledge questions raise issues of self-presentation. Respondents do not wish to appear foolish or ill-informed by giving obviously incorrect answers or admitting to not knowing something that everyone else knows. Much of this threat can be reduced by an introductory phrase such as "Do you happen to know" or "Can you recall, offhand." Offering "I don't know" as an answer category also reduces threat. These procedures indicate that a "don't know" answer is acceptable even if it is not the most desirable answer. The use of these threat-reducing phrases reduces the amount of guessing and increases the percentage of "don't know" answers. Conversely, if you wish respondents to give their "best guess," the phrases used above should be omitted, and respondents should be asked to give "your best guess," as in this Gallup question: "Just your best guess, what proportion of persons on welfare are 'chiselers,' that is, are collecting more than they are entitled to?"

The line between knowledge and attitude or opinion questions is often blurred. Earlier (in Figure 6.11, Questions 1 and 14), knowledge questions are asked in the guise of opinion questions. The question that asks respondents to guess about the proportion of welfare chiselers is really an attitude question in the guise of a knowledge question. Although a few respondents may actually know the correct proportion from reading news stories, most respondents will guess, and their guess will be based on their attitudes toward welfare programs in general.

Controlling for Overstatement of Knowledge

Respondents presented with a list of persons or organizations and asked whether they have heard or read something about them may find the question mildly threatening—especially if the list is long and includes many unfamiliar names (as in Figure 6.5, Question 1). Indicating that you have not heard anything about all or most of the names on a list suggests you are out of touch with current affairs. Since the answers to this question cannot be checked, there is a tendency for respondents to overclaim having heard about people and organizations. The easiest way to control for this is to ask an additional question about who the person is or what he or she does (as in Question 2, Figure 6.5) or what the company makes (as in Question 1, Figure 6.7).

In some cases, such additional qualifying questions may not be appropriate. For instance, in a study of knowledge about possible candidates for political office (such as president of the United States), the current position of a person may not be relevant, and the fact that he is a possible nominee may be evident from the context of the question. A solution in this case is to add the name of a "sleeper" or a person whom no one would be expected to know. For example, in a study conducted by NORC some years ago, the name of a graduate student was added to a list of civil rights leaders. About 15 percent of all respondents reported that they had heard of this graduate student. This suggested that several other actual civil rights leaders whose names were supposedly recognized by about 15 percent of the population might, in reality, be virtually unknown.

The same procedure can be used with companies and brands in marketing research to determine brand name awareness. Of course, when sleepers are used, it is important to avoid names of known persons and to make sure that the sleeper brand is not actually in use at a regional level or has not been used in the past.

Using Multiple Questions

It is well known that the reliability of individuals' scores on tests and scales increases with the number of items (up to a reasonable level). Similarly, more reliable measures of an individual's knowledge are obtained if multiple questions are used. Particularly with dichotomous or multiple choice questions, single questions are subject to high unreliability because of guessing. If knowledge is the key dependent variable, as in the National Assessment of Educational Progress, then it is evident that many questions must be asked to obtain reliable measures of knowledge. Fewer questions are needed if knowledge is to be used as an independent variable, and a single question may be sufficient if the knowledge question is to be used to screen out respondents who will not be asked additional questions. Note that in many of the examples given earlier, multiple questions are used.

The number of questions to ask also depends on the general level of respondent information on the topic. If most respondents know nothing or very little about an issue, it will only take one or two questions to determine that. If there is great variability in the amount of information respondents know, it is possible to order a series of questions from the easiest to the hardest. Interviews start with the easiest questions and the interviewer discontinues asking the questions in the series after the respondent answers two or three incorrectly. The logic of this method is similar to that of a Guttman scale (see Chapter Five).

Asking Numerical Questions

As we have already indicated, numerical questions are generally the most difficult for respondents to answer. If given a choice of

answers, most respondents will guess and choose an answer somewhat near the middle. For this reason, Payne (1951) suggested that
the correct answer be put at the top or bottom of the list of alternatives. Respondents, however, can be misled by this. We believe that
an even better procedure is not to offer alternatives to the respondent but to make such questions open-ended. There is no difficulty
in coding such responses since the data are numerical and can easily be processed without additional coding. The open question is
more likely to elicit a "don't know" response than the closed questions, but respondents who do volunteer an answer or guess will be
indicating knowledge or attitudes that are not distorted by the question stimulus.

Using Key Informants

Using key informants in social science is widespread in studies of
community power and influence, community decision making and
innovation, collective behavior, and the ecology of local institutions. Key informants can provide information that is not currently
available from census data or other published sources. Although
key informants are usually better informed than the general public, they cannot be expected to know everything. Information
informants provide may be distorted by their attitudes or roles in
the community.

  As an illustration in a study of what they called "community
informants," Houston and Sudman (1975) reported that church
informants mentioned a higher number of churches in the neighborhood than did other informants and the community organization informants mentioned more community organizations. These
unsurprising results are a function not only of the greater expertise
in their areas of specialization but also of somewhat different perspectives. Thus, the church informants tended to define a neighborhood's boundaries in terms of parish boundaries or of church
attendance patterns, the school informants used school boundaries,
and so on.

Clearly, it is necessary to use multiple key informants to obtain reliable information about a community. At a minimum, we would suggest that at least three or four key informants be used for each setting and that additional informants be added if the data are variable. The less informed the respondents, the larger will be the number of respondents required to obtain reliable information. If, instead of informants, residents are used to provide information on neighborhood ecology, a minimum sample of about ten would probably be required. Although the limits of key informant data must be recognized, key informants provide data that cannot be obtained so accurately and economically by any other procedure.

Using Nonverbal Procedures

As illustrated in Figure 6.11, Questions 12 and 13, not all knowledge questions and answers must be verbal. The use of nonverbal stimuli—such as pictures, maps, music, sounds, drawings, and other real-world objects—should always be considered along with standard questions in face-to-face interviewing. Both respondents and interviewers enjoy these questions as a change of pace from standard questions. Nonverbal procedures can be used as either stimuli or responses. Thus, in a test of classical music knowledge, respondents might be asked to listen to the start of Beethoven's Fifth Symphony and asked to identify the composer and composition, or they might be given the name of the composition and asked to hum a bit of it into a recorder. This latter procedure and other similar procedures that require recall are more difficult than the procedures that require respondents simply to recognize the nonverbal stimulus.

Self-Administered Knowledge Questions

As a rule, knowledge questions are not appropriate for self-administered surveys (except under controlled conditions on the computer, as with standardized tests), whether by mail or especially on the Web since the respondent will have the chance to look up the correct answer or to consult with others. Knowledge questions can be asked on the phone as well as face-to-face since the phone conversation prevents the respondent from seeking outside help. There are a few exceptions to this rule. The easiest knowledge question ("Have you heard or read about . . . ?") can be asked on a self-administered survey, although questions used to screen out respondents who do not know enough to have an informed opinion cannot be used on a self-administered survey.

Some questions that appear to be asking for attitudes but really are trying to tap into knowledge (such as the Wechsler items in the section on "Measuring Ability") can also be successful in self-administered versions. Finally, for purposes of obtaining information by using key informants in companies or communities, self-administered forms can be superior to personal interviews. In this situation, it may be desirable for the respondent to consult records and to discuss the questions with others. The resulting answers are likely to be more complete than immediate answers given in a personal interview.

Summary

Knowledge questions are used to evaluate educational achievement, to design and implement information programs or advertising campaigns, to determine public awareness of current issues and people, to measure ability, and to obtain community information. Knowledge questions vary in difficulty. The easiest questions ask whether a respondent has heard or read about a topic; the most difficult require detailed numerical information. Questions that are too easy or too difficult do not differentiate between respondents. Questions may also vary from the standard format of verbal questions by using pictures, maps, music and other sounds, or other physical objects. Most knowledge questions are asked in face-to-face or telephone interviews, but in selected cases they may be asked in self-administered interviews.

Topics discussed in this chapter include procedures for reducing threat, guessing, and the overclaiming of knowledge; ways of asking numerical questions; and procedures for increasing reliability by using multiple knowledge questions or multiple informants.

Additional Reading

There has been little formal research on use of knowledge questions in surveys. As may be evident from the examples in this chapter, the Gallup organization has been and continues to be one of the major users of such questions. Printed references to the collection of Gallup questions (Gallup, 2002, and earlier years) and the current Gallup Web site (www.gallup.com) can be used to find examples of knowledge questions and other types of questions. For detailed information on the National Assessment of Educational Progress as well as questions that have been used, consult the Web site of the National Center for Education Statistics (www.nces.ed. gov/nationsreportcard/).

For information on the use of data from key informants, see *Side by Side* (Bradburn, Sudman, and Gockel, 1971b). For methodological assessment of these data, see "A Methodological Assessment of the Use of Key Informants" (Houston and Sudman, 1975). For information on the use of knowledge questions to predict survey interviewer success, see *Reducing the Cost of Surveys* (Sudman, 1967, Chapter Eight).

Chapter Seven

Asking Questions that Evaluate Performance

It seems like it should be a simple question—"How well are my employees doing?" Despite its apparent simplicity, this ends up being a very difficult—and important—question for individuals and organizations and also for service providers and service recipients.

If done correctly, careful measurements of performance can have two important consequences. First, these measurements may be used diagnostically to improve or troubleshoot potential problems in employee performance. Second, these measurements may be used in a way that contributes to salary bonuses or promotion decisions. In some companies, employees are evaluated by superiors, peers, and subordinates. For example, a manager may be evaluated by top management, other managers, and direct employees, and a manager's employees may be evaluated by the manager, peer employees, or clients. In this chapter we offer suggestions for asking questions that can be used to evaluate the performance of employees, employers, students, and teachers.

Checklist of Major Points

1. If the process of developing, measuring, administering, and analyzing performance questions is seen as fair, it will contribute to cooperation and acceptance of the outcomes. Involve those people who will be evaluated and get their feedback on the instrument and the way the questions are worded.

2. Behaviorally anchored rating scales can be useful in contexts where it is feared that subjectivity could otherwise bias an evaluation.

3. A system similar to the one used to develop employee evaluations can be used to develop the instrument for manager or supervisor evaluations.

4. Customer evaluations can be very useful if they are developed for the purpose of evaluation and not marketing. In addition, they need to effectively separate out the service provided by the employee from more general biases and feelings a customer might have about the product or service.

5. Teaching evaluations should be generalizable (across all faculty) as well as having some specific parts that are unique to individual instructors. A two-part questionnaire can solve this.

6. Care must be taken with teaching evaluations that there is some consistency and carryover year-to-year to enable administrators to track improvement or progress in faculty.

Employee Rating Techniques

Not only is employee performance an overall measure of how well the company is doing, but it is also a basis for individual evaluation and rewards. Besides the issue of accuracy and fairness, another key issue in the process of rating and evaluating employees is related to the perception of fairness by the employees. This underscores the importance of process. If the process of developing, measuring, administering, and analyzing these questions (and data) is seen as fair, it greatly contributes to cooperation and reduces subversive efforts. The following steps are recommended in order to achieve this goal.

1. Begin by conducting a job analysis for each of the necessary evaluations. Although this task might seem onerous, it is less

so than it might seem. Well-documented job analyses can be used over time, and some jobs share similar responsibilities and can be grouped accordingly into a single set of responsibilities and task statements.

2. For each job, develop scales that are specifically related to performance. This includes defining the performance dimensions and listing statements of behavior that indicate the desired performance within each dimension.

3. Inform both managers and employees of the dimensions that will be evaluated and the purpose the data will serve. This is important to the earlier notion of perceived fairness. This helps gain both managerial and employee acceptance and active participation in the new rating system.

4. Select an employee evaluation format that is acceptable to the organization. Although there is little evidence suggesting any one format is superior to another, there are definitely strategic approaches to designing performance reviews that will be covered in this book. As a result, a number of appropriate scales and formatted alternatives can be developed, and the organization should select the format judged to be most acceptable by the majority of users. The selection might be based on polling for raters with respect to their preference. In the end, although scales are only different on the surface, if the performance dimensions and tasks have been communicated in a thorough manner, disagreements over the evaluation form will be minor or even irrelevant.

5. Make certain that managers are capable of accurately rating employees. Provide training to those who will be using the new forms and who are required to submit reports. It is also important to be certain that enough time has been provided for the evaluations to take place. The amount of time provided to the process can be seen as an indication of its importance. Rushed ratings may actually have a lower cost-benefit ratio to the organization than no ratings.

6. At regular and agreed-on intervals, make certain the evaluation system is working as planned. If the appraisal system was designed to make employees more skilled at satisfying customers, check to make sure that customers are more satisfied. If the system was designed to promote only those employees with managerial potential, make sure that new managers are effective and successfully handling their new responsibilities. In addition, check to make sure that managers and employees are satisfied with the new system; try to determine whether they are having any trouble using the system and how it might be improved.

7. Finally, allow the performance evaluation system the chance to change. The performance evaluation system is implemented in order to yield a product for the company—the ratings. But if the system is also a process, ensure that it endures by allowing it to change along with the organization.

A wide number of options are available for conducting employee evaluations, including questionnaires, checklists, individual interviews, observation interviews, group interviews, and diaries. (See Figure 7.1.) The focus of much of the rest of this chapter is on questionnaires and on modified versions of checklists.

One concern about ratings used to evaluate others is that they may be too subjective. That is, one person's evaluation of effectiveness may be different from another's. Although this can be addressed by issues of scaling, a statistical solution is not reassuring to those being rated. For this reason, behaviorally anchored rating scales were developed because they were perceived to be more objective by both employees and employers.

Behaviorally Anchored Rating Scales (BARS)

Many solutions to the recurring problems in performance measurement have been proposed. One of the more notable of these solutions has been behavioral-expectation scaling or behaviorally anchored rating scales (BARS). The BARS method was introduced in a study sponsored by the National League for Nursing (Smith and Kendall, 1963). The original BARS approach combined the Fels parent-behavior rating scales (Guilford, 1954, pp. 266–267) and Thurstone's attitude scales (Guilford, 1954, pp. 456–459). It uses graphic rating scales that incorporate specific behavioral descriptions using various points along each scale. (See Figure 7.2.) Each scale represents a dimension or factor considered to be an important part of work performance, and both raters and those being evaluated are typically involved in developing the dimensions and generating behavioral descriptions.

Although many variations of the BARS procedure have been introduced since its inception, the procedures that follow are true to the original ideals of BARS. A complete discussion of the various appraisal formats that have been introduced under the guise of BARS can be found in Bernardin and Smith (1981).

The BARS procedure was originally an iterative process that began by having a sample of the evaluating population (the raters) identify, define, and propose a first draft of scales they believed captured ideal behavior. This draft was then reviewed and modified by other raters until a final version was agreed on (Bernardin, 1977).

At this point, dimension-clarification statements are developed to anchor the high, middle, and low parts of the scale. Behavioral examples are then written for the high, medium, and low effectiveness for each dimension. Behavioral examples are then "retranslated" by a second group of people who are given a randomly ordered list of these high, medium, and low effectiveness examples and asked to choose the dimension to which each example is related. (An 80 percent successful retranslation is typically used.) Next, 7-point scales (1 = low effectiveness, 7 = high effectiveness) are used to rate the effectiveness of each behavioral example on the dimension for which it was written. Behavioral examples with large variances (in excess of 2.0) are eliminated in order to remove examples that are unreliable.

When using the BARS method, raters are instructed to record observed behaviors throughout the appraisal period and to indicate

Figure 7.1. Comparison of Methods for Collecting Job Analysis Data.

Method	Definition	Advantages	Disadvantages
Questionnaire	Obtains job function information through mailed survey. Employees are asked to describe the job in their own words. They complete the form independently from the workplace.	▪ Information can be pulled from a large sample. ▪ Works well with reasonably articulate employees. ▪ Superior to observations with jobs that require a minimum of quantifiable activity.	▪ Can be difficult to organize such a task. ▪ Employees liable to exaggerate duties performed. ▪ Responses may be hard to interpret. ▪ Responses may not be complete.
Checklist	Lists task statements. Employees are asked to identify tasks performed during their work. Usually relies on interviews or class standards to form basic list.	▪ Depends on recognition rather than memory. ▪ Information can be gleaned from a large sample. ▪ Critical tasks, frequency or performance, and time to perform can be identified easily.	▪ Information about sequences of tasks is not discovered. ▪ Varying definitions of tasks. ▪ Employees can be unreliable through boredom or loss of interest.
Individual Interview	Records information from managers and employees. Usually done on-site and using a standard form.	▪ Has been found to unearth more detailed and accurate information than other methods. ▪ It is generally considered the most reliable.	▪ Slow and time-consuming. ▪ Not practical with a large and widely spread-out office complex.
Observation Interview	Records information from managers and employees. The data is gathered on-site while employee engages in activities being discussed.	▪ Allows employees to continue working. ▪ Excellent when nature of job makes the activity overt.	▪ Slow data collection. ▪ Possible conflict with operational activities. ▪ Cost is higher than most other methods.

Group Interview	• Records information from a group of employees representative of job. Function work activity information is recorded on a standard form.	• Very cost effective in terms of work-hour costs. • If done with a brainstorming format, can produce large amount of data about job function.	• Depends heavily on employee's recall of work activities.
Diary	• Keeps a logbook of work activities while actually performing them.	• Perfect recall is not an issue. • Promotes accurate recording of time spent on activities and sequences.	• May not get a representative sample of job. • Relies on both verbal and written information.

Figure 7.2. Behaviorally Anchored Rating Scale (BARS) for Evaluating College Professors.

Organizational skills: A good constructional order of material moves smoothly from one topic to another; design of course optimizes interest; students can easily follow organizational strategy; course outline

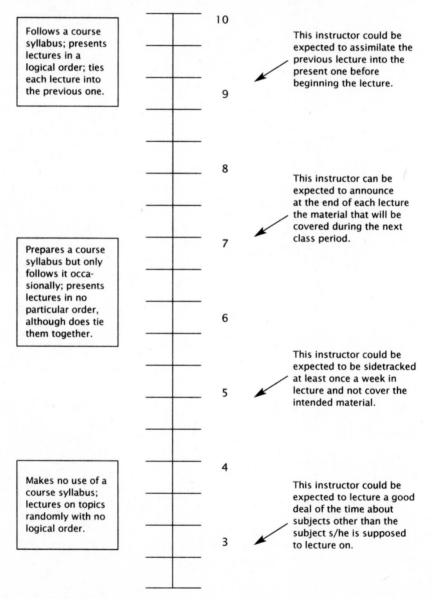

Follows a course syllabus; presents lectures in a logical order; ties each lecture into the previous one.

This instructor could be expected to assimilate the previous lecture into the present one before beginning the lecture.

This instructor can be expected to announce at the end of each lecture the material that will be covered during the next class period.

Prepares a course syllabus but only follows it occasionally; presents lectures in no particular order, although does tie them together.

This instructor could be expected to be sidetracked at least once a week in lecture and not cover the intended material.

Makes no use of a course syllabus; lectures on topics randomly with no logical order.

This instructor could be expected to lecture a good deal of the time about subjects other than the subject s/he is supposed to lecture on.

Source: Cardy and Dobbins, 1994.

the date and details of the incident on the scale. Scaling the effectiveness level of the observation is facilitated by a comparison with the series of illustrative behavioral "anchors" that defined the highest, lowest, and midpoint of each scale. Each rater was to decide what had been observed in relation to these specific examples. The rater could then use the examples as benchmarks when briefly noting what behavior had been observed. These anchoring illustrations were to be concrete, specific, and located at irregular intervals along the relevant scale according to effectiveness. The dimensions themselves would have been picked only after considerable discussion of organizational goals and objectives. (See the earlier section in this chapter on developing a rating system.) After a period of observing and recording incidents, the rater could, if needed, make a summary rating. This summary, plus the notes, could serve as a basis for discussion with the person being rated. It could also serve to measure performance.

Thus, to summarize the original BARS procedure, the sequence was as follows:

1. Observation

2. Inference

3. Scaling

4. Recording

5. Summary rating

The procedure is intended to define, to clarify, and to operationalize the implicit evaluative theory of the rater. In doing so, the BARS system encourages an evaluator to observe and to explicitly acknowledge the implications and interpretations of behavior. What sets the BARS method apart is that it can improve future observations, such as forced-choice or summated scales (Bernardin and Smith, 1981). The BARS method is effective because it creates a common frame of reference so that evaluators look for the same kinds of behaviors and interpret them more consistently and objectively.

In the end, the BARS method has proven to be a useful and accurate tool to evaluate the performance of individuals responsible for large groups of people over time. In addition, the BARS method, once defined for a particular audience, may be used over many iterations with only minor adjustments.

Employer Ratings

Although there is a long history of managers rating employees, there is a more recent trend of turning the tables and also having employees rate managers. The two processes have many similarities. (See Figure 7.3.) The general process of developing these scales varies only slightly from the process used to develop the instruments to evaluate employees.

Figure 7.3. Example of a Graphics Rating Scale with Numerical and Verbal Anchors.

INSTRUCTIONS

Circle the number corresponding to the value associated with your evaluation of the manager on the dimension below.

LONG-RANGE PLANNING

Forecasts with respect to manpower planning and costs; anticipates future problems and new trends; reviews with his people to constantly update them and uncover new information.

1	2	3	4	5
Unsatisfactory	Fair	Good	Very Good	Exceptional

Source: Beatty and Bernardin, 1984.

This section offers specific guidelines managers can use to implement appraisal systems of themselves and their managers. Much like the system for evaluating employees, the following steps are recommended for evaluating employers or managers:

1. Conduct a well-documented job evaluation for each of the managerial dimensions that are to be analyzed.

2. For each job, develop scales that are specifically related to performance. As with employee evaluations, this would also include defining the performance dimensions and listing statements of behavior that indicate the desired performance within each dimension.

3. Inform both managers and employees of the dimensions that will be evaluated and the purpose the data will serve. Besides giving the perception of fairness, this helps employees realize that their opinions and observations will be given weight and are worth their time and effort.

4. Select an employee evaluation format that is acceptable to the organization. It is best that one be used that is consistent with the evaluation format used to rate employees. This lessens the perception of there being a double standard.

5. Make certain that employees are capable of rating and have the appropriate time to complete ratings.

6. At regular and agreed-on intervals, make certain that the evaluation system is working as planned.

7. Finally, allow the performance evaluation system the chance to change. The performance evaluation system is implemented in order to yield a product for the company—the ratings. But if the system is also a process, ensure that it endures by allowing it to change along with the organization.

As with employee ratings, objectivity can be a concern. This is particularly the case if disgruntled employees see this as an opportunity for vindictiveness. Other employees might give dishonestly positive evaluations if they believe that an honest but negative evaluation would invite retaliation. Other times (see Figure 7.4), rating scales provide feedback but not diagnostic suggestions about what can be done differently. For this reason, checklists can be useful in that they are more tangible and point to specific behaviors that can be altered.

Figure 7.4. Example of a Checklist.

INSTRUCTIONS

Below you will find a list of behavioral items. Read each item and decide whether the item describes the person being evaluated. If you feel the item does describe the person, place a check mark in the space provided. If the item is not descriptive of the person, leave the space next to the item blank.

☐ Regularly sets vague and unrealistic program goals.

☐ Is concerned only with the immediate problems of the day.

☐ Develops work schedules that allow for the completion of projects.

☐ Is aware of needs and trends in his/her area of responsibility and plans accordingly.

☐ Follows up on projects to ensure immediate goals are achieved.

☐ Looks for new markets and studies potential declines in current markets.

☐ Anticipates and plans for replacement of key personnel in the event of corporate relocation.

Source: Adapted from Beatty and Bernardin, 1984, p. 93.

In the discussion of ratings, we have moved to recommending the use of surveys to accomplish higher-order goals of the organization. Many organizations survive because of the value they provide to customers, clients, or patrons. The ratings of these people are critical for organizational success.

Customer, Client, and Patron Ratings

One major drawback of performance appraisal systems is that they unintentionally shift employees' attention toward their manager and away from their customers. As a result, performance appraisal systems run the risk of only reinforcing those employee behaviors that are stressed by their manager. Behaviors that help ensure customer satisfaction may be ignored.

To help avoid this trap, client and customer ratings are becoming more common as organizations become more customer-oriented (Stahl and Bounds, 1991). In addition to controlled, formal surveying of target populations, most large companies now have continuous feedback mechanisms involving comment cards, toll-free hot lines, and on-line Web surveys. Important issues of sample bias are relevant, however, since it is thought to be primarily passionate people (happy or mad) who make the effort to participate in feedback. Recent efforts are being used to try to widen the participation level.

Franchises (such as fast food) have long been areas where quality and service can vary widely across units within the same chain. A mechanism used to assess service across a wide number of units is "mystery shoppers," people who are evaluating the company by simply behaving like a shopper (or diner) and whose identity is not known to those they are evaluating. The primary job of mystery shoppers is to frequent the franchised restaurants to ensure that food quality, timing, cleanliness, and other standards are being met. Many other retailers are beginning to develop and engage in similar activities.

A more detailed description of one customer appraisal system may clarify the manner in which they are used. One organization sends an appraisal form, such as that in Figure 7.5, to every customer who has a service performed by a company employee. These customer ratings are then summarized in a quarterly feedback report that provides average ratings on eight diagnostic dimensions as well as an overall customer satisfaction score. The report is given to both employees and their managers, and it provides information used to develop employees and make decisions about salary bonuses. This customer rating form then becomes a method of employee rating as well, thereby serving two purposes for the organization.

Collecting feedback from the customer's perspective is consistent with the basic tenets of total quality management (TQM) and with the notion that the customer is always right. It also reinforces to employees that their overreaching goal is to provide the ideal value that the typical customer seeks.

In many cases, customers are often in a better position to evaluate the quality of products and services offered than are managers or fellow employees. This third-party performance rating can be

Figure 7.5. Illustration of a Client Evaluation Scale.

MANAGEMENT SERVICES COMMENT CARD

This survey asks your opinion about specific aspects of the service you received. Your individual responses will remain confidential and will be compiled with those of other customers to improve customer service. Please use the following scale to indicate the extent to which you agree with the statement. Circle one response for each item.

1 = Strongly Disagree

2 = Disagree

3 = Neutral

4 = Agree

5 = Strongly Agree

If you feel unable to adequately rate a specific item, please leave it blank.

SERVICE/ATTITUDE

When serving me, this person was helpful.

1   2   3   4   5

This person was cooperative in meeting my requests.

1   2   3   4   5

This person was accurate.

1   2   3   4   5

This person was pleasant.

1   2   3   4   5

This person represents the company well.

1   2   3   4   5

CUSTOMER SATISFACTION

How would you rate your overall level of satisfaction with the service you have received?

1 = Very dissatisfied

2 = Dissatisfied

3 = Neutral

4 = Satisfied

5 = Very Satisfied

What specifically could be done to make you more satisfied with the service?

critical for accurate product or service ratings in an industry. Managers in a single organization may have limited information about how well products and services are produced and delivered by competitors or by the industry as a whole. On average, however, a customer is probably more aware of the range of features and benefits that are typically available. In the end, if customers are unhappy with a particular company's products or services, managers need to know the problems and the source before they can change the system and improve customer satisfaction (Bounds and Dobbins, 1991).

If a front-line employee consistently receives low customer ratings, then the individual may be a true detriment to the organization. In today's marketplace, ignoring such an employee's performance would be costly to the organization.

Unfortunately, the appraisal field has generally focused on the ratings of managers or supervisors and neglected customer feedback. In contrast, until recently, client customer evaluation systems were almost always designed by marketers who are interested in ways to generally change the service and product and who are less interested in the individual appraisal of employees. For instance, some employees believe that "secret shoppers" are hard-to-detect enemies out to take their job away, and that an institutionalized form of formal client feedback can only prevent them from receiving salary increases. Although it would be valuable to have consistent consumer ratings across time, this is seldom possible because of the ad hoc nature of most of these evaluations.

One key issue is whether customers who have interacted with an employee can make an accurate and unbiased rating of the employee's performance. In many contexts, there is an inherent conflict between the customer and the employee. For example, suppose a mechanic and customer are trying to agree on a mutually acceptable maintenance fee. The mechanic may think his efforts are worth more than the customer thinks. It can be difficult for such a customer to make unbiased ratings during such a conflict.

For appraisal systems to be effective, they need to distinguish employee performance aspects from system aspects. For example, if a person purchased a bicycle that continually has mechanical problems due to poor design, they would probably evaluate customer service at the bicycle shop as ineffective (because the bicycle is frequently being repaired). However, such a low rating may better reflect the poor quality of the bicycle than the quality of work at the service center.

Despite flaws, the client appraisals are likely to continue to grow in popularity across a wide range of organizations. Increasingly, these appraisals are serving as an effective organizational development tool that causes employees to recognize that they are ultimately accountable to customers and not just their boss or manager.

Teacher and Instructor Ratings

When most institutions (or training and executive education groups) decide to develop a teacher or instructor rating system, they generally believe their needs and situation are unique and that therefore they need to generate their own rating form. The key importance in developing a rating instrument is to clearly understand the purpose for which it is to be used. Such forms are usually developed with little thought about how such information can be used by a faculty member to improve the teaching-learning situation. Perhaps even less thought is given to how such information can be used by administrators to encourage and reward faculty improvement efforts.

Student feedback forms have been constructed by many different types of groups, such as student committees, faculty, administrators, and even special task force committees. As with employee evaluations, they are generally constructed without the benefit of advice and consultation with experts in questionnaire design, and this results in questionable and often problematic results. These questionnaires generally end up reflecting the thinking and biases of what one or two individuals regard as meaningful criteria of instructional effectiveness, and they are often not useful for all instructors and courses.

Types of Student Feedback Forms

The first and least generalizable type of rating form is the one made up by an individual instructor and tailored to fit a specific course. (See Figure 7.6 for an example.) Although the instructor might find this form provides useful feedback in improving his or her course, such forms are usually too idiosyncratic to use for more formal purposes of evaluation.

A second, more generalizable, type of rating form is one that is designed by having a required set of questions supplemented with additional questions more tailored to individual faculty and courses. At the minimum, most schools ask two standard questions of all students in all courses. These typically deal with the teaching effectiveness of the instructor and the quality of the course. For instance, two standard items could be measured on 5-point scales of "exceptionally low" to "exceptionally high," with the two standard statements all students answer being "Rate the instructor's overall teaching effectiveness" and "Rate the overall quality of this course." (1 = low; 5 = high).

In addition to a small set of standard questions, some schools allow faculty or department chairs to modify the questionnaires by selecting from a wide range of other questions that are more tailored to the topic or to the course. These types of evaluations are sometimes called "cafeteria questionnaires" and are becoming increasingly popular since they involve selecting individual items from a large menu of items. One example of such a pool of questions is the 560-item "question bank" of the Survey Research Laboratory (SRL) at the University of Illinois. This wide range of questions deals with topics such as course management (organization, assignments, grading, and workload), student outcomes (cognitive, affective, participation, and effort), instructor characteristics (communication skills, stimulation of thinking, warmth and concern for students),

Figure 7.6. Illustration of a Course Improvement Questionnaire.

COURSE IMPROVEMENT QUESTIONNAIRE

- At present, 12½% of the class time is spent in review, 12½% in taking and going over tests, and 75% of the time in regular instruction. Is this balance in emphasis about right? *(If you answered no, please specify the balance you'd prefer.)*

- About how often are you unable to understand why the answers to the learning exercises are correct? *(Note: this question is not asking if you answered the questions correctly, but rather how often you couldn't understand why the answer given was correct.)*

- How helpful would it be if, in the answer to each learning exercise, a reference was given to the page(s) in the book or to a portion of the lecture in which the relevant concepts are discussed?
  - ☐ Would be very helpful to me.
  - ☐ Would not be very helpful to me.

- Assuming the same total content covered is the same, would you prefer:
  - ☐ fewer objectives that are broader in scope?
  - ☐ more objectives that are more specific?
  - ☐ about the same number of objectives we now have?

- The number of learning exercises provided for each objective is usually:
  - ☐ too few (wish there were more).
  - ☐ too many.
  - ☐ about the right number.

- How do you feel about the use of several different forms of each quiz?

- Have you gone to see any of the three instructors for help outside of class time?
  - ☐ *If yes,* did you feel he/she was willing to spend sufficient time to help you with your difficulty?

- Is there something you wanted to get out of this course in statistics that has not yet materialized? *If yes, please describe what it is.*

- Please indicate any other suggestions you have for the improvement of this course.

Source: Millman and Aleamoni, 1981.

and so on. After instructors choose their items, items are inserted onto a printed answer sheet along with two standard items. The back of the questionnaire is reserved for open-ended responses. Figure 7.7 illustrates a subset of the SRL question bank questions used to evaluate an instructor's communication style.

Having only two standard questions is somewhat extreme. It is more typical for schools to have a larger standard section of items that apply to almost all courses and instructors with additional optional item sections that allow the instructor to select specific (or more diagnostic) items from the institutional pool. A more extreme version of this can be found at schools that provide a small number of standard forms (perhaps six to eight) that have some common questions but that are tailored differently for courses depending on whether they are primarily discussion-based, lecture-based, or lab-based.

Finally, the third type of rating form is one used for all instructors and all courses with no provision for additional items selected by the instructor. Such forms are typically sponsored by the student government association, and results are published campuswide. (Figure 7.6 is an example of such a form.) Although efficient, these forms do not offer the flexibility and diagnostic value of the more stylized forms. In these cases it might be best for faculty members to supplement these forms with their own questionnaire for diagnostic purposes only.[1]

It is important that an institution interested in implementing a feedback form for its students seek the advice of individuals who have experience in questionnaire design. This helps ensure a proper design and more reliable and valid measures from the outset. It also helps avoid questionnaires with too narrow applications and poorly defined responses.

Types of Items

The items used to evaluate learning can be classified in terms of (1) their content, (2) their level of inference, and (3) the type

Figure 7.7. Evaluation Items Related to Instructor Effectiveness.

(Rated on 5-point scales from "Almost Never" to "Almost Always")

_____ The instructor acted interested in the material.

_____ The instructor was well prepared.

_____ The instructor acted relaxed.

_____ The instructor looked at the class while speaking.

_____ The instructor enunciated well.

_____ The instructor lectures deemed to go smoothly, following a logical sequence of thought.

_____ The instructor used relevant examples.

_____ The instructor explained clearly and exploitations were to the point.

_____ The instructor emphasized important points by raising voice, repeating, etc.

_____ The instructor made you interested in the material.

_____ The instructor lectures were related to the reading assignments.

_____ The instructor gave clear explanations of abstract ideas.

_____ The instructor made clear the objectives for each lecture or series of lectures.

_____ The instructor followed an outline.

_____ The instructor stimulated your intellectual curiosity.

_____ The instructor seemed to have very recent information on the subject.

_____ The instructor answers to questions were relevant.

_____ The instructor varied pace of lecturing.

_____ The instructor presented material not in the reading assignments.

_____ The instructor's voice was animated.

_____ The instructor used humor effectively.

_____ The instructor answered all questions (or admitted didn't know the answer).

_____ The instructor encouraged questions during the lecture.

Source: Survey Research Laboratory, University of Illinois.

of response required. In discussions related to developing rating forms, it is easy to confuse the three and have seemingly conflicting opinions about issues that are essentially distinct. In developing such forms it is best to discuss these three dimensions separately.

1. *Content.* When deciding on the item's content, it is important to determine which elements of the course, instruction, and learning areas need to be addressed. Questions constructed for the course area should assess how well material was covered by instructors and understood by students. Questions constructed for the instruction area should assess instructor characteristics such as fairness, clearness, willingness to interact, clarity, and so on. Finally, those questions constructed for the learning area should address issues such as a student's satisfaction, perceived competency, and desire to continue study in the field.

2. *Inference.* If student ratings will be used to produce measures that require considerable inference beyond what is observed in the classroom (such as "partial" or "fair," "autocratic" or "democratic," "dull" or "stimulating"), then higher-inference measures are needed (Rosenshine, 1970). Students should apply these measures when they assess the instructor or the instruction.

If the purpose of the questions is to classify teaching behaviors according to relatively objective categories, then low-inference measures are needed. These measures are obtained as frequency ratings of the instructor on such scales as "gesturing," "variation in voice," "asking questions," or "praise and encouragement."

Ratings on high-inference items are particularly useful in exploring new ideas, and they have generally yielded higher correlations with overall instructor effectiveness than have the more specific, or low-inference, behavioral measures. Yet because the information in low-inference measures is easier to project to specific behaviors, it is easier to use in instructional improvement programs.

3. *Format.* The questionnaire's format can influence how carefully students respond to the items and how accurately they will respond with true feelings. Using open-ended (free-response) questions,

for instance, usually produces a colorful array of responses in the student's "own words," but provides very little information that can be used for formative evaluation. Instructors still value these responses because they can attach their own interpretation to these comments. Using closed-ended (limited-response) formats provides more accurate counts of the types of responses to each item. In many situations, the best approach is to use a combination of both closed-ended and open-ended responses.

Most student evaluation forms suffer from severe design problems. This is typically because they are designed by committees of students or administrators who have little questionnaire design experience and little regard for the unforeseen consequences of a poorly worded or inaccurate question.

The type of question being asked will typically determine the type of closed-ended responses the survey designer can provide. As with other surveys, if appropriate responses do not match each question, incongruous and unreliable responses will result. For instance, if a continuum-response format is used and only endpoints are anchored (for example, Very Poor 1–2–3–4–5–6–7 Very Good), it will tend to produce unreliable responses because it is not clear what the midpoint represents. It is important that each response point along the continuum be appropriate whenever an item is stated either positively or negatively. Another type of possible response scale requires elaborate behavioral descriptions along the continuum. (See the discussion of BARS earlier in this chapter.) If possible, items with common responses should be grouped together.

Selecting the Appropriate Items

One way to generate a questionnaire draft is to evaluate what other institutions are using and to adopt similar ideas. Many institutions have catalogues of questions (often called items) that have been tested previously. Care must be taken before adopting another set of survey items unless it is known whether the other institution considered the possible shortcomings discussed earlier and evaluated or tested the questionnaire accordingly. A second way to generate a questionnaire draft is to use a commercially available questionnaire. Commercial forms usually avoid the potential problems noted above but still need to be carefully matched to the requirements of the institution. Carefully analyze each question and other items before adapting the questionnaire for the institution.

If an institution has generated or obtained a pool of items rather than adopted an entire instrument, care must be taken when selecting items on a piecemeal basis. Use logical and empirical analysis to select individual items from a pool. Logical analysis requires form developers to make subjective judgments in selecting appropriate items, whereas an empirical analysis requires that studies be conducted to determine the usability of the items.

The last step in the design and construction of the items and the questionnaire is organizing the items in the questionnaire. Although there can be a fear of halo effects (favorably inflated responses) when putting such a questionnaire together, it is nonetheless best to make the questionnaire as simple and as easy-to-complete as possible. If you must choose between possible halo effects and simplicity, choose simplicity. For instance, although frequently reversing the endpoints on a scale might help reduce halo effects, it can sometimes lead to errors because it makes the questionnaire needlessly complex.

Questions need to be grouped, labeled, and organized for easy reading and answering, and according to how and where the responses should be placed. There should be some negatively worded questions, and they should begin to appear early in the questionnaire to avoid mistakes that might be due to a positive response-set bias. (That is, varying the wording keeps respondents from simply selecting the same response for every question.) Negatively stated items can be useful, but only if they can be stated negatively in a coherent manner. Most questionnaire items can be grouped into subscales. If the original grouping was done on a logical basis, then a statistical technique such as factor analysis can be used to confirm whether the grouped items represent a common construct. If you have questions about how to lay out the feedback form, consult a skilled questionnaire developer. Figure 7.8 shows a student-designed feedback form that has been successfully used to evaluate professors in a consistent manner.

Administrating Student Feedback Forms

Whenever possible, managing and directing a campuswide program of administering teacher evaluations should be the responsibility of either the institution's chief academic officer or of instructional development, evaluation, or testing personnel. The responsibility should not be given to students or faculty in individual departments or colleges. When students or faculty administer teaching evaluations, the application of the ratings becomes restricted, and the possibility of a lasting program with consistent benchmarks is reduced.

When Should Questionnaires Be Administered?

The manner in which the questionnaire is administered and collected can determine the quality of the resulting data. It is generally best to formally administer the questionnaires by providing a standard set of instructions and allowing enough class time to complete all the items. If the questionnaire is offhandedly administered without standard instructions and a designated time to fill it out, the students tend to place that same amount of effort in their responses. It is also worth noting that if students are permitted to take the questionnaire home to fill it out, and to return it at the next class meeting, only a particular type of student who is energetic and proactive will return it.

If the instructors administer their own questionnaires, they should read a standard set of instructions and leave the room after selecting a student to gather the completed questionnaires and deliver them to a central location. Students tend to hold back their true impressions of the course and instructor if they feel that the instructor will see them at the end of that class period or, in some cases, before the course has ended. The exception to this rule is when instructors have informed their students that their responses will be used in such a way that will improve the ongoing course.

Suggestions for Student-Administered Questionnaires

Student government representatives can administer the student rating questionnaires if the faculty or college administrators request them to do it and if they are qualified and organized enough to administer the questionnaires. Students administering the questionnaires should read a standard set of instructions and request that the instructor leave during the administration. If an administrator decides instead to designate a staff member to administer the student rating questionnaire, then the same procedure should be followed as suggested above. In general, this option should be avoided, as faculty and students tend to feel threatened if they know that an administrator is controlling and directing the administration of the questionnaires.

When the questionnaire is administered, students should be given all the necessary materials (forms and no. 2 pencils). Students should generally fill out the forms in their regular classroom near the end of a particular class session. One common mistake is to hand out the questionnaire on the last day of the course. One preliminary finding is that the closer to the final exam a questionnaire is administrated, the less consistent the evaluations of the students. In addition, many students do not show up on the last day of class.

It is critical that students understand that their frank and honest comments are desired. If students get the impression that the instructor is not really interested in their responses, they will not respond seriously. Along with providing an understanding of how these results are used, it is best to ask students to concentrate and to not talk as they are completing the evaluations. Not only does this underscore the seriousness of the evaluation, but it also decreases bias by not allowing students to discuss the course and instructor while filling out the questionnaires.

Figure 7.8. Teacher Evaluation Questionnaire.

Instructor: _____ Course Number: _____ Quarter: _____

Please fill in your responses below.

Student Input	*Scale*	*Response*
How much prior exposure did you have to the material in this course?	1 2 3 4 5 (None) (A Great Deal)	_____
Excluding class sessions, estimate the average number of hours per week spent in preparation of review.	Estimate on the line to the right:	_____
How often were you prepared for class?	1 2 3 4 5 (Rarely) (Always)	_____
How would you rate student interest throughout the course?	1 2 3 4 5 (Poor) (Excellent)	_____
How would you rate the quality of student participation in classroom discussions?	1 2 3 4 5 (None) (Excellent)	_____

Instructor Input	*Do not write here*	*Response*
Overall, did the instructor convey the course material clearly?	1 2 3 4 5 (Not Clear) (Very Clear)	_____
Overall, did the instructor convey the material in an interesting way?	1 2 3 4 5 (Not Interesting) (Very Interesting)	_____
Did the instructor provide instructive feedback on your performance?	1 2 3 4 5 (None) (A Great Deal)	_____

Evaluation of Course Content	*Do not write here*	*Response*
Did you take away useful tools, concepts and/or insights from the course?	1 2 3 4 5 (Very Few) (A Great Many)	_____
Given the objectives of this course, did the course challenge you?	1 2 3 4 5 (Not at All) (Very Much)	_____
How much did you get out of the course?	1 2 3 4 5 (Very Little) (A Great Deal)	_____

Evaluation of Course Content	*Do not write here*	*Response*

Would you recommend this course   1   2   3   4   5
to other students?   (Definitely Not)   (Definitely)   _____

Did you take advantage of T.A. sessions?   ☐ Yes   ☐ No

Comment on strengths and weaknesses of the instructor.

Please indicate what you consider to be the major strengths and weaknesses
of this course.

Please indicate one change you would make that would most improve
this course.

Please rank your teaching assistant on a score from 1-10 (10 being the highest)

T.A. name	*Ranking*

Was this a required course?   ☐ Yes   ☐ No

If so, would you have chosen to take this course?   ☐ Yes   ☐ No

Source: University of Chicago, 2003.

Finally, the amount of time it takes to administer a questionnaire in the classroom may represent only a portion of the actual time required to complete the process of using student ratings. There are significant time-related costs to analyze, print, and distribute these results (Millman, 1981). Given these costs, forms should provide the most reliable and valid feedback possible. An individual experienced in both education and instructional evaluation should pool student suggestions together into a final instrument. In this way the questionnaire can provide the same degree of precision and reliability that is merited given the costs involved and the consequences (such as performance evaluation) of the results.

Summary

Questions that evaluate performance follow the principles covered previously in this book. One of the main purposes of this chapter is to underscore the importance of the process of developing these questionnaires. If the process of developing, measuring, administering, and analyzing performance questions is seen as fair, it will contribute to cooperation and acceptance of the outcomes. It is critical to involve those people who will be evaluated and get their feedback on the instrument and the way the questions are worded. In some cases, this may result in different types of questions. (For example, BARS can be useful in contexts where it is feared that subjectivity could otherwise bias an evaluation.)

Instead of exclusively being used by managers to evaluate employees, performance-related questions are now increasingly used by employees to rate managers and by customers to rate employees. Within the past twenty years, student ratings of professors have been used increasingly to provide performance feedback and evaluation of teachers and professors. Given the increasing use of these questions, it is important we acknowledge some of their unique challenges.

Further Reading

The following books detail the process of developing performance appraisal surveys, obtaining institutional buy-in, and using surveys for evaluation.

Performance Appraisal: Assessing Human Behavior at Work (Beatty and Bernardin, 1984).

Performance Assessment Methods and Applications (Berk, 1986)

Performance Appraisal: Alternative Perspectives (Cardy and Dobbins, 1994)

Measurement-Based Evaluation of Teacher Performance (Coker, Medly, and Soar, 1984)

Evaluating Teaching (Doyle, 1983)

Improving Organizational Surveys (Edwards, Rosenfeld, and Thomas, 1993)

Handbook of Teacher Evaluation (Millman, 1981)

Questionnaire Design and Attitude Measurement (Oppenheim, 1966)

Development and Design of Survey Questionnaires (Pierre-Pierre, Platek, and Stevens, 1985)

Note

1. One way a diagnostic supplement can be added to these otherwise conventional forms is to make the supplement open-ended. Two effective questions that are relevant across courses and contexts are (1) "What are three things about the course or instructor that most helped you learn?" and (2) "What are three suggestions for improvement?" Although not everyone gives three answers for each question (and some give more), asking for three answers per question does prompt respondents to think past the first thought that comes to mind.

Chapter Eight

Asking Psychographic Questions

Psychographic and "lifestyle" research are sometimes referred to as activities, interests, and opinions (AIO) research because the questions often focus on these types of questions. This research resembles both motivation research and conventional research. It resembles motivation research because a major aim is to draw recognizably human portraits of consumers, but it also resembles more conventional research in that these portraits can be analyzed with standard statistical tools.

Our understanding of human behavior has evolved from viewing humans as an undifferentiated, homogenous population ("People think . . .") to viewing them on a more demographic basis ("So, what do women think about the new president?" or "What do the French think about biotechnology?"). Although this evolution represented some improvement in the accuracy and specificity of survey results, it is still difficult to predict human behavior, even when people are grouped by demographic characteristics. For instance, why is it that two neighbors with similar backgrounds, incomes, and educations can have different political beliefs, different types of cars, and different preferences for foods?

Psychographic and individual difference measures enable us to further segment populations to explain why different people behave in different ways. When the term *psychographics* was introduced by Emanuel Demby in the 1960s, it was generally defined as "the use of psychological, sociological, and anthropological factors, self-concept, and lifestyle to determine how the market is segmented by the propensity of groups within the market—and their reasons—to make a particular decision about a product, person, or ideology" (Demby, 1989, p. 21).

Perhaps the most obvious use of psychographic research is to draw portraits or profiles of target groups. Yet lifestyle and personality characteristics that are specific to certain people or behaviors must be defined and measured in order to be useful to researchers. For instance, it would be relevant to some researchers to identify a health-conscious segment, or it might be of interest to a clothing company to identify a fashion-conscious segment. In other words, personality and lifestyle characteristics, as with all measurement, must be defined by your objectives.

Checklist of Major Points

1. Asking psychographic questions can be used to help predict preferences and behavior.

2. Psychographic questions can be useful in developing segments that reflect people's thinking and behavior instead of simply their demographic makeup.

3. Psychographic segments can be used for three broad purposes: (1) examining predicted relationships, (2) creating personality clusters, or (3) creating generic segments for the purposes of trend-related research.

4. One way to generate psychographic measures is to use previously validated psychological constructs. Another approach is to generate ad hoc items relevant to the specific behavior of interest.

5. When developing psychographic measures, enlist the insights of experts and inside sources and conduct in-depth interviews with consumers.

6. The most useful questions are AIO statements that are measured on 7- or 9-point scales anchored with "Strongly Disagree" and "Strongly Agree."

7. It is important to include measures of behavior frequency (such as product usage) in the study of psychographics.

8. Pretest psychographic scales and use factor and cluster analysis to eliminate redundant or nondifferentiating questions.

What Are Some Examples of Psychographic Segments?

Psychographic questions are typically used to segment people by the way they think or behave. Segmenting people on this basis enables researchers to more clearly examine what these different segments prefer (such as brand preference) and what they do. For example, psychographic questions allow comparisons between healthy and unhealthy behaviors. A second reason to ask psychographic questions is to try to develop more general or generic segments that might be useful in examining trends and larger systemic patterns of behavior.

Let us first consider using psychographics to examine segment-related differences in preference or behavior, a practice that is becoming increasingly common. Using psychographic questions involves using one or two hypothesized characteristics (or personality traits) to explain differences in choice or behavior. For instance, one study hypothesized that a trait called "venturesome" was related to the probability that "venturesome" people would try new and different products. In turn, researchers found that people with this trait were more likely to choose a new and different flavor of toothpaste (Ultra Brite instead of Colgate) when compared to less adventuresome people.

Using Psychographic Questions to Help Predict Behavior

Using psychographics to predict behavior patterns is most widespread in the area of marketing research. Psychographics have been used to explain preferences that are based more on personality than on demographics. They explained, for instance, why Anheuser-Busch's Natural Light failed and Bud Light was a huge success. More common are studies of psychographic profiles that predict preferences for one brand versus another. A study of VCR purchasers compared those males who had purchased a higher-cost target brand to males who had purchased more affordable competing brands. After psychographically segmenting consumers into one of eight categories, the researchers found that those who purchased the higher-cost target brand were more likely to be "inconspicuous social isolates," "masculine hero emulators," or "sophisticated cosmopolitans." Those who preferred less expensive alternatives were characterized as either "silent conservatives," "embittered resigned workers," "highbrow Puritans," "rebellious pleasure seekers," or "work hard–play hard executives" (Weinstein, 1994, p. 122). Note that a considerable degree of creative license is used in defining the various psychographic segments.

One preference study wanted to predict what types of people preferred bitter beer, malt beer, or other types of beer. Cluster analysis was used to segment people into an "innovative, sports active, self-confident" psychographic segment or into a "self-absorbed, spontaneous, social drinking" segment. Researchers found that members of the first cluster tended to prefer bitter beers that were less malty and had less head creaminess (Wells, 1975). Clustering methods have also been used to examine behavior. In an attempt to group people by their food- and health-related tendencies and behaviors, one study (Glanz and others, 1998) identified seven clusters that could be used for segmentation purposes. These included (1) physical fanatics, (2) active attractives, (3) tense but trying, (4) decent do littles, (5) passively healthy, (6) hard-living hedonists, and (7) noninterested nihilists. Subsequent follow-up studies (Wansink, 2004) showed these lifestyle clusters related to certain behaviors with some group members. For example, decent do littles tended to be more interested in shelf stocking, cooking, and baking, and hard-living hedonists tended to be more interested in impulsive behaviors and tended to be more influenced by environmental factors (such as assortment size and packaging).

Using Psychographic Questions to Segment Respondents

In addition to using psychographic questions to segment consumers into potentially diagnostically useful groups, questions can be used to develop more general segments from which to examine trends and larger systemic patterns of behavior. One of the more widely known psychographic segmentation research programs (VALS, an acronym based on "values and lifestyles") is conducted by SRI Consulting (Gunter and Furnham, 1992). Although many psychographic studies focus on measures and characteristics that are uniquely related to a topic of interest (reducing binge drinking, determining taste profiles, understanding who is most likely to give donations to a college), the VALS study is conducted across categories and attempts to show more general psychographic segments that can be used across a wide number of people and topics. Their psychographic approach sorts people into one of eight different groups. A general description of people in each category is offered in Table 8.1.

These breakdowns are determined by cluster analyzing respondents' answers to questions regarding gender, age, education, and income along with the key psychographic questions noted in Table 8.2. Each of the scaled questions is answered using one of four categories: (1) Mostly disagree, (2) Somewhat disagree, (3) Somewhat agree, (4) Mostly agree.

A number of other syndicated lifestyle services use psychographic techniques to segment populations and predict trends. The Yankelovich Monitor (Gunter and Furnham, 1992) is an annual survey of fifty trends relevant to consumer marketing, such as personalization, health orientation, meaningful work, responsiveness to fantasy, and an emphasis on winning.

Another alternative to VALS is the List of Values (LOV), which is gaining favor among academics because it is in the public

Table 8.1. Eight Psychographic Segments
Used by VALS.

Values & Lifestyles

FULFILLEDS
mature, responsible, well-educated professionals; well informed about
world events; open to new ideas and social change; have high incomes
and are value-oriented.

BELIEVERS
conservative, predictable consumers favoring American products and
established brands; have modest incomes; lives centered on family,
church, and community.

ACHIEVERS
successful, work-oriented people deriving satisfaction from their jobs and
their families; politically conservative and respect authority; favor
established products that showcase their success.

STRIVERS
values similar to achievers but have fewer resources available; style and
appearance are important to them as they strive to emulate the people
they wish they were.

EXPERIENCERS
youngest segment with lots of energy to pour into physical and social
activities; avid consumers who spend heavily.

MAKERS
practical people who value self-sufficiency; focused on family, work,
and recreation with little interest in the outside world; unimpressed by
material possessions.

STRUGGLERS
lowest income and minimal resources; within their limited means, they are
brand-loyal consumers; struggle to make ends meet.

ACTUALIZERS
highest incomes and maximum resources; high self-esteem; image is
important as an expression of their taste, independence, and character;
tastes lean toward the finer things in life.

Source: SRI Consulting Business Intelligence, http://www.sric-bi.com/VALS/

Table 8.2. Examples of Psychographic Questions Used in Constructing VALS Profiles.

1. I am often interested in theories.
2. I like outrageous people and things.
3. I like a lot of variety in my life.
4. I love to make things I can use everyday.
5. I follow the latest trends and fashions.
6. Just as the Bible says, the world literally was created in six days.
7. I like being in charge of a group.
8. I like to learn about art, culture, and history.
9. I often crave excitement.
10. I am really interested only in a few things.
11. I would rather make something than buy it.
12. I dress more fashionably than most people.
13. The federal government should encourage prayers in public schools.
14. I have more ability than most people.
15. I consider myself an intellectual.
16. I must admit that I like to show off.
17. I like trying new things.
18. I am very interested in how mechanical things, such as engines, work.
19. I like to dress in the latest fashions.
20. There is too much sex on television today.
21. I like to lead others.
22. I would like to spend a year or more in a foreign country.
23. I like a lot of excitement in my life.
24. I must admit that my interests are somewhat narrow and limited.
25. I like making things of wood, metal, or other such material.
26. I want to be considered fashionable.
27. A woman's life is fulfilled only if she can provide a happy home for her family.
28. I like the challenge of doing something I have never done before.
29. I like to learn about things even if they may never be of any use to me.
30. I like to make things with my hands.
31. I am always looking for a thrill.
32. I like doing things that are new and different.
33. I like to look through hardware or automotive stores.
34. I would like to understand more about how the universe works.
35. I like my life to be pretty much the same from week to week.

Source: SRI Consulting Business Intelligence, http://www.sric-bi.com/VALS/

domain and relates closely to consumer behavior and to trends (Kamakura and Novak, 1992). Consistent with research on values in social psychology, the LOV approach focuses on psychographic segments that are composed of different empirically validated constructs such as self-respect; security; warm relationships; sense of accomplishment; self-fulfillment; being well respected; sense of belonging; and sense of fun, enjoyment, or excitement (Weinstein, 1994).

What Psychographic Questions Should I Ask?

There are two basic approaches to deciding what psychographic measures to use. One involves using previously validated items, and the second involves developing situation-specific items.

The most easily justified (but perhaps less creative) way to approach psychographic or individual difference measures is to use those that have been validated in the literature and are known to be related to whatever is being studied. The advantage to this approach is that the original scales can be used, they will have been validated, and there will be some notion as to what one might expect. Table 8.3 gives a small sample of some individual difference measures that have been shown to successfully differentiate be-

Table 8.3. Some Examples of Individual Difference Variables.

Need for cognition	Detail-oriented	Curiosity
Aggression	Anxiety	Problem-solving
Need Achievement	Need Affiliation	Popularity
Self-centered	Involvement	Health-conscious
Motivation	Prevention-focused	Introverted
Innovator	Emotional	Social Desirability
Moral Judgment	Risk Taking	Obsessive
Rational	Self-monitoring	Conformity
Suggestibility	Need for Approval	Locus of Control
Impulsivity	Dogmatisms	Delay of Gratification
Masculinity-Femininity	Dependency	

tween different behaviors in various fields. All of these characteristics have scales associated with them that can be easily adapted to different uses.

As shown in the example that follows, questions are most often asked as either Likert questions or semantic differential questions.

Likert Questions

1. I consider myself to be detail-oriented.

$$1 - 2 - 3 - 4 - 5 - 6 - 7 - 8 - 9$$

Strongly Disagree   *Strongly Agree*

Semantic Differential Questions

2. I consider myself to be . . .

$$1 - 2 - 3 - 4 - 5 - 6 - 7 - 8 - 9$$

Not Detail-Oriented   *Detail-Oriented*

Another approach is to force people to rank a set of statements from most to least agreement in order to suppress "yea-saying." This ranking approach can also force discrimination among items that might otherwise have been marked on the same scale position. When rating measures are taken, people are usually divided into high and low categories based on median splits or into top-third and bottom-third splits.

Although the two questions noted in the example use 9-point scales, 4-point scales are often seen (recall the VALS example) and may be more appropriate for verbal and electronic formats. More discussion of this can be found at the end of this chapter and in the discussion of response formats in Chapter Five.

There are additional ways to ask psychographic questions. Some researchers prefer to present two personality or AIO statements to respondents and ask them to indicate which comes closer to their views. Other researchers prefer to ask respondents to rank a set of statements from most to least agreement. These alternatives can force discrimination among items that might otherwise be marked at the same scale position. But they are often difficult to administer and difficult for respondents to handle.

Seven Steps to Generating Psychographic Questions

When conducting psychographic research, one can either begin with a large, highly diversified collection of statements (a "shotgun" approach) or a more limited number of multi-item scales that focus on specific, well-identified psychological constructs.

Some notable researchers (Wells, 1975) prefer the more exploratory shotgun approach because of its ability to generate novel, unexpected, and potentially interesting or useful relationships. Using a limited number of multi-item scales reduces the range of topics researchers can cover and often prevents respondents from generating insightful observations. Although the latitude afforded by the shotgun approach can provide some tempting and interesting findings, ultimately the more idiosyncratic these measures are, the more difficult it is to justify any interesting findings related to them. Discoveries obtained with idiosyncratic measures are also more difficult to replicate.

With this caveat in mind, how would you go about generating and isolating psychographic or individual difference variables that might be interesting for a particular project? The approach is similar to the general steps you use in formulating questions described in earlier chapters.

1. *Scan the literature.* Look for constructs that might be mentioned (even parenthetically) as containing characteristics that influence attitudes or behaviors in the domain in which you are interested. This literature can be academic or popular.

2. *Talk to relevant experts in this area.* These may be researchers, salespeople, consumers, or what we simply call "inside sources"—that is, those people whose expertise is based on their frequent interaction with the people you are interested in. For instance, a study attempting to understand (and deter) binge drinking interviewed bartenders to try to develop personality profiles of those most predisposed to binge drinking. Similarly, a study of men who

spent a lot of money on business shoes used shoe shiners in airports to get a better idea as to how a "Cole-Haan" man differed from an "Allen-Edmunds" man (Wansink, 1994c).

3. *Conduct in-depth interviews or focus groups.* When possible, conduct in-depth interviews or focus groups with the individuals in these areas that you most want to profile. The more extreme or "fanatical" people are regarding your domain of interest, the more useful will be their insights. You can begin by having them describe themselves and others who have similar preferences. The goal here is to gain more confidence that some of the criteria you have defined will relate to some subsegments of the population you are studying.

4. *Focus on AIO statements that are measured on scales.* The most effective psychographic studies have developed viable lifestyle segmentation profiles by beginning with a large number (several dozen) statements related to activities, interests, and opinions (AIO). These statements may or may not directly relate to the behavior of focus, but they should at least have a hypothesized indirect or an interactive effect on the behavior. A study involving car purchases used statements such as "My family knows I love them by how well I take care of them," "My choice of car affects how I feel about myself," and "Advertisements for automobiles are an insult to my intelligence" (Weinstein 1994, p. 120).

These AIO statements are typically asked on 7- or 9-point scales that are anchored with "strongly disagree" and "strongly agree," but have also been used with 4-point scales anchored with "mostly disagree" and "mostly agree." In general, because measuring dispersion is critical in developing segments, there is good reason to use more detailed scales. This is particularly important if smaller samples are being used.

5. *Include important behaviors.* In addition to AIO information, it is also critical to include a number of behaviors that may be related to the behavior of interest. These questions tend to ask about how often respondents engage in relevant behaviors. Although knowing the frequency that respondents use various products is often useful,

the frequency that people have dinner parties, drink wine with dinner, exercise, and read nonfiction books has also been useful in helping develop various psychographic profiles (Wansink, 2003a).

6. *Conduct a pilot study and use multivariate analysis.* When it is clear what some of the potentially distinguishing criteria are, conduct a pilot study. The results from this study can be analyzed (through factor analysis, cluster analysis, and mean comparisons) and used to reduce unneeded questionnaire items before conducting your main study.

7. Name the psychographic segments descriptively. After a reasonably accurate set of segmentation profiles have been identified, it is useful to give descriptive names to these profiles. Although simply naming them Segment[1], Segment[2], and so on is often used in academic circles, it hinders one's ability to interpret the data efficiently. For example, a recent study of influential cooks (Wansink, 2003a) defined segments such as "competitive cooks," "innovative cooks," "traditional cooks," "stockpiling cooks," "guilty cooks," and so on. These definitions were useful in identifying which segments of cooks were most likely to adopt healthy new cooking methods and ingredients, and which ones were most likely to be influential in disseminating these new ingredients through word-of-mouth.

Example: A Psychographic Soup Story

One example of using psychographic questions involves a study done for a soup company (Wansink and Park, 2000a). Over many years, this soup company had promoted all its soups in a generic manner. There had recently been evidence, however, that different types of people preferred different types of soups. The company reasoned that if it could make some basic generalizations as to what types of people preferred what types of soups, it could use this information to promote its soups in a more tailored manner. For example, if health-oriented, outdoorsy people tended to prefer vegetable soup, the company could develop a more tailored "vegetable soup ad" that could be placed in magazines these people might read; the ad could tout health benefits and perhaps even display robust, outdoorsy people. To this end, the soup company wanted to have psychographic and lifestyle profiles of its most popular soups.

In conducting this research, the first step was to search the academic literature for evidence of individual difference and personality variables related to different tastes—and to locate the scales used to measure these items. Following this, researchers searched the popular press for clues about potentially defining characteristics worthy of further examination.

The second step was to consult sources that might have insider knowledge or a unique perspective in the area of soup preferences. Because of their frequent contact with soup eaters, experienced waitresses at diners were thought to be inside sources worth consulting. The researchers contacted thirty-two of these waitresses (each with an average of eight years of experience) and asked them such questions as "If your soup of the day is chicken noodle, what kind of person would order that soup?" The majority of the waitresses had a number of opinions about each type of soup lover, ranging from the way they walked and talked, to what they wore and talked about, and even to whether their clothes had cat hair on them. After these interviews, a number of converging insights emerged. For instance, waitresses often noted that people who frequently ordered chicken noodle seemed to be the most friendly and the most upbeat, and they stayed the longest for lunch. The waitresses also noted that those who instead frequently ordered tomato soup often mentioned a pet (or had pet hair on their clothes), and they were likely to read a paperback if eating lunch alone.

The third step involved in-depth interviews with people who were self-proclaimed fanatics of one flavor of soup. These people were interviewed and asked to describe themselves and to differentiate themselves from people who preferred other types of soup. In addition, questions related to the first two steps of the search were explored.

The fourth step involved developing the questionnaire. In all, the background literature, the waitress interviews, and the in-depth interviews suggested a number of personality characteristics or constructs that might differentiate each of the eight types of soup lovers. (See Figure 8.1 for a partial list.) For each of these criteria, measures were found in the literature or were formed on the basis of qualitative research or through the insights of the inside sources (the waitresses). The completed questionnaire was pretested, and the final (reduced) version was next used on a sample of 1,002 North American adults. Figure 8.1 gives an idea of what types of variables related most strongly to which type of soup user.

Figure 8.1. Lifestyle and Personality Variables Used to Differentiate Soup Preferences.

Lifestyle	Personality
Active Lifestyle (Vegetable) • I am outdoorsy • I am physically fit • I am a workaholic • I am socially active	**Mentally Alert (Clam Chowder)** • I am intellectual • I am sophisticated • I am creative • I am detail oriented • I am witty • I am nutrition conscious
Family Spirited (Chicken Noodle) • I am family-oriented • I am a churchgoer • I am pretty traditional	**Social (Chili)** • I am fun at parties • I am outgoing • I am not shy • I am spontaneous • I am a trendsetter
Homebody (Tomato) • I enjoy spending time alone • I am a homebody • I am a good cook • I am a pet lover	**Athletic (Cream Soups)** • I am athletic • I am competitive • I am adventurous
Intellectually Stimulated Pastimes (French Onion) • I am a technology whiz • I am a world traveler • I am a book lover	**Carefree (Minestrone)** • I am down-to-earth • I am affectionate • I am fun loving • I am optimistic

Source: Wansink and Park, 2000a.

The final analyses were cross-validated with an independent sample. People with extreme preferences were found to have much in common. For example, people with extreme preferences consumed the same flavor of soup 70 percent of the time. Furthermore, each soup lover has a blend of different tastes. The typical tomato soup lover tended to be a book lover, a pet lover, stubborn, and to possess a strong sense of family; the typical chicken noodle soup lover tended to be more of a home lover and churchgoer, and a bit less creative (Wansink and Park, 2000b). These clusters were then used to determine how the different soups should be differentially promoted—in what magazines and using what message strategy.

Structuring Psychographic Questions and Analyzing Answers

One type of psychographic question asks respondents to indicate the extent to which they agree with various statements about their personality (such as those noted in Tables 8.1 and 8.2). A common way to formulate the question is to use an odd-interval, 9-point scale ranging from 1 = strongly disagree to 9 = strongly agree. Often the midpoints are not identified, and respondents are left to interpolate these values.

A second method is to use a more abbreviated scale (such as done in the VALS example mentioned earlier in the chapter). Here an even-interval, 4-point (or 6-point) scale is presented with the points identified as being mostly disagree, somewhat disagree, somewhat agree, and mostly agree. Although it does not provide a midpoint or the wide range of the 9-point scale, this format is well suited for use in many modes—paper-and-pencil, telephone, or electronic.

Wells (1975) notes that when the sample is large and the responses well scattered, the simplest way to analyze AIO data is by ordinary cross-tabulation. But when the sample is small and the responses are highly skewed, a simple cross-tab will have many empty cells. In such cases, it is best to group scale steps to embrace reasonable numbers of respondents. Once the significant relationships have been found, the problem is to organize and understand them. Factor analysis is useful at this point.

It has been said that the relationships between psychographics and preferences for products or behavior are only superficial manifestations of more basic demographics. Yet two products with very similar demographic profiles can sometimes turn out to have usefully different psychographic profiles, and a demographic group in itself means little unless you have a clear picture of its lifestyle implications. Although correlations between psychographic variables and preferences seldom get higher than .3 or .4 (Wells, 1975), the same is true of the relationships between demographics and product preference.

Summary

The last twenty years have improved our understanding of consumers along with our ability to process larger and more complex amounts of data. As a result, it is increasingly common to use psychographic questions to segment and profile people based on how they think and act rather than simply on the basis of demographic criteria. Although much of the early work on psychographics has been exploratory and oriented toward specific ad hoc problems or segmentation efforts, the growing number of studies will help standardize future efforts.

• Using psychographic AIO questions along with behavior-related questions can be a fresh and useful way to better understand people and why they behave as they do. Essentially, the use of these questions can help blend an investigation that might be more sociological and help it also benefit from a psychological vantage point.

Additional Reading

Consumer Profiles: An Introduction to Psychographics (Gunter and Furnham, 1992)

"Value-System Segmentation: Exploring the Meaning of LOV" (Kamakura and Novak, 1992)

"Developing and Validating Useful Consumer Prototypes" (Wansink, 1994b)

"Profiling Nutritional Gatekeepers: Three Methods for Differentiating Influential Cooks" (Wansink, 2003a)

"Accounting for Taste: Prototypes that Predict Preference" (Wansink and Park, 2000a)

"Methods and Measures that Profile Heavy Users" (Wansink and Park, 2000b)

"Profiling Taste-Motivated Segments" (Wansink and Westgren, 2003)

Market Segmentation (Weinstein, 1994)

"Psychographics: A Critical Review" (Wells, 1975)

Chapter Nine

Asking Standard Demographic Questions

This chapter has a different format than earlier chapters. Rather than offering a wide range of examples and then some advice on what to consider in wording questions, the chapter provides a limited number of examples of demographic questions that can be used under most circumstances.

⸰ The demographic questions we present come from a variety of sources, but primarily from the U.S. Census Bureau questions used in the Decennial Census and on the Current Population Survey. These questions are worth your attention because they have received significant testing, and using questions identical to those used by the U.S. Census allows you to compare the characteristics of your sample to U.S. Census estimates. This can help you determine if your sample is biased and how your sample could be weighted to represent the population.

We give our recommended questions in a different typeface, along with a discussion of the issues related to that question. Although we do discuss major modifications you can make, we do not discuss minor changes in format that might be appropriate for different modes of questionnaires. We give a sample source for each question, but it should be recognized that each question has been used in many different questionnaires.

Checklist of Major Points

1. A researcher can spend a lot of time reinventing the wheel when trying to determine how to ask demographic questions.

It is best to adopt the questions used in this chapter and to conservatively modify them to fit your needs.

2. Determine what level of precision you need for your demographic questions. The examples in this chapter will give most researchers more precision than they might need. Follow the examples provided in this chapter, and adjust them based on the level of precision your study requires.

3. Demographic questions are almost always asked at the end of an interview, after the substantive questions. One exception to this general rule is when they are asked at the beginning of the survey in order to screen—for example, you might want to screen for people over the age of fifty-five—or to balance a particular sample, or to ask questions separately about all household members. Questions that occur at the end of the survey (except for questions about race and ethnicity) can be asked in any order.

4. It is also important to note that a respondent can also be asked about other people in the household and can serve as an informant. This is most common with demographic questions. In this type of question, the word *you* would be used when referring to the respondent, but the name of each person in the household would be inserted in repeated questions. That is, a questionnaire would not ask only "When is your birthday?" it would ask, "When is your/(NAME's) birthday?" For each person or "name" in the household the question would be repeated. In this chapter, we are using an abbreviated form for questions; in reality, the word "NAME" would be inserted in many of the questions used in the field.

Asking About Household Size and Composition

Researchers are often interested in who lives in a household and their relationships to one another, either for substantive reasons or in order to have information necessary to weight the data.

Household composition questions are difficult to ask efficiently and may cause rapport problems if they come at the beginning of the interview.

> How many people were living or staying in this house, apartment, or mobile home last night (DATE)?

> Include in this number: foster children, roommates or housemates, and people staying here last night who have no other permanent place to stay. This also includes people living here most of the time while working, even if they have another place to live.

Do not include in this number:

College students living away while attending college

People in a correctional facility, nursing home, or mental hospital last night

Armed Forces personnel living somewhere else

People who live or stay at another place most of the time

In this question by the U.S. Census Bureau, it is evident from the list of inclusions and exclusions that household listing is by no means an easy task. A significant number of people have no permanent address, but float from place to place and are likely to be overlooked in a household listing. Others (such as children at college and family members on long-term assignment away from home) are still likely to be included. The question deals with the total number of people because this is a less sensitive question than immediately asking for names (which, if required for future reference, is usually done next). Respondents tend to deliberately conceal the presence of some people, such as welfare recipients, illegal aliens, and unmarried partners, because they fear legal consequences or loss of benefits.

Please give me the first names (or initials) of all the people who were living or staying here last night (DATE). Start with the

person or one of the people living here who owns, is buying,
or rents this house, apartment, or mobile home. (If there
is no such person, start with any adult living or staying here.)

Even in the earlier edition of this book, the term *head of house-hold* was considered to be a subjective term; it currently is not used at all. Instead, it has been replaced with an operational definition based on the people who own or rent the dwelling. Respondents may often ask the interviewer, "Why do you want first names or initials?" The typical reply by an interviewer would be "Because I have some questions to ask about each household member, and referring to them by first name or initials will keep us from getting confused." Of course, if there are no specific questions about individual household members, first names should not be requested.

If the composition of the household is of interest, the following question should be asked for each person in the household.

(For all household members except Person 1) How are you/
is (NAME) related to (NAME PERSON 1)?

Husband or wife

Natural-born son or daughter

Adopted son or daughter

Stepson or stepdaughter

Brother or sister

Father or mother

Grandchild

Parent-in-law

Son-in-law or daughter-in-law

Other relative (Specify)

If Not Related to Person 1:

Roomer, boarder

Housemate, roommate

Unmarried partner

Foster child

Other nonrelative

This is a basic U.S. Census question. It should be pointed out that the number of nontraditional households has increased rapidly since our earlier edition, and the detailed relationship and non-relationship categories are clearly needed.

⏵ Asking About Gender

What is your/(NAME's) sex?

☐ Male   ☐ Female

Sometimes a person's gender is obvious from his or her name or voice, but sometimes the name or the voice is not diagnostic. If initials are used, an interviewer has more leeway in asking the gender question because most people will recognize it as merely a formality.

⏵Asking About Age

To accurately capture a person's age and to minimize the chance of error, the U.S. Census Bureau asks two questions.

1. **What is your age as of (DATE)?**

2. **What is your date of birth? (MONTH/DAY/YEAR)**

The U.S. Census Bureau has found the way to get the most accurate age reports is to ask for both age and date of birth. One can be checked against the other at the time of the interview, and any discrepancy can be resolved quickly. Checking age against birth date may reduce the likelihood of a careless mistake or a coy attempt to stay at age thirty-nine for yet another year.

It is not clear how strong this bias is, or how often mistakes are made. As a result, in most studies where age is only one of many independent variables and not of critical importance, we do not believe it is essential to ask two questions. For most purposes, a single question asking year of birth is sufficient. Sometimes researchers use five- or ten-year age categories in the question, but it is more accurate and just as easy to code age into single-year intervals initially and to combine later if necessary. If only a single question is asked, year of birth is superior to asking age because respondents concerned about their ages find year of birth less threatening.

In what year were you/was (NAME) born?

Asking About Race and Origin

1. Are you/is (NAME) Spanish/Hispanic or Latino?
   ☐ No   ☐ Yes

2. What is your race? *(Multiple answers possible)*

   ☐ White

   ☐ Black, African American, or Negro

   ☐ American Indian or Alaska Native

   ☐ Asian

   ☐ Other *(Specify)* _____

These two U.S. Census questions about Hispanic origin and race reflect the current ruling by the U.S. Office of Management and Budget that these questions should be asked separately. To reduce confusion about the racial question, it is important to ask the Hispanic (or more general ethnicity) question first. Yet many Hispanics consider the race question confusing and answer "Other" after they have already checked Hispanic in the first question.

Many nongovernment researchers simply combine these two questions into a single question with Spanish-Hispanic-Latino as one of the racial categories. It has long been recognized that there is no scientific basis for this classification and that it should be based on what the person considers himself or herself to be. A corollary to this is that interviewers should always ask the question; interviewers' observations are not reliable. In recent years, an increasing number of people consider themselves to be members of multiple racial groups. The current question allows them to indicate all of these groups.

The U.S. Census coding of these questions breaks them down into subcategories, but if you need further breakdowns we suggest you ask an open-ended question—for example, "What is your/ (NAME's) ancestry or ethnic origin? (multiple answers possible)."

The answer categories will depend on the distribution of responses. Many respondents will simply say "American." Many Jewish people will not give a country of origin but will simply say "Jewish." For illustrative purposes, we give the code categories used by the General Social Survey, with slight modifications. If you think there will be a low incidence of a particular country of origin, leave that choice off the list and make sure there is an "Other" choice. The list that follows contains an "Other" choice.

Africa	German	Serbian
American	Greek	Slovak
American Indian	Hungarian	Spanish
Arabian	Indian	Swedish
Austrian	Irish	Swiss
Belgian	Italian	West Indies (Hispanic)
Canadian (French)	Japanese	West Indies (Non-Hispanic)
Canadian (Other) _____	Jewish	Other Hispanic
Chinese	Lithuanian	(Central and South
Croatian	Mexican	America) _____
Czech	Norwegian	Other Asian _____
Danish	Polish	Other European _____
Dutch (Holland/	Portuguese	
Netherlands)	Puerto Rican	
English or Welsh	Romanian	
Filipino	Russian or former	
Finnish	Soviet Union	
French	Scottish	

∂ Asking About Marital Status

What is your marital status? Are you:

☐ Now married

☐ Widowed

☐ Divorced

☐ Separated

☐ Never married

Avoid using the term "single," as in popular speech this often means divorced, separated, or never married. "Separated" should mean living apart from a spouse because of marital discord; it does not include couples living apart because the husband is in the Armed Forces, working in a different city, or something similar.

A significant number of people currently live together and share household income and expenses who are not legally married. NORC defines this population as "living as married." Depending on your needs, you might put this group in a separate category, combine it with the "now married" group, or omit it entirely.

⬥ Asking About Education

1. Are you now attending or enrolled in school?

2. *(If Yes):* Is that full-time or part-time?

   ☐ Yes, full-time student

   ☐ Yes, part-time student

   ☐ No

3. *(If Yes):* What grade or level are you attending?

   ___ year in school

4. What is the highest number of years of school you/(NAME) completed?

   ___ years completed

5. What is the highest degree you/(NAME) received?

☐ None

☐ Elementary school diploma

☐ High school diploma or the equivalent (GED)

☐ Associate degree

☐ Bachelor's degree

☐ Master's degree

☐ Professional degree (MD, DDS, DVM, LLB, JD, DD)

☐ Doctorate degree (Ph.D. or Ed.D.)

There are two important reasons for including education questions in general population surveys. They not only identify household members who are currently enrolled in educational programs but also help ascertain the education levels of household members who have completed their educations. To get a complete measure of educational levels, it is necessary to determine the highest degree received because, for example, a person may have received a high school diploma by passing a GED examination while having completed less than eight years of formal schooling. The years of school completed and the degrees received are sometimes combined into a single complex question, but asking separate questions makes the task easier for the respondent.

If education is not a key variable, you might ask either Question 4 or Question 5, recognizing that you lose some precision by not asking both questions. Also note that Question 4 refers to years of school completed and not years of school attended. The recommended questions are geared to the American educational system and do not identify people who have had special training, including vocational and on-the-job training. If such information is needed, a follow-up question might be asked—for example, respondents could answer "yes" or "no" when asked "Besides what you've told me about regular schooling, did you ever attend any other kind of school, such as vocational school?"

Asking About Employment-Related Issues

1. Last week did you do any work for either pay or profit?

   ☐ Yes *(Ask Q. 2)*   ☐ No *(Ask Q.3–Q.7.)*

2. How many hours did you work last week?

   ___ hours

3. *(If No):* Last week were you on layoff from a job?

   ☐ Yes   ☐ No *(Skip to Q.5.)*

4. Have you been informed that you will be recalled to work within the next six months or given a date to return to work?

   ☐ Yes *(Skip to Q.7.)*   ☐ No

5. Last week were you temporarily absent from a job or business because of vacation, temporary illness, a labor dispute, or some other reason?

   ☐ Yes   ☐ No

6. Have you been looking for work during the last four weeks?

   ☐ Yes *(Ask Q.7.)*   ☐ No

7. Last week, could you have started a job if offered one, or returned to work if recalled?

   ☐ Yes   ☐ No

This series of questions has two purposes. First, it helps determine whether an individual is currently employed. Second, it helps determine if unemployed individuals are or are not in the labor force (actively seeking a job). If you are interested only in employment status and not in labor force status, only Questions 1 and 2 are needed. In the Current Population Survey, which measures the unemployment rate, these questions are typically not asked of anyone who is under fifteen years old.

Asking About One's Occupation

Ask open-ended questions to learn more about a person's occupation. An example follows.

1. **For whom did you work?**

2. **What kind of business or industry was this?**
   (Need not be asked if obvious from Q.1.)

3. **What kind of work were you doing?**

4. **What were your most important activities or duties?**

Obtaining accurate information on a person's occupation is a complex task requiring coding of four open-ended questions. Since this coding requires substantial training and experience, the alternative of having either the respondent or interviewer code occupation is a serious mistake because it leads to frequent and often serious misclassifications. We believe that if occupation is important to your research, you should ask all the questions and code them carefully. If occupation is only one of many dependent variables you will be studying, you might well be better off to eliminate it entirely.

We give some examples of why the questions are needed. Strictly speaking, Question 1 is not needed, but most people when asked about their work first report for whom they work. Suppose in response to Question 1, the respondents say they work for Busey (which is a bank). This is insufficient to identify the business. The next question would then determine that Busey is a bank. If the response to Question 1 had been Busey Bank or the University of Illinois or the U.S. Army, then Question 2 would not be needed. Even with Questions 1 and 2 one does not know if the respondent is a bank manager, a teller, a guard, or a janitor.

Questions 3 and 4 are also insufficient by themselves. For example, laborers' work varies with the type of industry in which they are employed. Question 3 is insufficient because many jobs may have the same title. For example, respondents who say they are engineers may (1) design bridges or airplanes or computers, (2) operate a railroad locomotive, (3) tend an engine in a nuclear power plant, or (4) maintain a school building. Similarly, respondents who say they are road construction workers could be foremen if they supervise a road gang, machine operators if they operate a bulldozer, or laborers if they use a pick and shovel.

Even asking these four questions may be insufficient if the answers given are vague. Interviewers will need to be trained to ask follow-up probes. For instance, if factory workers say they operate a machine, ask "What kind of machine do you operate?" Nurses would be asked whether they are registered nurses or practical nurses. Teachers would be asked "At what level do you teach?" to distinguish between college and elementary school teachers.

Asking About Mobility

Sometimes it is necessary to know how long someone has lived in the same location. One useful way to ask this is as follows:

1. Did you live in this house or apartment five years ago?
   (Do not ask for children under five years old.)

   ☐ Yes   ☐ No *(Ask Q.2.)*
2. Where did you live five years ago?

The detail used in coding Question 2 depends on what level of detail is required for your research. For many purposes, it may be sufficient to code as different country, different state in the United States, and different address in the same state.

Asking About Income

Income questions continue to be the most difficult demographic question to ask. Some people overreport their income because of a social desirability bias, and other people systematically underreport their income. Sometimes this is intentional, and sometimes it happens because people may not know how much each family member earns or because they simply forget to report all sources of income. The U.S. Census Bureau tries to remind respondents of other income sources, but this detailed and time-consuming questioning leads to a much higher refusal rate on this topic because of the time and intrusiveness involved. Currently, as high as 20 percent of respondents do not answer all parts of detailed income questions. Less detailed income questions still have 5 to 10 percent of the answers missing.

We present three versions of the income question. The first is the detailed version used by the U.S. Census Bureau, which reduces underreporting but increases nonresponse. The second is a version using branching that was adapted for telephone interviewing, but is now widely used in many face-to-face surveys. The third version is used on self-administered surveys and on some face-to-face surveys as well.

1a. Did you receive any money in wages, salary, commissions, bonuses, or tips during (YEAR)?

☐ Yes   ☐ No

1b. *(If Yes):* How much did you receive from all jobs before deductions for taxes or other items?

$ _____

2a. During (YEAR) did you receive any money from own nonfarm businesses or farm businesses, including proprietorships and partnerships?

☐ Yes   ☐ No

2b. *(If Yes):* How much did you receive? Report net income after business expenses.

$ _____

3a. Did you receive any money from interest, dividends, net rental, or income from estates and trusts?

☐ Yes ☐ No

3b. *(If Yes):* How much did you receive?

$ _____

4a. Did you receive any money from Social Security or Railroad Retirement?

☐ Yes ☐ No

4b. *(If Yes):* How much did you receive?

$ _____

5a. Did you receive any money from retirement, survivor, or disability pensions not including Social Security?

☐ Yes ☐ No

5b. *(If Yes):* How much did you receive?

$ _____

6a. Did you receive any money from Supplemental Security Income (SSI)?

☐ Yes ☐ No

6b. *(If Yes):* How much did you receive?

$ _____

7a. Did you receive any money from public assistance or welfare payments from the state or local welfare office?

☐ Yes ☐ No

7b. *(If Yes):* How much did you receive?

$ _____

8a. Did you receive any money regularly from any other source such as alimony, child support, veteran's payments, or unemployment compensation?

☐ Yes ☐ No

8b. *(If Yes):* How much did you receive?

$ _____

9. What was your total income during (YEAR)? If loss, enter amount of loss as a negative number.

$ _____

Note that although this is a detailed series of questions, it still combines multiple sources of income in each subquestion rather than asking about each income source separately. Still, this series can be time-consuming when asked about each household member fifteen years and older.

The next version simply requires respondents to answer "yes" or "no" to a small number of income splits. Most typically, the first split is at or near the estimated median income at the time the study is being conducted, which will, of course, change over time. For purposes of this example, we shall use a median split of $40,000.

1. What was the approximate annual income from employment and from all other sources for all members of your household, before taxes in (YEAR)?

a. Was it $40,000 or more, or less than that?

☐ Yes *(Ask b)*   ☐ No, less than $40,000 *(Ask e)*

b. Was it $50,000 or more, or less than that?

☐ Yes *(Ask c)*   ☐ No, less than $50,000 *(Stop)*

c. Was it $60,000 or more?

☐ Yes *(Ask d)*   ☐ No, less than $60,000 *(Stop)*

d. Was it $75,000 or more?

☐ Yes   ☐ No

e. Was it less than $40,000?

☐ Yes *(Ask f)*   ☐ No *(Stop)*

f. Was it less than $30,000?

☐ Yes *(Ask g)*   ☐ No *(Stop)*

g. Was it less than $20,000?
  ☐ Yes *(Ask h)*   ☐ No *(Stop)*

h. Was it less than $10,000?
  ☐ Yes   ☐ No

One can obtain still finer splits of the sample by asking more questions, but normally asking four yes-no questions is sufficient to get a reasonable distribution from a general population sample. If you were surveying an upper-income population, starting at the median would lead to underestimates of income (Locander and Burton, 1976). In this case the preferred splits start at the high end and work down.

a. Was it more than $100,000?

b. *(If No):* Was it more than $75,000?

c. *(If No):* Was it more than $50,000?

d. *(If No):* Was it more than $40,000?

[And so on]

Low-income households, in contrast, tend to overreport if the questioning starts at the median. For surveys of low-income households, it is better to start at the lower end and work up.

a. Was it less than $5,000?

b. *(If No):* Was it less than $10,000?

c. *(If No):* Was it less than $20,000?

d. *(If No):* Was it less than $30,000?

[And so on]

The final version asks respondents simply to choose a category. As with the branching version, the specific categories will change with inflation.

Would you please tell me the letter on the card that best represents your total household income in (YEAR) before taxes? This should include wages and salaries, net income from business or farm, pensions, dividends, interest, rent, and any other money income received by all members of the household.

a. Less than $5,000

b. $5,000–$9,999

c. $10,000–$14,999

d. $15,000–$19,999

e. $20,000–$29,999

f. $30,000–$39,999

g. $40,000–$49,999

h. $50,000–$59,999

i. $60,000–$79,999

j. $80,000–$99,999

k. $100,000 and over

Asking About Religion

The U.S. Census Bureau does not ask questions about religion. Therefore, we recommend those questions asked by the General Social Survey (GSS), a survey sponsored by the National Science Foundation and conducted by NORC. The GSS (2000) uses a rather detailed procedure to ask people about religious preference. Religious preference should not be confused with religious participation. For example, religious preference is not necessarily related to membership in a congregation or to regular attendance at a place of worship.

1. What is your religious preference? Is it Protestant, Catholic, some other religion, or no religion?

- ☐ Protestant
- ☐ Catholic
- ☐ Jewish
- ☐ Muslim
- ☐ Other *(Specify)* _____
- ☐ None

2. (If Protestant): What denomination is that, if any?
   - ☐ Baptist
   - ☐ Episcopalian
   - ☐ Evangelical
   - ☐ Lutheran
   - ☐ Methodist
   - ☐ Presbyterian
   - ☐ Other *(Specify)* _____
   - ☐ Nondenominational

3. (If Jewish): Are you Orthodox, Conservative, Reformed, or something else?
   - ☐ Orthodox
   - ☐ Conservative
   - ☐ Reformed
   - ☐ Something else *(Specify)* _____

4. (If Christian Orthodox): Is that Russian, Greek, Armenian, or something else?
   - ☐ Russian
   - ☐ Greek
   - ☐ Armenian
   - ☐ Other *(Specify)* _____

As noted, the question on religious preference should not be confused with questions dealing with participation. People who are unaffiliated and never attend church may report that they prefer a specific religion. If religious participation or beliefs are being studied, this will require more specific questions. The GSS asks the following two behavior questions.

Are you, yourself, a member of a church, synagogue, or mosque?

☐ Yes   ☐ No

How often do you attend religious services?
☐ Never
☐ Less than once a year
☐ About once or twice a year
☐ Several times a year
☐ About once a month
☐ 2–3 times a month
☐ Nearly every week
☐ Every week
☐ Several times a week

For some purposes, it may be useful to obtain information on the religion in which a person is raised. In that case, the following question might be asked:

What religion, if any, were you raised in? Was it Protestant, Catholic, Jewish, Muslim, some other religion, or no religion?

Summary

A researcher can spend a lot of time reinventing the wheel when trying to determine how to ask demographic questions. It is best to adopt the questions used in this chapter and modify them to suit your research questions. For the most part questions are stated in order to provide a reasonably extreme or fine-grain level of precision. The questions can easily be made less complex if this degree of precision is not needed.

Part Three

Drafting and Crafting the Questionnaire

Chapter Ten

Organizing and Designing Questionnaires

Since the first edition of this book was published, there have been substantial changes in the way surveys are conducted. Although many surveys are still traditionally conducted over the telephone or in person with paper and pencil, an increasing percentage of surveys are conducted by interviewers with computer assistance. This includes Web-based surveys, e-mailed questionnaires for large surveys, and one-on-one interviews conducted with personal digital assistant (PDA) devices. Because researchers use traditional paper-and-pencil methods and also computer-assisted approaches, this chapter is split into three parts: (1) a discussion of general formatting issues that apply to both methods, (2) a discussion of formatting issues related to computer-assisted interviews, and (3) a discussion of formatting issues related to paper-and-pencil surveys.

General Formatting Issues

Why is formatting important? The format of a questionnaire determines how easy it is for interviewers, respondents, and data processing personnel to read and understand the questions and the kind of answers required. Thus, the quality of the data becomes heavily influenced by the questionnaire format (Sanchez, 1992). A general principle to follow in formatting is that the respondent's needs must receive top priority, the interviewer's needs next highest priority, and the data processing staff's needs the lowest priority (since they are not subject to the stresses of the interview). Ideally, the questionnaire should be formatted to meet all of these needs simultaneously. One of the major advantages of computer-assisted interviews is that the format of the questionnaire can be altered to do this.

Typefaces

The simple rule is that the type should be sufficiently large and clear as to cause no strain in rapid reading for all potential respondents. Some inexperienced researchers believe they can make their forms appear shorter and easier by using smaller typefaces, but any print that causes respondents or interviewers to feel eyestrain should be avoided. We generally recommend using 12-point type for questions, although 10-point type is also readable in many fonts (particularly sans serif fonts). Instructions to the interviewer that are not to be read to the respondent should be distinguished by a different typeface. One way of doing this is to put the questions in bold type and instructions in nonbold type, or the other way around. Another way is to capitalize or italicize all letters in instructions. In computer-assisted interviewing, color can be used to distinguish instructions from questions.

Most current data processing programs do not require any processing instructions on the questionnaire; they are either programmed into the data entry process (such as skips) or organized into the data file. If, however, any processing instructions are needed, they can be put into a different and smaller typeface than the question and interviewer instructions; most data entry personnel can handle smaller-sized type more easily than interviewers or respondents can, since data entry is removed from the demands of the interviewing situation.

Interviewer Instructions

When giving instructions to interviewers or respondents, the general rule is to put these instructions at the point in the questionnaire where they will be used. Instructions are placed just *before* the question if they deal with who should answer, whether only one or multiple answers are possible, or how the question should be administered, such as with cards or other special forms. Instructions should be placed just *after* the question if they relate to how the answer should be recorded or how the interviewer should probe. Probing instructions tell the interviewer what to do or say to determine that the answer is complete and can be interpreted and coded.

In addition to these instructions on the questionnaire, careful researchers also prepare separate question-by-question written or computer instructions for interviewers. These are used both in the interviewer training and for review and reference purposes. The separate instructions do not replace the instructions found on the questionnaire and are used to cover what the interviewer should do in a few unusual cases. The instructions found on the questionnaire are included so that interviewers do not need to rely on their memory. In computer-assisted interviewing, these detailed instructions may be stored in the computer so that the interviewer may access them anytime during an interview.

Numbering of Questions

Standard programs for computer-assisted interviewing require that all questions be numbered. Even for paper questionnaires, there are several good reasons to number the questions. First, numbering questions can alert either the respondent or the interviewer that a question has been skipped. Thus, a respondent who answers Question 2 and then starts to read Question 4 realizes that Question 3 has been skipped and goes back to it. Second, a small number of questions will suggest to potential respondents that the task is not too difficult and will not take too much of their time if they agree to participate. Finally, follow-up debriefings have indicated that some people find satisfaction in seeing they have answered a certain number of questions and are progressing through the questionnaire at a satisfactory rate.

If data processing is required, numbered questions serve as important reference points in communications between the researcher and data processing personnel, and they provide important reference points when describing the findings. Main questions are usually numbered consecutively with standard Arabic numerals from 1 to *n*. Subparts of questions usually follow some sort of outlining procedure. Thus, a question with three parts is usually identified by *A, B, C* (or by *a, b, c*). To further identify questions as subparts, they are usually indented. Subparts of subparts are usually identified by numbers placed in parentheses [(1), (2), (3)] and are further indented.

Advance Preparation for Data Processing

Computer-assisted interviewing requires researchers to make data processing decisions before the study is fielded. Even with paper questionnaires, we would strongly advise you to do as much advance preparation as possible for data processing before you print the questionnaire. If you wait until the interviewing is completed and then discover there are problems in processing the results or analyzing the data, problems can be difficult to solve. Advance preparation saves substantial amounts of time and money later and, even more important, it can help eliminate questions that may not provide the kinds of data anticipated. Even experienced researchers often revise or eliminate several questions in this stage of questionnaire preparation.

The major activity in advance preparation for data processing is to precode all closed-ended questions. Precoding simply involves assigning a code number to every possible answer to a closed-ended question. If there are more than ten answers (including "don't know" and "no answer"), it is necessary to use two or sometimes three-digit precodes. If two-column precodes are used, the first nine codes are 01, 02, . . . , 09 and not 1, 2, . . . , 9. Similarly, if three-digit precodes are used, the numbers are written 001, 002, 003, and so on, not 1, 2, 3.

Precoding.   In precoding, provision should always be made for "no answer" and "don't know" possibilities. These categories need not always appear on the questionnaire and should not appear on self-administered questionnaires. In addition, "no answer" and "don't know" responses must use distinct numbers in their precodes. Some organizations, for example, routinely use 8 and 9 codes for "don't know" and "no answer" or 88 and 99 for these codes in two-column precodes. Thus, if there are eight possible answers, excluding the "don't know" and "no answer" categories, it will be necessary to use two columns instead of one.

The same precodes need not be used for the same answer categories of different questions. For processing purposes, different codes make it easier to detect errors in data entry. Care should be taken, however, not to confuse the interviewer or respondent. If confusion could possibly result, the same codes should be used for a series of questions. In the common case of a series of yes-no questions, changing the precodes does not seem to confuse interviewers or respondents, and does reduce the likelihood of data entry errors. The following example shows how you could replace precodes for a series of yes-no questions.

	Yes	No	replace with	Yes	No
Q.a.	1	2		1	2
Q.b.	1	2		3	4
Q.c.	1	2		5	6

Assigning Numbers to Precodes. Problems with data analysis may be minimized if you think carefully about the actual numbers you assign as precodes. The following example shows three format options. The category "stay the same" could come in the middle or come at the end.

A. During the last few years, has your financial situation been getting better, getting worse, or has it stayed the same?

B. During the last few years, has your financial situation been getting better, has it stayed the same, or has it been getting worse?

C. During the last few years, has your financial situation been getting worse, has it stayed the same, or has it been getting better?

There is no clear-cut rule to indicate whether it is better to have the middle category actually in the middle of the question or at the end. A decision here depends on your general feeling about how easily the question reads. In some situations, it seems more natural to have the middle category in the middle. In this question, it seems somewhat better to us to have the contrast between "getting better" and "getting worse" together (version A).

| | Order of Response Categories | | |
	A	B	C
Getting better . . .	1	1	3
Getting worse . . .	2	3	1
Stayed the same . . .	3	2	2
Don't know	8	8	8

Code from Low to High. Although it may not matter whether you ask the middle category in the middle position of the question or not, having the numerical codes arranged in the same order as the response categories given in the questionnaire poses a potential problem. For analytical purposes these response categories are regarded as running from better to worse in a continuum, with "stayed the same" as a middle position. Yet if the categories are given numerical precodes, which will then be used in the analysis, and if these precodes follow the order of presentation of the categories, the middle category may turn out to be the highest number. If you have access to computer programs that produce tabulations with the response categories labeled, there is less chance of confusion during the analytical stage. However, if the numerical code should print out without the response label—or, more important, if you wish to combine answers to this question that are ordered from better to worse or good to bad—some sort of recoding will have to be done to transpose the numbers. If you forget to recode, you get meaningless data and misleading results.

There are two simple ways to prevent this problem from occurring. First, the response categories can be printed in the order in which they are scaled rather than in the order in which they were asked. Second, the numerical codes can be given in the right scale order even though they are not in proper numerical sequence. These two alternatives are shown in versions B and C in the previous example.

Note also that on short 5- or 7-point scales the category "don't know" is sometimes coded numerically as an 8. If possible, the number used for "don't know" should be one that is separated numerically from the last substantive response category by two or more digits (say an 11 or 12) to avoid confusing it with a substantive answer.

Questionnaire constructors have an overwhelming tendency to code response categories numerically, beginning with 1 and proceeding sequentially as far as is needed. In several instances, however, serious consideration should be given to some other sequence. In questions where the response categories have an implicit numerical direction (for example, "high," "medium," "low," or "above average," "average," "below average") it is better to give a higher number code to the response category that has the higher implicit numerical value. It is confusing to the analyst to have a set of response categories "high," "medium," "low" with "high" coded as 1 and "low" coded as 3. That is, it is better that 1 equal "low" and 3 equal "high." Otherwise, it is too easy to forget that the high number actually means the "low" category and vice versa.

Numerical categories should be given considerable attention when you intend to combine responses into an overall scale, particularly when the numerical codes for the response categories are to be added up. In these cases, it is vital that the numerical codes be scaled in the same direction for all questions that you want to combine. If there are two questions, each with three response categories, and the response category in Question 1 is coded 1 and the item to which it is to be added from Question 2 is coded 3, you cannot combine these without first recoding one of the questions in the proper order. Paying attention to matters of numerical precoding before you begin to ask questions will save considerable time and confusion during the analytical phase.

Coding Open-Ended Questions

It is a difficult, complex, and expensive task to plan for the coding of open-ended questions. This is one reason why they are usually only used in pilot studies. Unfortunately, a small test cannot provide the full range of answers that will be obtained from a much larger sample. Some provision must be made for coding unanticipated answers either during the field period or after interviewing is completed.

If the open-ended question has only a single dimension, then only a single set of codes will be required. Some open-ended questions, however, will be coded and analyzed in multiple dimensions. Thus, an open-ended response might be coded on such dimensions as favorability, relation to respondent, and subject of comment. Each of these dimensions will need its own set of codes.

A more complex problem occurs when respondents are asked for and may provide multiple answers to the same question, such as "What are the three or four main things a school should try to teach children?" In this case, a straightforward procedure is to prepare (and update) a list of all possible items and then for a respondent to code each item as follows:

Mentioned first   1

Mentioned later   2

Did not mention   3

The codes distinguish between "mentioned first" and "mentioned later," since the item mentioned first may be the most salient, although it may also be an item that was cued by earlier parts of the questionnaire. (See the discussion in Chapter Five.) With this coding scheme, it is necessary to look only in a single location to determine the proportion of respondents who think that reading is one of the most important things a school can teach.

Fitting Questions on the Page or Screen

A question, including all its answer categories, that can fit on a single page should never be split between two pages or two screens. The interviewer or respondent is likely to assume that the question has ended at the end of the page and thus will answer on the basis of an incomplete question. If the question and its answer categories do not fit comfortably on the page, they should be moved to the next page and the amount of space between earlier answers increased. In computer-assisted interviewing, the standard procedure is to put only one question at a time on the screen.

Occasionally, questions may require more than one page because the list of possible answers is long, such as brand names for a product purchase, or country of origin for parents or grandparents. For such questions, interviewers need to receive special instructions on the number of pages or screens that the question covers. Such multipage questions or screens would not be appropriate for self-administered questionnaires except with well-educated and professional respondents. In this case, there is usually a separate sheet with all the categories, and respondents are asked to enter the proper code on the main questionnaire. For a computer-assisted interview, respondents are asked to click on the selected response. When the list of answer categories is long, the answers must be arranged in a logical sequence, most typically in alphabetical order.

A final note of caution: a long question with a number of subparts should not be followed by a short question at the end of the page or screen. Such a question is frequently omitted in error. Care should be taken with how the questions are placed.

Single Questions on a Line and Vertical Answer Formats

In a misguided effort to make a questionnaire appear shorter, researchers sometimes have two or more columns of questions or put two or more answer categories on the same line. Such a format interferes with standard English reading patterns of left to right and top to bottom. It is often found that interviewers or especially respondents will answer the questions in the first column and forget to answer the questions in the other columns.

We believe that having the answers to an individual question in a single column reading down is easier for interviewers, respondents on self-administered questionnaires, and for data processing personnel than having the answers read across. Reading across could cause confusion as to where to record the answer. Figure 10.1 shows how readers might not know whether to record their answer on the blank line before or after the answer category.

Some organizations do not follow this recommended format, but they do try to be sure to include substantial space between the answer categories. Most researchers find the vertical format superior since it gives the questionnaire a more open look with more blank space. Thus, it appears easier to complete. With paper questionnaires, the vertical answer format also provides the interviewer or respondent with space for writing additional comments or responses to open-ended questions.

Scale Formats

As discussed in Chapter Five, scales may be verbal, numerical, or both, and they can be presented either horizontally (such as on a semantic differential scale) or vertically (such as on a ladder scale). On interviewer-administered face-to-face interviews, it is helpful to have the scale answers on a separate card the respondents can refer to, but it is not necessary for self-administered questionnaires. Phone surveys require special procedures that are discussed in the next chapter.

Figure 10.1. Unacceptable Formats of Commonly Asked Questions.

Q.22 Your sex: _____ Male _____ Female

Q.23 Your present marital status: _____ Never Married _____ Married _____ Separated _____ Widowed

Q.24 Number of children you have in each age group: _____ Under five years _____ 5-13 _____ 14-18 _____ 19-25 and over

Q.25 Your present age: _____

Q.26 Do you own (or are you buying) your own home? _____ No _____ Yes

Q.27 Did you serve in the armed forces? _____ No _____ Yes (Year entered _____, Year discharged _____)

Q.28 Are you presently: _____ Employed _____ Unemployed _____ Retired _____ Full-time homemaker

Q.29 Please describe the usual occupation of the principal earner in your household, including title, kind of work, and kind of company or business. (If retired, describe the usual occupation before retirement.)

Q.30 What was your approximate net family income, from all sources, before taxes, in 1970?
Less than $3,000 _____   10,000 to 12,999 _____   20,000 to 24,999 _____
3,000 to 4,999 _____   13,000 to 15,999 _____   25,000 to 29,999 _____
5,000 to 6,999 _____   16,000 to 19,999 _____   Over $30,000 _____
7,000 to 9,999 _____

Q.31 What is the highest level of education that you have completed?
No formal education _____   _____ Some college
Some grade school _____   _____ Completed college. . . major _____
Completed grade school _____   _____ Some graduate work
Some high school _____   A graduate degree . . . degree and
Completed high school _____   major _____

Q.32 What is your religious preference? _____ Protestant denomination _____ Jewish _____ Catholic _____ Other_____ (Specify) _____ None

Q.33 How frequently did you attend religious services in a place of worship during the past year? _____ Regularly _____ Occasionally _____ Only on special days _____ Not at all

Q.34 Which do you consider yourself to be? _____ Republican _____ Democrat _____ Independent _____ Other _____ (Specify) _____ None

Q.35 Which of these best describes your usual stand on political issues? _____ Conservative _____ Liberal _____ Middle of the road _____ Radical

Source: Dillman, 1978.

If you are using existing scales developed by other researchers, the same format should be retained in the version seen or used by the respondent, since changing the format may change response distributions. The format of the interviewer questionnaire need not be identical to what the respondent sees.

On a card, verbal responses would usually be listed vertically as follows:

_____ Strongly Agree

_____ Agree

_____ Disagree

_____ Strongly Disagree

If several successive questions use exactly the same answer categories, you can save space on paper questionnaires by listing the answers across. Interviewers and most respondents seem to have no trouble with this format. This is not necessary for computer-assisted surveys, where space is not an issue.

Thank You

Researchers are fortunate that most people are still willing to donate their time and energy to taking surveys. These respondents deserve to have the process made interesting and enjoyable to them, and they also deserve a sincere "thank you" at the end of the interview. This would be automatic for most interviewers, but it is best to end each questionnaire with a printed thank you. In some cases additional degrees of personalization are appreciated, such as by graphically reproducing the first-name signatures of a number of people on the research team.

Following the interview, it is also appropriate for respondents who want additional information on the type of studies being done to be directed to a Web site that gives more general information. In academic-sponsored research, offering respondents the follow-up ability to learn more about the research (or similar types of research) has been well received by Institutional Review Boards.

Computer-Assisted Interviewing

Researchers unfamiliar with computer-assisted interviewing may wonder why this methodology has gained such rapid and widespread use. We first discuss the capabilities of computer-assisted systems, then discuss how computers change the questionnaire design process. We shall be using the following widely accepted abbreviations for various kinds of computer-assisted interviewing:

CATI   computer-assisted telephone interviewing

CAPI   computer-assisted personal interviewing
(face-to-face)

CASI   computer-assisted self-administered interviewing

Capabilities of Computer-Assisted Interviewing Methods

Computer-assisted interviewing methods have been growing in popularity for a number of reasons, including: (1) ease of interviewee response that doesn't depend on an interviewer; (2) improved quality of responses through elimination of skip errors; (3) elimination of interviewer bias; (4) shorter turn-around times; (5) simple integration of images, sound, and video; and (6) automatic data entry.

Perhaps the most welcome benefit of computers during interviews is that they eliminate clerical errors caused by interviewers during the stress of the interview. Concern for interviewer errors is a function of the complexity of the interview and the memory effort required by the interviewers at various points of the interview. Specifically setting up skip protocols is something the computer can do very well.

Skip Instructions. As discussed in the previous chapter, many surveys have significant amounts of branching with a question or series of questions being asked or not asked, depending on the answer to a previous question. In paper interviews, the complexity of such skips is limited by interviewer memory. Even with simple skips, significant interviewer errors occur, with questions being skipped that should not have been skipped, and questions being asked that should not have been asked.

In computer-assisted interviewing, the researcher programs the skips into the computer as part of the questionnaire design process. The instructions may be very complex involving answers from several earlier parts of the interview that are far removed from the current question. The computer executes the skips perfectly each time, so that the respondent is never asked a question that should not be asked and never misses a question that should be asked. This benefit was an initial motivation for computer-assisted interviewing and is still a major reason for its use.

Randomization of Answer Choices or Question Order. As was pointed out in Chapter Five, the position of an answer, whether first, last, or in the middle, as well as the order of a question in a group of related questions, may impact how the question is answered. A common procedure for measuring the effect of the position of an answer or the order of questions is to randomize positions and orders. Full randomization can easily be done with computer-assisted interviewing, whereas paper questionnaires are typically limited to two or to a small number of alternative versions.

Importing and Updating Information from Earlier in the Interview. Computer-assisted interviews allow for information from earlier in the interview to be automatically available in later questions. For example, as part of the household enumeration, you may obtain the first name of all household members. Suppose one of the adults is named Harry. A later question may then ask "Did Harry go to the emergency room of a hospital in the past year?" If the answer is "yes," the follow-up question might be "What was the reason for that visit?" The answer given might be "He broke his leg."

A question later in the survey might ask "When Harry broke his leg, did he lose any time from work?" Fill-ins are possible in paper surveys, but unless the questions are contiguous they may strain an interviewer's memory.

Rostering. It is often the case that a series of questions, such as health questions, need to be asked about every household member or about a series of events such as purchases. Rostering permits the researcher to enter the question into the computer only once and to indicate about whom or what the question will be asked. The computer will automatically replicate the question for each separate use, and, if required, prepare a table showing all the answers in a single roster.

Revising the Questionnaire. When pretesting a computer-assisted questionnaire, a researcher may find it necessary to modify the wording in a questionnaire. This is far easier to do on a computer than using printed questionnaires. If the computers are networked, as with CATI, changes can be made almost instantly. For CAPI questionnaires that are programmed in the field using disks, it is necessary to prepare and ship the revised disks, but even here this is easier than having to reprint all the questionnaires. Note, however, that adding questions, reordering the questionnaire, or changing skip instructions may be a very complex process with CATI if the earlier versions had complex skip instructions or if programmers are needed to make the changes.

Play Sound Segments as Part of the Interview. Audio-CAPI has become an important method for obtaining sensitive information from respondents who have trouble reading. For example, it is well known that respondents are more willing to admit to contranormative behavior such as drug use on a self-administered interview than they are to interviewers. A sizable number of drug users, however, have difficulties reading. One solution is to have respondents sit at a computer and wear earphones. The questions are shown on the screen, but simultaneously spoken to the respondent through the earphones. The same computer skipping of questions as was discussed above is possible with audio-CASI. There are other uses of sound such as testing reactions to television programming and advertising. Most of these uses were impractical or far more difficult before audio-CASI.

Timing the Study. For planning future studies, it is useful to know how long an interview lasts as well as the length of time required for specific sections and individual questions. This information can be obtained automatically in computer-assisted interviewing. With a little custom programming, it is also possible to obtain measures of response latency for individual questions. The primary measure of interest is the amount of time between when a question is asked and when the respondent begins to answer it. This is a measure of the cognitive effort required by the respondent to answer the question and can be useful in determining how much thought has been put into the question and as a surrogate code of salience (as with questions related to memory).

Editing and Data Processing. A major benefit of computer-assisted interviewing is that almost all editing and data processing are done directly on-line while the interview is in progress. If the respondent enters an unacceptable answer such as "4" where only "1" to "3" are possible, the program automatically rejects this answer and asks for another code to be entered. If a series of numbers must add to a total or a series of percentages to 100 percent, the computer can alert the interviewer or respondent if the data are not consistent. If a very unlikely answer is entered, such as $2,000 for the purchase of a book or $1,000,000 for family income, respondents may be asked "Are you sure you mean this?"

Once the interview is completed, the data go directly into a data file and the researcher can look at cumulative data files on a daily basis. Once the interviewing for a study is completed, the marginal tabulations are immediately available and the data are ready for editing and analysis.

Sample Control. A major function of all networked CATI programs is to keep track of sample outcomes and schedule callbacks as necessary. Since this is not part of the questionnaire design process, we do not discuss this function further, but it is an additional incentive for using CATI programs if follow-up calls are required.

Issues in Computer-Assisted Interviewing

Although computer-assisted interviewing solves many of the clerical problems associated with traditional paper interviews, it creates some new issues. First, computer-assisted interviewing demands that all aspects of data processing, data entry, data editing, and data analysis be developed before the study is fielded. We believe that advance preparation and thinking are vital for paper questionnaires as well, but with paper questionnaires it is possible to delay editing and analysis plans until the study is fielded and sometimes until the fieldwork is completed. Although this may delay the completion of the study, it will not necessarily affect the interviewing.

• It generally takes longer to do all the programming necessary to field a study using computers than it does to field a paper survey. This is especially true for complex studies involving many skips and other uses of the computer's special capabilities. Simple studies can be rapidly programmed.

There were early claims that computer-assisted interviewing would save money by eliminating the data processing functions, but this has not proved to be the case. Generally, when comparisons have been made of total costs of similar studies, computer and paper surveys cost about the same. The costs are, of course, distributed quite differently. For studies with small sample sizes, it is probably more cost-efficient to use paper than computers because initial computer set-up costs are high regardless of the sample size. For larger studies, computers can generally be more cost-effective. It is important, however, not to evaluate your choice solely on the basis of cost. Critical issues of sample representativeness and data quality should also be considered. (See Sudman and Wansink, 2002, for a more complete discussion.)

The powerful ability of the computer to execute complex skip instructions also has some problems attached to it. The more complex the skip instructions, the greater the possibility that an error will creep into the programming so that questions are skipped improperly, or that certain patterns of responses cause the computer to freeze.

The only solution, if the complex skips are required, is to spend the time to test how the questionnaire flows, under a wide variety of different answer patterns. This adds to the development time of the questionnaire, but saves much agony later. Even with substantial testing, some bugs may remain that will not be caught until the main survey; however, if the frequency and importance of these bugs is very low, they may usually be ignored or corrected during the field period.

You should also be aware that complex skips and branching possible with CATI might make it more difficult to analyze your data and to obtain simple margins. With complex branching, the same variable will have different names depending on the branch taken, and these differently named variables will need to be combined for final analysis, which is not always a simple task.

Furthermore, conducting a survey partly on CATI and partly with a paper-and-pencil questionnaire is messy. You cannot simply print out the CATI questionnaire and expect the interviewer to follow it. Also, merging data from a paper-and-pencil version with data from CATI interviews can be tricky. Instead of planning a mixed-mode study, think hard and creatively as to whether all parts can be either computer-assisted such as CATI and CAPI or all parts be done on paper. This will save you a lot of later-stage headaches.

Software for Computer-Assisted Interviewing

A wide variety of software packages can be used with computer-assisted interviewing. You will need to decide which software best meets your needs. We can make no general recommendations since no one software package dominates its competitors for all situations. It is probably not cost-effective to buy a software package for a single study, however, unless that study is very large and complex. For smaller single studies we would suggest that you use either an existing field organization that already has computer capabilities or an on-line version of standard programs (which are available at reasonably low-cost monthly rates), or stick with a paper questionnaire.

If you have the name of questionnaire software, you can almost certainly obtain more information by going to the developing company's Web site. Three software packages that are widely used and that have Web sites are as follows:

Blaise for Windows
Mailing address:
Westat
1650 Research Blvd.
Rockville, MD 20850
Attn: Blaise Services-RE 330-S
Web site: westat.com/blaise

Blaise for Windows is a survey processing system software suite developed by Statistics Netherlands and distributed and supported in the United States and Canada by Westat.

CASES (Computer-Assisted Survey Execution System)
Mailing address:
Software Support Services
CSM Program, University of California
2538 Channing Way, #5100
Berkeley, CA 94720
Web site: cases.berkeley.edu

CASES was developed at the University of California, Berkeley, and is used by several U.S. government agencies, as well as university research centers.

Ci3 Sawtooth Technologies
Mailing address:
Sawtooth Technologies
1007 Church Street, Suite 402
Evanston, IL 60201
Web site: sawtooth.com

Ci3 is widely used by many smaller research organizations. It is priced lower than Blaise or CASES and does not contain all the features that make these other programs attractive to large users.

Many other simpler (and cheaper) programs are available. We suggest you use Web search engines and the search term *computer questionnaires* to obtain additional information.

Web-Assisted Interviewing (WAI)

It is now possible and practical to conduct surveys through the Web. These surveys have many positives and some negatives as well. Generally, Web-assisted interviews (WAIs) are considered easier, more efficient, and less error prone than paper—and even computer-assisted surveys. However, if researchers are not careful, WAIs can introduce coverage and sampling errors (Couper, Traugott, and Lamias, 2001).

Eight main types of Web-based survey methods have been identified: (1) Web surveys as entertainment, (2) self-selected Web surveys, (3) volunteer panels of Internet users, (4) intercept surveys, (5) list-based samples of high-coverage populations, (6) mixed-mode design with choice of completion method, (7) prerecruited panels of Internet users, and (8) probability samples of full population (Couper, Traugott, and Lamias, 2001). A brief discussion of the main benefits and faults of each method follows.

1. *Web surveys as entertainment.* These surveys are generally for entertainment purposes and are not of real value. We mention them only for your general knowledge. Most often, surveys as entertainment are polls that have no set population in mind. Typically these polls are not asking anything of scientific value. Good examples of these are question-of-the-day surveys.

2. *Self-selected Web surveys.* This is the most popular form of Web survey and comes in the form of pop-up windows that allow Web visitors to link to the survey. These surveys have some value, but often do not limit who visits, or how many times. Although these types of surveys are not considered scientific, some broad generalizations can be made about them.

3. *Volunteer panels of Internet users.* Participants in these surveys are recruited from pop-up advertisements or from well-frequented sites. Some demographic information is collected through an initial form, and this information becomes the bulk of lists that can be accessed for future survey participants. When asked to participate, respondents often need to use a special code and therefore cannot forward the survey or have someone else fill it out.

4. *Intercept surveys.* These surveys typically ask a randomly selected interval of visitors (every tenth visitor, for example) to fill out a survey as they enter or exit the Web site. Coverage problems are avoided by only asking site visitors to fill out the survey. This approach does incorporate problems of timing (when to solicit participation) and nonresponse (low response rates).

5. *List-based samples of high-coverage populations.* This survey starts with a list of possible respondents who already have Web access. Respondents are then invited to participate. Problems of noncoverage are generally avoided with this method, but the problem of nonresponse is a major concern. Surveys using this method generally have less of a response rate than comparable mail surveys.

6. *Mixed-mode design with choice of completion method.* This method of Web survey is often posed as a choice among different response methods (Web, phone, mail), to groups of people who have

long histories with a company or service. Problems of nonresponse can generally be expected, and this method may not be cost-effective unless your survey population is relatively large.

7. *Prerecruited panels of Internet users*. This type of survey uses a panel that is put together using probability sampling methods. Often, telephone interviews are used first to form lists of interested participants. They are then invited to fill out the Web-based survey through an electronic invitation and specific access protocols. Coverage is usually not a concern, but nonresponse can be large.

8. *Probability samples of full population*. This is the only method that has some chance of obtaining a sample that contains the full population, rather than those with Web access only. This approach employs a panel design that starts with a phone or mail survey, but then provides (if needed) the equipment for Web-based surveys in the future. Besides being expensive, probability sampling of full populations tends to elicit low initial response rates and nonresponse in general. However, this method can solve the coverage issue of the other methods; that is, it does not restrict the sample to those who already have Web access.

Although many of these methods do not compare favorably with the validity of paper-based or computer-assisted surveys, their popularity and continuous improvement cannot be denied. Over time, they will continue to become more advanced and more widely accepted. With an increase in the sourcing software for computer-based surveys, it is now possible and relatively simple to outsource the design and production of a questionnaire designed for a computer or World Wide Web application. Many sources are available, including free services. These include freepolls.com, GammaPoll (gammapoll.com/gp/en/index.cfm), mypoll.net, pollhost. com, pulsepoll.com, webpollcentral.com, and XML Polls. In addition, more companies can be found by accessing a search engine and using the search term *Web surveys*.

PDA-Assisted Interviewing (PDAAI)

Developments of the PDA are also influencing the way one-on-one survey research is being done. PDAs are increasing in popularity among survey researchers because they are becoming more accepted by respondents, are easy to program, and are portable, efficient, inexpensive, and easy to use.

As of 2002, for example, more than twenty million Palm handhelds have been sold, and the company now offers models that retail for as little as $99; competing models are also now available from Sony, HP, Dell, AlphaSmart, Toshiba, and Handspring (recently purchased by Palm). Not only are PDAs reasonably easy to program, but a number of companies offer custom programming services.

Portability of the PDA platform is another reason why it has advantages over paper-based surveys. Respondents can access the survey stored on their PDA any time of the day and can complete it over the course of many days. Respondents rarely lose their PDA or damage it so badly that it cannot be salvaged. Because it is worn or carried on the body, respondents will not say they did not have the access to the survey.

Efficiency is another key selling point if the PDAAI format is used. Not only do today's PDAs cost less than they used to, they also require few energy resources. Most run for weeks, months, or years on AAA or rechargeable batteries. Surveys deployed in the field do not have to be concerned about running out of power or finding a source on-site. Besides the power benefits, PDAs are also very fast at storing information and at accessing survey questions. Data is saved even if the device is turned off by accident.

Finally, PDAAI is easy to use. Although many people still have trouble navigating today's computer software, most find it easy to navigate the PDA system. PDA device interfaces are intuitive enough that most users can complete a survey with little or no help from interviewers. This means that large groups of respondents can complete the survey with only a minimum of instruction, or none at all.

Paper Questionnaires

Simple paper questionnaires are likely to be relatively free of clerical errors, even when the data are input manually. Data entry problems occur, however, if a questionnaire involves complicated skipping or if it requires information from earlier questions to be incorporated into later questions. Then, careful formatting of the questionnaire can help reduce, but not totally eliminate, clerical errors.

Using Booklet Format

We recommend using paper questionnaires in a booklet format (folded and saddle stapled) for four reasons. First, booklets prevent pages from being lost or misplaced. When questionnaires are fastened with only a single corner staple, rear pages may get torn off during the interview or when being coded. Second, a booklet makes it easier for the interviewer or respondent to turn the pages. Third, a booklet makes it possible to use a double-page format for questions about multiple events or persons. Finally, for a self-administered questionnaire a booklet looks more professional and is easier to follow.

To conserve paper, to make the questionnaire look smaller, and to reduce mailing costs, the questionnaire should be printed on both sides of the pages. If the questionnaire is not in booklet form, it is easier for interviewers and respondents to forget the backs of pages and miss them entirely.

Appearance of Self-Administered Questionnaires

Although clarity is important in all questionnaires, the appearance of the questionnaire can have an important effect on cooperation on mail and other self-administered paper questionnaires. The general rule is that the questionnaire should look as easy as possible to the respondent and should also look professionally designed. All self-administered questionnaires should be printed on paper of sufficient quality that the print or writing on the reverse side cannot be seen. Forms that are blurred or blemished in any way or that are difficult to read because the ink is too light should not be used.

Dillman (1978) argues that the front and back covers of self-administered questionnaires need particular attention. He suggests that the front cover should contain a study title, a graphic illustration, any needed directions, and the name and address of the study sponsor. We would agree with these requirements for general population samples where a booklet form is used. For samples of special populations such as professional groups and for short two-page questionnaires, we believe the illustration may be omitted. If an illustration is used, it should be neutral. An outline map of the state being studied would be one such example. As Dillman (p. 150) points out: "A view of a pristine wilderness area on the questionnaire cover would be highly inappropriate for a study seeking to determine the relative priorities for economic growth versus environmental preservation."

The back cover of a questionnaire is usually blank and can be used for additional comments by the respondent. For some studies the mailing label is placed on the back cover and the questionnaire is sent in a window envelope. The mailing label ensures that the respondent's name is on the completed questionnaire, so that for follow-up procedures it is possible to determine who has returned a questionnaire. On a study of about 40,000 college graduates, only five objected to this procedure and scratched out their names. If any of the information being obtained is sensitive or confidential, however, this procedure should not be used. Instead a code number should be placed on the first page of the questionnaire.

Use of Blank Space

Perhaps the most common mistake many researchers make when constructing a questionnaire is to crowd questions together in the hopes of making the questionnaire look short. Although length is important, the respondent's perception of the difficulty of the task is even more important on self-administered questionnaires. A less cluttered questionnaire with substantial white space looks easier to fill out and generally results in higher cooperation and fewer errors by either respondents or interviewers. Additional white space also allows for less confusion for both the interviewer and the reader.

On open-ended questions, sufficient blank space must be provided. Even though additional blank space is provided elsewhere (for instance, on the back cover), the answer will usually be no longer than the space provided for it. Respondents on self-administered questionnaires, as well as interviewers recording responses, use the amount of space available as an indication of what is expected. We do not recommend the use of lines for open-ended questions. Lines make the questionnaire look more crowded and serve no useful function. However, if a short answer (one or two words or a number) is required, a single line should be used.

Using Colored Paper

There is no evidence that the use of particular colors of paper has any effect on response to mail questionnaires or is easier for interviewers to use. Either white or pastel colors are acceptable. Dark-colored papers that are difficult to read should never be used. If colored paper is used, the ink color should contrast sufficiently from the paper so that the questionnaire can be read easily. In the end, the questionnaire must be usable and this also means it must be clean and easily followed.

The use of different colors may help interviewers and data processing personnel when several different forms are being used in the same study, and different-colored paper may be used for different subparts of the questionnaire. Typically, the forms and parts are also identified by title and letter or number codes, color being used as a supplementary memory device to reduce error.

Asking Identical Questions About Multiple Household Members or Events

We have already pointed out that asking the same question about all household members or events is easily handled in computer-assisted interviewing using the rostering capabilities of the program. Such questions on paper forms are very difficult for respondents and are prone to significant errors by interviewers even after careful interviewer training.

If used, however, these questions are usually formatted by having the question on the left and a series of parallel columns for each household member or event. If necessary, this series can extend to facing pages. This format is sometimes shifted ninety degrees, that is, the questions appear across one page or two facing pages, and the persons or items are listed from top to bottom at the left. This format would be used instead of the other when the number of persons or items exceeds the number of questions asked about each.

Some studies may require either more questions or more items than can fit on two facing pages. Although the number of questions is known in advance, the number of items (persons or events) will vary from household to household. Again, this situation lends itself to computer-assisted interviewing. If paper is used, two basic strategies are possible: using supplementary forms or making the basic form larger. Thus, even though most households have fewer than six members, some may have as many as twelve or more. The basic form could be made sufficiently large to record information about twelve members, or the basic form could have room for only six household members and supplementary forms would be used for additional members. Supplementary forms are more flexible and reduce the size of the basic paper form, but they can sometimes get separated. They also require that the interviewer be able to locate the necessary forms while the interview is in progress. Although one supplementary form is not too difficult to handle, the task becomes more burdensome if the interviewer must sort among several supplementary forms during an interview to find the one required. Multiple supplementary forms should be avoided, if at all possible; if they cannot be avoided, color-coding these supplements helps the interviewer find the right form.

Using Skip Instructions

We have already pointed out the major value of computer-assisted interviewing to reduce skip errors, but here we discuss methods for reducing skip errors if paper is used. There are two ways in which interviewers (and respondents) can be instructed on questions that are to be skipped: (1) by verbal instructions or (2) by arrows that point to the next question. Both methods have been found satisfactory by researchers who use them.

What is important for paper questionnaires is that the instruction be placed immediately after *the answer* so that the interviewer or respondent will not forget or miss the instruction. The most common mistake is to put the skip instruction after the question but before the answer. The skip instruction is much more likely to be forgotten or ignored if it is in this position.

The other common error is to place the skip instruction only at the beginning of a subsequent question when there are intervening questions. An instruction such as "If respondent answered yes to Q.6, ask Q.10; otherwise skip to Q.11," requires the interviewer or respondent to look back and locate the answer to Q.6. This backward flow should be avoided because it is likely to cause errors. A useful precaution is to put the skip instruction after the response to the filter question and to put the appropriate response categories before the follow-up questions. Although not strictly necessary, this double procedure confirms that the skip instruction has been followed properly.

Skip instructions should always be worded positively, not negatively. An error is less likely to be made if interviewers are told to skip when an answer is given, rather than when an answer is not given. One place, however, where skip instructions should be avoided is in asking about multiple household members or events. Interviewers instructed to skip if a designated response is given about any household member or event may skip immediately and thus forget to ask about any remaining household members or events, or forget to skip entirely.

Using the Questionnaire to Plan New Studies

The length of an interview is based on the ending time minus the beginning time. The times should be recorded on a paper interview with the beginning time at the top of the first page of the question-naire and the ending time at the bottom of the last page. Some-times, intermediate times are also recorded to obtain the length of individual sections. (This information is obtained automatically in computer-assisted interviewing.) This provides useful information for estimating the cost and timing of future studies using the same or a similar questionnaire. It is difficult or impossible to estimate the time required to conduct an interview simply on the basis of the number of pages or questions.

There should also be some place for interviewers to record any problems they had with the questionnaire since such comments can be helpful in planning new studies and in interpreting the results of the present one. The space for comments may be on a separate interviewer report form or on the questionnaire. These comments are a supplement to and not a substitute for interviewer debriefings that are held after a study to obtain interviewer experiences.

Summary

Each mode of survey has its advantages and disadvantages relative to the others. A basic summary of some of these advantages and dis-advantages are noted in Table 10.1. Too often, the mode of a survey is dictated by what a person or institution is most comfortable with. People who are used to Web-based surveys will have a bias toward conducting additional surveys in this manner. People who are

Table 10.1. Advantages and Disadvantages of Various Survey Methods.

Dimension	Computer	Paper	PDA	Telephone	Web-Based
Clerical	Generally less clerical work than paper due to the automatic recording through computer programs	More clerical effort required than any other form due to the individual attention needed for every survey	Much like computer surveys, this form can remove a lot of the clerical requirements, due to its electronic format	Between computers and paper forms as the responses over the phone can be recorded by hand, or on computer	One of the easiest of all as the responses are collected and sorted as they come in
Pre-Field Completion	Computer surveys can allow changes to the survey design after pre-field, as long as a specific computer program has been written	This is an important step in a paper survey as the copying requirements, time & expense are not something that be incurred can repeatedly	Pre-field is important due to the special program that is written for the PDA format	Testing here is important, but not nearly so much as other forms. Interviewers can change questions or procedure rather simply.	Somewhat important here, but having a competent Web-programmer would alleviate some requirements
Programming	Requirements for programming here can be small or large. It depends on the amount of special software needed for the survey.	Not really applicable, can easily be avoided	A specific program for the PDA survey must be written and given to each PDA user. This can be costly.	There is some programming expense based on how the responses are recorded. If it is via computer, it can be expensive.	Again, a competent Web programmer would be needed for this format to work well; otherwise, data could be lost
Skips	Can be handled easily	Can become confusing for the survey participant and the data coder	Limited by the technology of the PDA; however, many new PDAs are very advanced	Limited by the skill and training of the interviewer. Also depends on the intelligence of the interviewee.	The Web-based survey format can handle the skips well, but the interviewee must be able to easily understand the progression

Fill-Ins	Easily done with a good software program	Possible, but not very smooth	Possible through the program that is written for the survey	Possible, but can be hard to do depending on the skill of the interviewer	Easily done with the right program
Interviewer Skills	Generally does not affect the collected data	Generally does not affect the data, but could be a hindrance when giving directions or assistance	Generally not a problem	Can be a large concern if the interviewer pool is not well trained	Generally not a problem
Set-Up Costs	Can be high based on the software used and the intricacy of the survey	Generally the cheapest method to begin, but can be costly due to paper and people requirements	Expensive based on the need for a special program to be written	Fairly cheap, but can be expensive due to phone charges and data coding	Can be cheap with an inexpensive Web programmer, but could also become costly due to delays or poor Web sites
Blank Space	Generally not a concern	Can be a confusing part of a paper survey. Care must be taken to avoid problems.	Generally not a concern	Generally not a concern	Generally not a concern
Data Collection	Much simpler through the use of a computer-based survey	Can be one of the most costly parts of the survey	Not the best method, but still easier than paper	Fairly personal intensive, depending on the collection method—computer or paper	Much simpler through the use of Web-based surveys

accustomed to and who have the operational capacity for paper questionnaires will conduct them this way. Recently, we have even seen that once an organization invests in PDAs, it has a bias in amortizing the expense by believing many subsequent surveys should also be used with PDAs.

. The critical considerations are what type of data are being collected (complex versus simple, or straightforward versus conditional skips), who the population is (probability or convenience-based), and how much control is needed over the process. The higher the need for control, the more critical it is that an interviewer be present and possibly that the questionnaire be done on paper. The same benefits of speed and efficiency that are a blessing to electronic modes of data collection are also their curse in the hands of a self-paced, careless respondent.

Chapter Eleven

Questionnaires from Start to Finish

Throughout the book we have focused on tactics related to how specific questions of a specific nature should be asked. In this chapter, we explain the general process of compiling these questions into an efficient sequence that elicits accurate answers from the first to last question. For some, this can serve as a quick reference guide; for others it can be useful as to how one should start and proceed with crafting their questionnaire. A second purpose is to remind researchers that a good questionnaire is the end product of a sequence of procedures that all play a role in the final quality. Assuming that all other recommendations in this book are followed, a questionnaire can still suffer if the steps in this chapter are omitted.

The next section lists the steps we believe are critical in preparing a questionnaire. Some readers may be surprised to see that there are actually more steps involved after the first draft is finished than before. As in golf, follow-through is critical in preparing an effective questionnaire.

Steps in Preparing a Questionnaire

1. Decide what information is needed. Conduct focus groups if needed to explore the topic to find out what information is required.

2. Search data archives for existing questions and scales on the topics of interest.

3. Draft new questions or revise existing questions.

4. Put the questions in sequence.

5. Format the questionnaire.

6. Precode the possible responses.

7. Use pretest interviews and solicit peer feedback of draft questionnaires.

8. Revise the draft and test the revised questionnaire on yourself, friends, or coworkers.

9. Prepare simple interviewer instructions for pilot testing; revise questionnaire if the instruction writing or interviewer training uncovers any problems.

10. Pilot-test on a small sample of respondents (twenty to fifty) similar to the universe from which you are sampling.

11. Obtain comments from interviewers and respondents in writing or at interviewer debriefings.

12. Eliminate questions that do not discriminate between respondents or that do not appear to provide the specific kind of information required.

13. Revise questions that cause difficulty.

14. Pilot-test again if revisions are substantial.

15. Prepare final interviewer instructions; revise questionnaire if the instruction writing uncovers any problems.

16. During interviewer training and initial interviewing, be alert for possible new problems; in very serious cases, interviewing may need to be stopped until new instructions can be issued to interviewers.

17. After interviewing is completed, analyze interviewer report forms and debrief interviewers and coders to determine whether there were any problems that would affect analysis.

18. Use the experience gained on one questionnaire for future planning.

The Testing Procedure

Of the eighteen-step process we have listed, the first six steps were discussed earlier in this book. Yet possessing scientific knowledge of the survey-design process is only the first step in being able to design a successful questionnaire. Ultimately, every questionnaire must be tested and refined under real-world conditions. Testing takes the form of pretest interviews and of soliciting peer feedback of draft questionnaires (step 7).

Conducting Pretest Interviews

Even after years of experience, no expert can write a perfect questionnaire. Among the three authors, we have more than one hundred years of experience in questionnaire construction, and we have never written a perfect questionnaire on the first or second draft, nor do we know any professional social scientists who claim they can write questionnaires that need no revision. We do, however, know many beginners who have spent all of their limited resources sending out a first draft of a questionnaire, only to dishearteningly discover that some key questions were misunderstood and not answered in a usable way. It is even more important for researchers with limited resources to pilot-test their questionnaires before spending all their money. If you do not have the resources to pilot-test your questionnaire, don't do the study. At least pretest your questionnaire with ten to twelve colleagues or (better yet) with representatives from the population you will be surveying. Such a pretest will help you determine if the questionnaire is gathering the data you need and whether it is convenient and clear for respondents to fill out. Additionally, a pretest will often suggest problems you were unaware of, and it can help you avoid costly mistakes.

Ask respondents if the questions were straightforward and whether the format made logical sense. In reviewing the answers to the questionnaire, you will get a good idea if people are responding in ways that seem reasonable. This may involve no more than informal, open-ended interviews with several of your respondents. Furthermore, it is even better to ask respondents to criticize a preliminary version of the questionnaire. Doing so will help you more critically determine the relevance of the questions and the extent to which you may have difficulty obtaining useful responses. For example, you might discover that respondents are likely to be offended by a certain type of question, or that a line of questions is not useful, or that a question leads to misinterpretations of the issue being examined.

The order of the steps of questionnaire development is intended to minimize the costs of revisions. Obtaining peer evaluation and testing the revised questionnaire on friends and coworkers should not require out-of-pocket funds, since these steps would normally be taken by the questionnaire designer and any other project staff. We have generally found that it is always useful for questionnaire designers to play the roles of respondents and answer their own questions. Surprisingly often, persons who write questions will find that they cannot answer them as written.

At both NORC and SRL, a process called the "group mind" is used. Coworkers of the questionnaire designer, who have been given a draft of the questionnaire earlier, meet in a group session to tear it apart. Although the process is always a humbling experience for the writer, it is also a rapid, efficient method of improving the questionnaire.

Follow Up Pretests with a Pilot Test

At this stage many of the problems will have been noted and corrected, but not all. Since the earlier evaluation has been by persons similar to the questionnaire writer, new problems may be discovered when the questionnaire is pilot-tested on respondents similar to those who will be sampled in the main study. In addition, unless the questionnaire is self-administered, this stage will require interviewers. It will be necessary to prepare instructions for these interviewers and to train them on how the questionnaire should be asked. In this process the trainer will often find ambiguities in the questionnaire that must be corrected before training can continue.

The pilot test procedure is not identical to the main study. The sampling is generally loose, and interviewers are given some flexibility. If, however, the main study will be conducted with respondents who might have trouble with some of the words or ideas in the questionnaire, such respondents must be included in the pilot sample. Also, the interviewers typically discuss the questionnaire with the respondents after the pilot-testing interview is over, to discover whether any of the questions were unclear or difficult to answer. It is also very helpful for questionnaire writers or field supervisors to observe some pilot-test interviews, since they may find questions that are being misinterpreted by interviewers and respondents. For complex studies it is always useful to meet with interviewers after the pilot study to learn what problems they and the respondents had. For more simple studies, this information can be obtained in interviewer reports and from the comments written on the questionnaire.

Pilot testing of mail and other self-administered questionnaires must be conducted a little differently. The preferred procedure is to mail or give the questionnaire to respondents, with no indication that the questionnaire is not in its final version. After the questionnaire is returned, telephone or face-to-face interviews are conducted with some or all of the respondents, to determine whether they had any difficulties in understanding or answering the questions.

The process just described should not be confused with a field trial of a preliminary version of the questionnaire. Although such field tests can be desirable, they have different purposes and should always follow the more informal review process just described. A field trial will be desirable or necessary if there is substantial uncertainty in what the response rate of the questionnaire is likely to be.

That is, if a field trial of a mailed questionnaire yields an unsatis-factory response rate, design changes or different data-gathering procedures must be undertaken.

Using Pilot-Test Results

A major problem with many studies is that insufficient time is allowed to use the results of the pilot study to correct the question-naire. The pilot study can be used to indicate questions that need revision because they are difficult to understand, and it can also indicate questions that may be eliminated. For example, a question that is to be used as an independent variable to explain some other behavior or attitude will be useless if all or virtually all respondents answer in the same way. Additionally, open-ended questions may yield answers that are impossible to code into theoretically mean-ingful dimensions.

The pilot test will also provide useful information on how long it takes to conduct the interview. If the interview or subsections of it turn out to be much too long, some questions may need to be dropped to stay within time and budget constraints. (Note, how-ever, that pilot-test interviews may take somewhat longer than reg-ular interviews because interviewers increase their speed as they become more experienced with a questionnaire.) The pilot test will also indicate whether the questionnaire is ordered correctly. Thus, you might learn that the first question asked is too difficult for the respondent and gets the interview off to a bad start, or that early questions are changing the context in which later questions are being answered.

If too many substantial revisions are required as a result of the pilot test, it is sensible to pilot-test the revisions. If you do not test your revisions, you may find that they cause new and serious prob-lems. After a number of questions have been omitted from the ques-tionnaire, it is important to retest in order to accurately estimate the new length of time it takes to conduct the interview. Therefore, you should be sure to leave enough time in the schedule for the second pilot test.

It is difficult to make any general recommendations about the optimal time to begin programming questionnaires into your CAPI or CATI system if you are using computer-assisted interviewing. Setting up complex questionnaires with many skip instructions takes considerable time and usually involves specialists. Therefore you should start setting up the questionnaire after you have a draft you are fairly satisfied with and before you have finished all of the pretesting and revisions. When all the revisions have been completed, it will then be necessary to revise the computer program to make sure all revisions have been incorporated into the CAPI or CATI program. It will also be necessary to check the skip instructions to make sure that any contingencies among questions that were altered in the revisions are also altered in the final program. Be sure to allow yourself enough time to ensure that the revised programs work correctly.

Last-Minute Revisions and Post-Interview Evaluations

After the final pilot test, it is unlikely many serious problems will remain. Nevertheless, even at this stage, a problem may arise that did not come up during pretesting. If such a problem surfaces during the writing of the final interviewer instructions, you can still revise the questionnaire. Sometimes, if the questionnaire has already been printed, you may need to supplement the questionnaire with an insert sheet. Such inserts should be used only for the most serious situations, since they may create new problems of their own. You can handle minor problems that surface during the actual interviewer training or interview by revising or expanding interviewer instructions or by ignoring the problems and editing or treating the data as missing during the analysis.

After the interviewing is completed and the data are collected, it is always useful to analyze interviewer reports of problems and to debrief the interviewers. The debriefing may alert the survey analyst that some questions must be discarded or treated cautiously because of unexpected problems. It may also be very useful in helping to improve the design of future questionnaires.

Concluding Remarks

The process described in this chapter may appear too complex for very simple questionnaires. Most questionnaires, however, require not only careful initial design but also careful follow-through to ensure that the respondent, interviewer, data processors, and analyst are all able to perform their roles. Also, the final stages typically involve only a small section of the questionnaire if the questionnaire has been carefully designed. In addition, the questionnaire continues to improve at every stage of the design process.

An inexperienced questionnaire writer who follows the steps recommended in this chapter will be able to create an effective questionnaire and experience the same success as an experienced questionnaire writer.

A final word of caution. Even well-worded and well-designed questionnaires may be unsatisfactory if they do not obtain the information required to achieve the research objectives. There is no reason why research objectives cannot be achieved if they are formulated before the questionnaire is designed. Waiting until the data are collected before formulating the research problem can destroy the value of even the best-designed questionnaire.

After the hard and careful work of preparing a questionnaire, it is always enormously satisfying to listen to interviews, read the questionnaires and the tabulations, and see that the questionnaire has obtained the data that were needed. We hope you have a rewarding experience.

Chapter Twelve

Asking Questions FAQs

Survey designers frequently have questions about how best to design a survey. This chapter summarizes questions asked by people working in survey research and questions asked by graduate students conducting research and taking survey research courses.

What Questions Should I Ask?

Some questionnaires give the impression that their authors tried to include every conceivable question related to the topic. Others appear to have been drafted by various members of a committee and patched together. Strong efforts should be made to avoid such fishing expeditions, because they yield long, frustrating, and annoying questionnaires that have many questions relevant to very few. Respondents can resent having to complete this kind of survey and may feel that it does not deserve their full attention. Excessively long surveys result in poor response rates, careless answers, and useless results.

The first step in deciding what questions to ask involves precisely defining what information is needed and writing the fewest number of questions to obtain it. (See Chapter One.) Secondary or peripheral "Wouldn't it be interesting to know?" questions should be avoided. Because well-defined goals are the best way to ensure good questionnaire design, many problems can be traced back to the design phase of the project. Being able to express the goals of a questionnaire in a few clear and concise sentences will help keep the design of the questionnaire focused.

To help define your goals, you may find it useful to explicitly state how you intend to use the information before you design the study. Although seemingly obvious, the planning is apparently seldom done, given the number of wasted "Wouldn't it be interesting to know?" questions found on surveys. One way to develop purposeful questions is to read each question and ask "How am I going to use this information?" If the information will be used in a decision-making process, keep it. If not, toss it. If you are not going to use a question related to income or ethnicity, do not ask it. It is even useful to formulate the plan you will use to do statistical analysis after the data is collected.

With these caveats in mind, one way to improve a survey and the impact of its results is to involve other experts and relevant decision makers in the questionnaire design process. Expert feedback generally helps improve the questionnaire.

Are There Words I Should Avoid Using?

A number of words can be particularly misleading or unclear, or can signal a potential problem with the way a question is worded. (See Chapter Two.) One common mistake is to include modifying adjectives and adverbs that are somewhat unclear, such as *usually, often, sometimes, occasionally, seldom,* and *rarely*. These words have highly variable meanings, as do such words as *many, most, numerous, a minority of, a substantial majority, a considerable number of, a large proportion of, a significant number of,* and *several*. Other adjectives produce less variability and generally have more shared meaning. These include *a small number of, not very many of, almost none, hardly any, a couple, a few, almost all, virtually all, nearly all, a majority of, a consensus of,* and *lots*.

Four other words can serve as warnings or red flags that you might have a problem with a particular question.

1. *And.* The word *and* can signal that you might be combining two questions and asking them as one question. To make cer-

tain you're asking only one question at a time, avoid using the word *and* in your question.

2. *Or.* Similar to the word *and,* the word *or* is often associated with a double question or with a false dilemma. ("Do you prefer the Republican or the Democratic candidate for governor?") Be careful whenever you use the word *or* in a question.

3. *If.* The word *if* is often associated with confusing directions or with skip patterns. If you need to use a skip pattern, be sure your questions are clearly numbered so that you can direct respondents properly.

4. *Not.* Avoid using *not* in your questions if you're having respondents answer "yes" or "no" to a question. Using the word *not* can lead to double negatives and confusion.

What Makes a Good Question?

A good question is one that yields a truthful, accurate answer. When a respondent is concerned about the consequences of answering a question in a particular manner, there is a good possibility that the answer will not be truthful. Anonymous questionnaires that contain no identifying information are more likely to produce honest responses than those identifying the respondent. If your questionnaire does contain sensitive items, be sure to clearly state your policy on confidentiality. (See Chapter One.)

A Good Question Asks for Only One Answer on Only One Dimension

The objective here is to make certain you are not asking a "double-barreled" question. (See Chapter Five.) An example of a double-barreled question is "Are sales reps polite and responsive?" Although the sales reps may be polite, they may not be responsive, or vice versa. If this is the case, the respondent will be forced to rate one attribute inaccurately. Consequently, data interpretation will be questionable.

The purpose of a survey is to find out information. A question that asks for a response on more than one dimension will not always provide the information you are seeking. Each question should be about one topic. Do not include questions that require a single response when two would be more appropriate. For example, "Do you agree that smoking and drinking are detrimental to health?" should be broken into two different questions, as should "Do you like the texture and flavor of the snack?" If a respondent answers "no," then the researcher will not know if the respondent dislikes the texture or the flavor or both. A good question asks for only one "byte" of information.

A Good Question Can Accommodate All Possible Answers

Multiple choice items are the most popular type of survey questions because they are generally the easiest for a respondent to answer and the easiest to analyze. Asking a multiple choice question that does not accommodate all possible responses can confuse and frustrate the respondent, however. (See Chapter Five.) For example, consider the following question:

What type of computer do you own?
☐ IBM-type PC   ☐ Apple

Clearly, there are many problems with this question. What if the respondents don't own a computer? What if they own a type of computer that is neither an IBM-type of PC or an Apple? What if they own both an IBM-type of PC and an Apple? There are two ways to correct this kind of problem. One way is to ask respondents to list all of the computers they own. Another way would be to allow "neither" or "both" as answers. If we assume for the purposes of our example that the only types of computers are IBM-type computers and Apple computers, our question might read as follows:

Do you own an IBM-type of PC?

☐ Yes   ☐ No

Do you own an Apple computer?

☐ Yes   ☐ No

Do you own both?

☐ Yes   ☐ No

Do you own neither?

☐ Yes   ☐ No

A Good Question Has Mutually Exclusive Options

alternative interpretations,

A good question leaves no ambiguity in the mind of the respondent. There should be only one correct or appropriate choice for the respondent to make.

For example, a question like "Where did you grow up?" could have the following answers: (A) Farm, (B) Country, and (C) City. A person who grew up on a farm in the country would not know whether to select choice A or B, and a person who grew up in the suburbs may have no appropriate answer. This question would not provide meaningful information. Furthermore, it is unclear what is meant by "grow up." If respondents were born on a farm but moved to the city in the sixth grade, where did they grow up? The response alternatives must contain all possible meaningful answers.

A Good Question Produces Variability in Response

When a question produces no variability in responses, we learn very little. If a question is not sensitive enough to detect actual variability, we will be unable to perform any statistical analysis on the item. Consider the following example:

What do you think about this instructor? *(check one)*

☐ It's the worst course I've ever taken.

☐ It's somewhere between the worst and best.

☐ It's the best course I've ever taken.

Since almost all responses would be choice B, very little information is learned. Design your questions so that they are sensitive to differences among respondents. For example, the question "Are you against the unlawful discharge of firearms within the city limits?" would have little variability in response and should probably not be asked.

A Good Question Follows Comfortably from the Previous Question

Writing a questionnaire is similar to writing anything else. Transitions between questions should be smooth. Questions should be grouped so that they are similar and easier to complete. Questionnaires that skip from one unrelated topic to another feel disjointed and require too much effort of respondents; such questionnaires are less likely to produce reliable responses and high response rates.

When Should I Ask Ranking Questions?

Asking respondents to rank a long series of items (by their importance, for instance) can be very difficult. (See Chapter Five.) It is feasible, however, to have people rank either the three most favored items or the three least favored items. Another method is to ask for explicit comparisons in a sequential manner, as in the following example:

> Following are three colors for an office wall: yellow, white, and light green.
>
> Which color do you like best?
> ☐ Yellow   ☐ White   ☐ Light green
>
> Which color do you like second best?
> ☐ Yellow   ☐ White   ☐ Light green
>
> Which color do you like least?
> ☐ Yellow   ☐ White   ☐ Light green

Ranking questions are also useful when you are asking respondents to rate items for which the general level of approval is high. Consider the following 4-point scale of importance used to rate selected attributes of a product: (1) No importance, (2) Low importance, (3) Moderate importance, (4) High importance.

Respondents may tend to rate almost every attribute topic as highly important. It then becomes difficult to separate topics of greatest importance from those of least importance. Asking respondents to rank items according to importance in addition to rating them will help resolve this problem. If there are too many items for ranking to be feasible, you can ask respondents to return to the items they have rated and indicate three or four items they consider "most important."

How Should I Order My Categories?

When response categories represent a progression between a lower level of response and a higher one, it is usually better to list responses from the lower level to the higher level and from left to right. For example: (1) Never, (2) Seldom, (3) Occasionally, (4) Frequently. The least confusing way to list questions is to associate greater response levels with larger numbers. (See Chapter Five.)

In addition, start with the end of a scale that is least socially desirable. (See Chapter Three.) Otherwise, the respondent may choose a socially desirable answer without hearing or reading the entire set of responses. For socially undesirable behavior, it is better to ask whether respondents have ever engaged in the behavior before asking whether they currently engage in that behavior. For socially desirable behavior, it is better to ask about current behavior first rather than ask about their usual or typical behavior.

What Scale Should I Use . . . 4-Point or 7-Point?

Your choice of scale for your question will shape the information you collect. (See Chapter Five.) In the research field, there is much discussion as to how many points and what kinds of scale labels (anchors) make up the most effective measurement tool. Each scale has variations, some more reliable than others.

Even-numbered scales (4-point or 6-point scales) can more effectively discriminate between satisfied or dissatisfied customers because there is not a neutral option. Carefully consider whether a clear division between positive and negative responses is necessary or whether a midpoint will be more appropriate. Although scales without midpoints are often used when measuring personality characteristics, our general bias is toward odd-numbered scales.

The number of points for your scale should be determined by how you intend to use the data. Although 7- to 9-point scales may seem to gather more discriminating information, there is debate as to whether respondents actually discriminate carefully enough when filling out a questionnaire to make these scales valuable, particularly in phone interviews. Many researchers nevertheless collect such information using scales with many points, even if in the end they summarize that information as simply "disagree," "neutral," and "agree."

Once the number of points on a scale has been decided, determine the labels for each scale point. With scales with few points, every point can be labeled. Other researchers prefer to label or define only the end points. This provides a scale with equal-appearing intervals between each scale point, with only numbers labeling the intervals. This format is particularly common with large scales.

How Many Response Categories Should I Have?

No more than necessary. Recall from Chapter Nine that a typical question about marital status might ask a person to check a box to indicate whether he or she is (1) Never married, (2) Divorced, (3) Married, (4) Separated, or (5) Widowed. Unless marriage is a focus of the study, distinguishing among these categories will not be particularly useful. If such a question is primarily asked to distinguish between married versus single households, it would be better to have only two response categories, "Married and living with spouse" and "Other."

It is also a good idea to avoid scale-point proliferation—for example, (1) Never, (2) Rarely, (3) Occasionally, (4) Fairly often, (5) Often, (6) Very often, (7) Almost always, (8) Always. These types of answers can annoy or confuse the respondent because of the hairsplitting they entail. In contrast to category proliferation, which seems usually to arise somewhat naturally, scale-point proliferation takes some thought and effort.

Although sensory research traditionally uses 9-point scales, psychometric research has shown that most subjects cannot reliably distinguish among more than six or seven levels of response. For attitude-related work, four to five scale points may be quite sufficient to stimulate a reasonably reliable indication of response direction.

What About Open-Ended Questions?

One potentially valuable part of any survey questionnaire consists of the open-ended questions. These are questions that don't restrict answers to prescribed categories. (See Chapter Five.)[1]

When evaluating service satisfaction, for instance, open-ended questions can point to the service issues that are most important to customers. Although customers might rate a number of service aspects as low or high, it will be the vehement comments or the effusive ones that will show what is really important to them.

Often valuable information from open-ended questions is wasted because researchers pay attention only to the most commonly mentioned open-ended answers and not to the unique ones. Open-ended questions can uncover uncommon but intelligent opinions, but if surveyors focus only on frequent responses, they will continue to be unaware of these ideas.[2] (See Appendix D for an example of a brief open-ended survey.)

How Should the Questions Be Ordered?

There are two key considerations when ordering questions. (See Chapter Ten.) First, questions should be ordered so as to minimize the effect of respondents' answers on subsequent questions. (See Chapter Four.)

Second, questions should be ordered in a way that motivates respondents to complete the questionnaire. Start with fact-based questions and then go on to opinion-based questions. Begin with interesting and nonthreatening questions that are easy to answer. People generally look at the first few questions before deciding whether or not to complete the questionnaire. If the first questions are too threatening or "boring," there is little chance that the person will complete the questionnaire. Make respondents want to continue by putting interesting questions first. In addition, place the most important questions in the first part of the mail questionnaire. Respondents often send back partially completed questionnaires, and if the important questions are toward the front, these partially completed questionnaires will still contain important information.

Try to order questions in a way that holds respondents' interest. Try to provide variety in the type of items used. Varying the questioning format will also prevent respondents from falling into "response sets." Still, it is important to group items into coherent categories so that all items flow smoothly from one to the next.

How Do I Know My Questionnaire Is Complete?

Pretest your questionnaire with a small group of colleagues or with people from the population you will be surveying. (See Chapter Eleven.) This pretest allows you to determine if the questionnaire is gathering the data you need and is convenient for respondents to fill out; it can also help you avoid costly mistakes.

It can be useful to ask a group of test respondents to criticize a preliminary version of the questionnaire. The purpose of these activities is to determine relevance of the questions and the extent to which there may be problems in obtaining responses. For example, it might be determined that respondents are likely to be offended by a certain type of question, that a line of questioning is not useful, or that a question is misunderstood.

Notes

1. For example, if three people report "I hate my boss," "I detest my boss," and "I loathe my boss," we would probably combine these responses into a single category, such as "Dislike of Supervisor." Many researchers would code these answers into three categories: "Hate of Supervisor," "Detestation of Supervisor," and "Loathing of Supervisor." Using trivial differences to classify data contributes to inaccurate coding. For example, identical responses by two different people may be classified in different categories by the same coder—or two different coders may classify the same response in different categories.

2. A reason frequently given for using open-ended questions is to capture unsuspected information. This reason is valid for brief, informal questionnaires given to groups made up of less than fifty respondents. When surveying small groups, a simple listing of the responses to each question usually conveys their overall character. However, in the case of a larger sample, it is necessary to categorize responses to each question in order to analyze these responses. This process is time-consuming and introduces error. It is far better to determine the prevalent categories in advance and ask the respondents to select among those offered. In most cases, obscure categories that apply only to very small minorities of respondents should not be included. A preliminary open-ended questionnaire sent to a small group of people is often a good way to establish the prevalent categories in advance.

Bibliography and Recommended Readings

Alwin, D., and Krosnick, J. "The Measurement of Values in Surveys: A Comparison of Ratings and Rankings." *Public Opinion Quarterly*, 1985, *49*, 535–552.

American Marketing Association. *The Technique of Marketing Research*. New York: McGraw-Hill, 1937.

Andersen, R., Kasper, J., Frankel, M. R., and Associates. *Total Survey Error: Applications to Improve Health Surveys*. San Francisco: Jossey-Bass, 1979.

Ash, P., and Abramson, E. "The Effect of Anonymity on Attitude Questionnaire Response." *Journal of Abnormal and Social Psychology*, 1952, *47*, 722–723.

Baddeley, A. D. *Human Memory: Theory and Practice*. Mahwah, N.J.: Erlbaum, 1990.

Bailey, K. D. *Methods of Social Research*. New York: Free Press, 1978.

Barton, A. J. "Asking the Embarrassing Question." *Public Opinion Quarterly*, 1958, *22*, 67–68.

Beatty, R. W., and Bernardin, H. J. *Performance Appraisal: Assessing Human Behavior at Work*. Boston: Kent, 1984.

Becker, S. L. "Why an Order Effect?" *Public Opinion Quarterly*, 1954, *18*, 271–278.

Belson, W. A. "Respondent Understanding of Survey Questions." *Polls*, 1968, *3*(1), 1–13.

Belson, W. A. *The Design and Understanding of Survey Questions*. Aldershot, England: Gower, 1981.

Belson, W. A., and Duncan, J. A. "A Comparison of the Checklist and the Open Response Questioning Systems." *Applied Statistics*, 1962, *11*, 120–132.

Belson, W. A., Millerson, B. L., and Didcott, P. J. *The Development of a Procedure for Eliciting Information from Boys About the Nature and Extent of Their Stealing*. London: Survey Research Centre, London School of Economics and Political Science, 1968.

Berk, Ronald A. (ed.). *Performance Assessment Methods and Applications*. Baltimore: Johns Hopkins University Press, 1986.

Bernardin, H. J., and Smith, P. C. "A Clarification of Some Issues Regarding the Development and Use of Behaviorally Anchored Rating Scales." *Journal of Applied Psychology*, 1981, 66, 458–463.

Bingham, W.V.D., and Moore, B. V. *How to Interview.* (4th ed.) New York: HarperCollins, 1959.

Blair, E. A., and Burton, S. "Cognitive Processes Used by Survey Respondents to Answer Behavioral Frequency Questions." *Journal of Consumer Research*, 1987, 14, 280–288.

Bradburn, N. M. *The Structure of Psychological Well-Being.* Hawthorne, N.Y.: Aldine de Gruyter, 1969.

Bradburn, N. M., Sudman, S., and Gockel, G. L. *Racial Integration in American Neighborhoods: A Comparative Survey.* NORC Report No. III-B. Chicago: National Opinion Research Center, 1971a.

Bradburn, N. M., Sudman, S., and Gockel, G. L. *Side by Side: Integrated Neighborhoods in America.* Chicago: Quadrangle, 1971b.

Bradburn, N. M., Sudman, S., and Associates. *Improving Interview Method and Questionnaire Design: Response Effects to Threatening Questions in Survey Research.* San Francisco: Jossey-Bass, 1979.

Brown, R. W. *Against My Better Judgment: An Intimate Memoir of an Eminent Gay Psychologist.* Binghamton, N.Y.: Haworth Press, 1996.

Burns, N., Kinder, D. R., Rosenstone, S. J., Sapiro, V., and the National Election Studies. *American National Election Study, 2000: Pre- and Post-Election Survey* [Computer file]. 2nd ICPSR version. Ann Arbor: University of Michigan, Center for Political Studies [producer], 2001; Interuniversity Consortium for Political and Social Research [distributor], 2002.

Campanelli, P., Martin, E., and Rothgeb, J. "The Use of Respondent and Interviewer Debriefing Studies as a Way to Study Response Error in Survey Data." *The Statistician*, 1991, 40, 253–264.

Campbell, A., and others. *The American Voter.* Hoboken, N.J.: Wiley, 1960.

Cannell, C. F., Marquis, K. H., and Laurent, A. *A Summary of Studies of Interviewing Methodology.* Vital and Health Statistics, Series 2, No. 69. Rockville, Md.: National Center for Health Statistics, 1977.

Cannell, C., Miller, P., and Oksenberg, L. "Research on Interviewing Techniques." In S. Leinhardt (ed.), *Sociological Methodology.* San Francisco: Jossey-Bass, 1981.

Cannell, C. F., Oksenberg, L., and Converse, J. *Experiments in Interviewing Techniques.* NCHSR Research Report 78-7. Hyattsville, Md.: National Center for Health Services Research, 1977.

Cantril, H. *Gauging Public Opinion.* Princeton, N.J.: Princeton University Press, 1944.

Cantril, H. *The Pattern of Human Concern.* New Brunswick, N.J.: Rutgers University Press, 1965.

Cardy, R. L., and Dobbins, G. H. *Performance Appraisal: Alternative Perspectives.* Cincinnati, Ohio: South-Western, 1994.

Cash, W. S., and Moss, A. J. *Optimum Recall Period for Reporting Persons Injured in Motor Vehicle Accidents.* Vital and Health Statistics, Series 2, No. 50. Rockville, Md.: National Center for Health Statistics, 1972.

CBS News/The New York Times. *CBS News/New York Times Monthly Poll no. 1, January 1994* [Computer file]. 2nd ICPSR version. New York: CBS News [producer], 1994. Ann Arbor, Mich.: Inter-university Consortium for Political and Social Research [distributor], 2000.

Clark, J. P., and Tifft, L. L. "Polygraph and Interview Validation of Self-Reported Deviant Behavior." *American Sociological Review,* 1966, *31,* 516–523.

Coker, H., Medly, D. M., and Soar, R. S. *Measurement-Based Evaluation of Teacher Performance.* New York: Longman, 1984.

Colombotos, J. "Personal Versus Telephone Interviews: Effect on Responses." *Public Health Reports,* 1969, *84,* 773–782.

Converse, J. M., and Presser, S. *Survey Questions: Handcrafting the Standardized Questionnaire.* Thousand Oaks, Calif.: Sage, 1986.

Converse, J. M., and Schuman, H. *Conversations at Random: Survey Research as Interviewers See It.* Hoboken, N.J.: Wiley, 1974.

Couper, M., Traugott, M., and Lamias, M. "Web Survey Design and Administration." *Public Opinion Quarterly,* 2001, *65,* 230–253.

Crabtree, S. "New Poll Gauges Americans' General Knowledge Levels." [Poll release, Gallup Poll News Service]. Princeton, N.J.: Gallup Organization, 1999.

Davis, J. A., Smith, T. W., and Marsden, P. V. *General Social Survey 1998: Culture Module.* Chicago: National Opinion Research Center, 2000.

Demby, E. H. "Psychographics Revisited: The Birth of a Technique." *Marketing News,* Jan. 2, 1989, p. 21.

Dillman, D. *Mail and Internet Survey: The Tailored Design Method.* (2nd ed.) New York: Wiley, 2000.

Dillman, D. *Mail and Telephone Surveys: The Total Design Method.* Hoboken, N.J.: Wiley, 1978.

Doyle, K. O. *Evaluating Teaching.* Toronto: Lexington Books, 1983.

Edwards, J. E., Rosenfeld, P., and Thomas, M. D. *Improving Organizational Surveys.* Thousand Oaks, Calif.: Sage, 1993.

Eisenhower, D., Mathiowetz, N., and Morganstein, D. "Recall Error: Sources and Bias Reduction Techniques." In P. P. Biemer and others (eds.), *Measurement Errors in Surveys.* Hoboken, N.J.: Wiley, 1991.

Erdos, P. L., and Morgan, A. J. *Professional Mail Surveys.* New York: McGraw-Hill, 1970.

Fee, J. "Symbols and Attitudes: How People Think About Politics." Unpublished doctoral dissertation, School of Social Sciences, University of Chicago, 1979.

Ferber, R. *The Reliability of Consumer Reports of Financial Assets and Debts*. Studies in Consumer Savings, no. 6. Urbana: Bureau of Economic and Business Research, University of Illinois, 1966.

Fischer, R. P. "Signed Versus Unsigned Personal Questionnaires." *Journal of Applied Psychology*, 1946, *30*, 220–225.

Forsyth, B., and Lessler, J. "Cognitive Laboratory Methods: A Taxonomy." In P. P. Biemer and others (eds.), *Measurement Errors in Surveys*. Hoboken, N.J.: Wiley, 1991.

Fowler, F. "How Unclear Terms Affect Survey Data." *Public Opinion Quarterly*, 1992, *56*, 218–231.

Fraisse, P. *The Psychology of Time*. New York: HarperCollins, 1963.

Fuller, C. "Effect of Anonymity on Return Rate and Response Bias in a Mail Survey." *Journal of Applied Psychology*, 1974, *59*, 292–296.

Gallup, G. H. *The Gallup Poll: Public Opinion, 1935–1971*. (3 vols.) New York: Random House, 1972.

Gallup, G. H. *The Gallup Poll. Public Opinion, 1972–1977*. (2 vols.) Wilmington, Del.: Scholarly Resources, 1978.

Gallup Organization. *Gallup Opinion Polls, 1965–2003 Cumulative Codebook*. Princeton, NJ, 2003. (For more information about Gallup Opinion Polls, please call, 1-800-888-5493.)

Gallup Organization. "Support for Invasion of Iraq Remains Contingent on U.N. Approval." [Poll analysis]. [http://www.gallup.com/poll/releases/pr021112.asp]. Nov. 12, 2002.

Glanz, K., and others. "Why Americans Eat What They Do: Taste, Nutrition, Cost, Convenience, and Weight Control Concerns: Influences on Food Consumption." *Journal of the American Dietetic Association*, 1998, *98*, 1118–1126.

Greenberg, B. G., and others. "The Unrelated Question Randomized Response Model: Theoretical Framework." *Journal of the American Statistical Association*, 1969, *64*, 520–539.

Grice, P. "Logic and Conversation." In P. Cole and J. Morgan (eds.), *Syntax and Semantics*, Vol. 3: *Speech Acts*. Orlando: Academic Press, 1975.

Groves, R. M. "Measurement Errors Associated with the Questionnaire." In *Survey Errors and Survey Costs*. Hoboken, N.J.: Wiley, 1989.

Groves, R. M., and Kahn, R. L. *Surveys by Telephone: A National Comparison with Personal Interviews*. Orlando: Academic Press, 1979.

Guilford, J. P. *Psychometric Methods*. (2nd ed.) New York: McGraw-Hill, 1954.

Gunter, B., and Furnham, A. *Consumer Profiles: An Introduction to Psychographics*. London: Routledge, 1992.

Haley, R. "Benefit Segmentation: A Decision-Oriented Research Tool." *Journal of Marketing*, 1968, *32*, 30–35.

Harris, L., and Associates. (For queries about Harris Poll questions in text, write to Louis Harris and Associates, 630 Fifth Avenue, New York, NY 10020.)

Hastings, E. H., and Hastings, P. K. (eds.). *Index to International Public Opinion*, *1978–1979*. Westport, Conn.: Greenwood Press, 1980.

Hirsch, A. *What Flavor Is Your Personality?* Naperville, Ill.: Sourcebooks, 2001.

Hochstim, J. R. "A Critical Comparison of Three Strategies of Collecting Data from Households." *Journal of the American Statistical Association*, 1967, *62*, 976–989.

Horvitz, D. G., Shaw, B. V., and Simmons, W. R. "The Unrelated Question Randomized Response Model." In E. Hasho (ed.), *Proceedings of the American Statistical Association*. Washington, D.C.: American Statistical Association, 1967.

Houston, M. J., and Sudman, S. "A Methodological Assessment of the Use of Key Informants." *Social Science Research*, 1975, *4*, 151–164.

Hyman, H. H., and Sheatsley, P. B. "The Current Status of American Public Opinion." In J. C. Payne (ed.), *The Teaching of Contemporary Affairs: Twenty-First Yearbook of the National Council for the Social Studies*. Washington, D.C.: National Council for the Social Studies, 1950.

Johnson, C. E., Jr. *Consistency of Reporting of Ethnic Origin in the Current Population Survey*. U.S. Bureau of the Census Technical Paper No. 31. Washington, D.C.: U.S. Government Printing Office, 1974.

Kahn, R. L. "A Comparison of Two Methods of Collecting Data for Social Research: The Fixed-Alternative Questionnaire and the Open-Ended Interview." Unpublished doctoral dissertation, School of Social Science, University of Michigan, 1952.

Kahn, R. L., and Cannell, C. F. *The Dynamics of Interviewing: Theory, Technique, and Cases*. Hoboken, N.J.: Wiley, 1957.

Kamakura, W. A., and Novak, T. P. "Value-System Segmentation: Exploring the Meaning of LOV." *Journal of Consumer Research*, 1992, *23*, 119–132.

Kidder, L. H. *Selltiz, Wrightsman and Cook's Research Methods in Social Relations*. (4th ed.) Austin, Tex.: Holt, Rinehart and Winston, 1981.

King, F. W. "Anonymous Versus Identifiable Questionnaires in Drug Usage Surveys." *American Psychologist*, 1970, *25*, 982–985.

Kinsey, S., and Jewell, D. "A Systematic Approach to Instrument Development in CAI." In M. Couper and others (eds.), *Computer Assisted Survey Information Collection*. Hoboken, N.J.: Wiley, 1998.

Krosnick, J., and Fabrigar, L. "Designing Rating Scales for Effective Measurement in Surveys." In L. Lyberg and others (eds.), *Survey Measurement and Process Quality*. Hoboken, N.J.: Wiley, 1997.

Laumann, E. O., Gagnon, J. H., Michael, R. T., and Michaels, S. *The Social Organization of Sexuality: Sexual Practices in the United States*. Chicago: University of Chicago Press, 1994.

Locander, W. B., and Burton, J. P. "The Effect of Question Form on Gathering Income Data by Telephone." *Journal of Marketing Research*, 1976, *13*, 189–192.

Loftus, E., and Marburger, W. "Since the Eruption of Mt. St. Helens, Has Anyone Beaten You Up? Improving the Accuracy of Retrospective Reports with Landmark Events." *Memory and Cognition*, 1983, *11*, 114–120.

Martin, E., DeMaio, T., and Campanelli, P. "Context Effects for Census Measures of Race and Hispanic Origin." *Public Opinion Quarterly*, 1990, *54*, 551–566.

McCourt, K., and Taylor, D. G. "Determining Religious Affiliation Through Survey Research: A Methodological Note." *Public Opinion Quarterly*, 1976, *40*, 124–127.

McCready, W. C., and Greeley, A. M. *The Ultimate Values of the American Population*. Thousand Oaks, Calif.: Sage, 1976.

McIver, J. P., and Carmines, E. G. *Unidimensional Scaling*. Thousand Oaks, Calif.: Sage, 1981.

Marquis, K. H., and Cannell, C. F. *Effect of Some Experimental Interviewing Techniques on Reporting in the Health Interview Survey*. Vital and Health Statistics, Series 2, No. 41. Rockville, Md.: National Center for Health Statistics, 1971.

Means, B., and Loftus, E. "When Personal History Repeats Itself: Decomposing Memories for Recurring Events." *Applied Cognitive Psychology*, 1991, *5*, 297–318.

Menon, G. "The Effects of Accessibility of Information in Memory on Judgments of Behavioral Frequencies." *Journal of Marketing Research*, 1993, *20*, 431–440.

Menon, G. "Are the Parts Better Than the Whole? The Effects of Decompositional Questions on Judgments of Frequent Behaviors." *Journal of Marketing Research*, 1997, *34*, 335–346.

Menon, G., Bickart, B., Sudman, S., and Blair, J. "How Well Do You Know Your Partner? Strategies for Formulating Proxy-Reports and Their Effects on Convergence to Self-Reports." *Journal of Marketing Research*, 1995, *32*, 75–84.

Menon, G., Raghubir, P., and Schwarz, N. "Behavioral Frequency Judgments: An Accessibility-Diagnosticity Framework." *Journal of Marketing Research*, 1995, *22*, 212–228.

Mieczkowski, T. (ed.). *Drug Testing Technology: Assessment of Field Applications*. Washington, D.C.: CRC Press, 1999.

Miller, P. "Alternative Question Forms for Attitude Scale Questions in Telephone Interviews." *Public Opinion Quarterly*, 1984, *48*, 766–778.

Millman, J. *Handbook of Teacher Evaluation*. Thousand Oaks: Sage, 1981.

Minneapolis Star Tribune, Oct. 1988.

Moser, C. A., and Kalton, G. *Survey Methods in Social Investigation*. New York: Basic Books, 1972.

Murray, J. R., and others. *The Impact of the 1973–1974 Oil Embargo on the American Household*. NORC Report No. 126. Chicago: National Opinion Research Center, 1974.

National Opinion Research Center. *General Social Surveys, 1972–2002: Cumulative Codebook*. Chicago: National Opinion Research Center, 2003. (For queries about other NORC questions in text, write to NORC, 1155 E, 60th St., Chicago, IL 60637, http://www.norc.uchicago.edu. Please mention year given in parentheses.)

Nesbary, D. *Survey Research and the World Wide Web*. New York: Allyn & Bacon, 1999.

Neter, J., and Waksberg, J. "Effects of Interviewing Designated Respondents in a Household Survey of Home Owners' Expenditures on Alterations and Repairs." *Applied Statistics*, 1963, *12*, 46–60.

Neter, J., and Waksberg, J. "A Study of Response Errors in Expenditures Data from Household Interviews." *Journal of the American Statistical Association*, 1964, *59*, 18–55.

Neter, J., and Waksberg, J. *Response Errors in Collection of Expenditures Data by Household Interviews*. U.S. Bureau of the Census Technical Paper No. 11. Washington, D.C.: U.S. Government Printing Office,[M1] 1965.

Noelle-Neumann, E. *Umfragen in der Massengesellschaft: Einführung in die Methoden der Demoskopie*. Munich: Rowohlt Deutsche Enzyklopadie, 1963.

Noelle-Neumann, E. "Wanted: Rules for Wording Structured Questionnaires." *Public Opinion Quarterly*, 1970, *34*, 191–201.

Norman, D. A. (ed.). *Models of Human Memory*. Orlando: Academic Press, 1970.

NPD Research. *National Purchase Diary Panel*. Floral Park, N.Y.: NPD Research, 1977.

Oksenberg, L., Cannell, C., and Kalton, G. "New Strategies for Pretesting Survey Questions." *Journal of Official Statistics*, 1991, *7*(3), 349–365.

Opinion Research Corporation. (For queries about ORC questions in text, write to ORC, North Harrison Street, Princeton, NJ 08540.)

Oppenheim, A. N. *Questionnaire Design and Attitude Measurement*. New York: Basic Books, 1966.

Ornstein, R. E. *On the Experience of Time*. New York: Penguin Books, 1970.

Parry, H. J., and Crossley, H. M. "Validity of Responses to Survey Questions." *Public Opinion Quarterly*, 1950, *14*, 61–80.

Payne, S. L. *The Art of Asking Questions*. Princeton, N.J.: Princeton University Press, 1951.

Pennings, J. M., Wansink, E. B., and Meulenberg, M. E. "A Note on Modeling Consumer Reactions to a Crisis: The Case of the Mad Cow Disease." *International Journal of Research in Marketing*, 2002, *19*(2), 91–100.

Petty, R. E., and Cacioppo, J. T. *Attitudes and Persuasion: Classic and Contemporary Approaches*. Boulder, Colo.: Westview Press, 1996.

Petty, R. E., and Krosnick, J. A. (eds.). *Attitude Strength: Antecedents and Consequences*. Mahwah, N.J.: Erlbaum, 1995.

Pierre-Pierre, P. K., Platek, R., and Stevens, P. *Development and Design of Survey Questionnaires*. Ottawa: Minister of Supply and Services, 1985.

Plummer, J. T. "How Personality Makes a Difference." *Journal of Advertising Research*, 1984, 24(6), 27–31.

Presser, S., and Blair, J. "Survey Pretesting: Do Different Methods Produce Different Results?" In P. V. Marsden (ed.), *Sociological Methodology*, 1994.

Rea, L. M., and Parker, R. A. *Designing and Conducting Survey Research: A Comprehensive Guide*. San Francisco: Jossey-Bass, 1997.

Reinmuth, J. E., and Geurts, M. D. "The Collection of Sensitive Information Using a Two-Stage, Randomized Response Model." *Journal of Marketing Research*, 1975, *12*, 402–407.

Robinson, J. P., Athanasiou, R., and Head, K. B. *Measures of Occupational Attitudes and Occupational Characteristics*. Ann Arbor: Survey Research Center, University of Michigan, 1969.

Robinson, J. P., Rusk, J. G., and Head, K. B. *Measures of Political Attitudes*. Ann Arbor: Survey Research Center, University of Michigan, 1968.

Robinson, J. P., and Shaver, P. R. *Measures of Social Psychological Attitudes*. (Rev. ed.) Ann Arbor: Survey Research Center, University of Michigan, 1973.

Rokeach, M. *The Nature of Human Values*. New York: Free Press, 1973.

Roper Public Opinion Research Center. *Survey Data for Trend Analysis: An Index to Repeated Questions in U.S. National Surveys Held by the Roper Public Opinion Research Center*. Storrs: Roper Public Opinion Research Center, University of Connecticut, 1974.

Roper Public Opinion Research Center. *Survey Data for Trend Analysis*. Storrs: Roper Public Opinion Research Center, University of Connecticut, 1992.

Roper Public Opinion Research Center. *Survey Data for Trend Analysis*. Storrs: Roper Public Opinion Research Center, University of Connecticut, 1994.

Rosenshine, B. "Evaluation of Classroom Instruction." *Review of Educational Research*, 1970, *40*, 279–300.

Roshco, B. "The Polls: Polling on Panama." *Public Opinion Quarterly*, 1978, *42*, 551–562.

Rugg, D. "Experiments in Wording Questions: II." *Public Opinion Quarterly*, 1941, *5*, 91–92.

Salant, P., and Dillman, D. A. *How to Conduct Your Own Survey*. Hoboken, N.J.: Wiley, 1994.

Sanchez, M. E. "Effects of Questionnaire Design on the Quality of Survey Data." *Public Opinion Quarterly*, 1992, *56*, 206–217.

Schaeffer, N. C. "Conversation with a Purpose—or Conversation? Interaction in the Standardized Interview." In P. P. Biemer and others (eds.), *Measurement Errors in Surveys*. Hoboken, N.J.: Wiley, 1991.

Schonlau, M., and others. *Conducting Research Surveys Via E-Mail and the Web*. Santa Monica, Calif.: RAND, 2002.

Schuman, H., and Presser, S. *Questions and Answers in Attitude Surveys: Experiments on Question Form, Wording, and Context*. Orlando: Academic Press, 1981.

Schuman, H., Presser, S., and Ludwig, J. "Context Effects on Survey Responses to Questions About Abortion." *Public Opinion Quarterly*, 1981, *45*, 216–223.

Schwarz, N. " Attitude Measurement." In N. J. Smelser and P. B. Baltes (eds.), *International Encyclopedia of the Social and Behavioral Sciences*. New York: Pergamon Press, 2001.

Schwarz, N., and Sudman, S. *Answering Questions: Methodology for Determining Cognitive and Communicative Processes in Survey Research*. San Francisco: Jossey-Bass, 1996.

Shanahan, J., Scheufele, D., and Lee, E. "The Polls—Trends: Attitudes About Agricultural Biotechnology and Genetically Modified Organisms." *Public Opinion Quarterly*, 2001, *65*, 267–281.

Sharp, L. M., and Frankel, J. "Correlates of Self-Perceived Respondent Burden: Findings from an Experimental Study." Paper presented at the annual meeting of the American Statistical Association, Detroit, Michigan, Aug. 10–11, 1981.

Shaw, A., and others. *Conceptualization and Measurement of Health for Adults in the Health Insurance Study*, Vol. 3: *Mental Health*. Santa Monica, Calif.: RAND, 1978.

Sherrick, B. J., and others. "Farmers' Preferences for Crop Insurance Attributes." *Review of Agricultural Economics*, 2003, *25*(2), 415–429.

Shober, M., and Conrad, F. "Does Conversational Interviewing Reduce Survey Measurement Error?" *Public Opinion Quarterly*, 1997, *61*, 576–602.

Singer, E. "Informed Consent." *American Sociological Review*, 1978, *43*, 144–161.

Sirken, M. G. *Designing Forms for Demographic Surveys*. Chapel Hill: Laboratories for Population Statistics, University of North Carolina, 1972.

Slamecka, N. J. *Human Learning and Memory*. New York: Oxford University Press, 1967.

Smith, P. C., and Kendall, L. M. "Retranslation of Expectations: An Approach to the Construction of Unambiguous Anchors for Rating Scales." *Journal of Applied Psychology*, 1963, *47*, 149–155.

Smith, T. W. "Situational Qualifications to Generalized Absolutes: An Analysis of 'Approval of Hitting' Questions on the General Social Survey." *Public Opinion Quarterly*, 1981, *45*, 224–230.

Smith, T. W. "The Polls—A Review: The Holocaust Denial Controversy." *Public Opinion Quarterly*, 1995, *59*, 269–295.

Social Science Research Council. *Basic Background Items for U.S. Household Surveys*. Washington, D.C.: Center for Coordination of Research on Social Indicators, Social Science Research Council, 1975.

Stahl, M., and Bounds, G. (eds.). *Competing Through Customer Value*. Westport, Conn.: Greenwood Press, 1991.

Statistics Canada. *Perspective Canada: A Compendium of Social Statistics*. Ottawa: Information Canada, 1974.

Stouffer, S. A. *Communism, Conformity, and Civil Liberties*. New York: Doubleday, 1955.

Sudman, S. *Reducing the Cost of Surveys*. Hawthorne, N.Y.: Aldine de Gruyter, 1967.

Sudman, S., and Bradburn, N. M. *Response Effects in Surveys: A Review and Synthesis*. Hawthorne, N.Y.: Aldine de Gruyter, 1974.

Sudman, S., Bradburn, N. M., and Schwarz, N. *Thinking About Answers: The Application of Cognitive Processes to Survey Methodology*. San Francisco: Jossey-Bass, 1996.

Sudman, S., and Ferber, R. *Consumer Panels*. Chicago: American Marketing Association, 1979.

Sudman, S., Finn, A., and Lannom, L. "The Use of Bounded Recall Procedures in Single Interviews." *Public Opinion Quarterly*, 1984, 48, 520–524.

Sudman, S., and Lannom, L. B. *Health Care Surveys Using Diaries*. NCHSR Research Report 80-48. Hyattsville, Md.: National Center for Health Services Research, 1980.

Sudman, S., and Wansink, B. *Consumer Panels*. (2nd ed.) Chicago: American Marketing Association, 2002.

Sudman, S., and others. "Understanding the Cognitive Processes Used by Women Reporting Cancer Prevention Examinations and Tests." *Journal of Official Statistics*, 1997, 13, 305–315.

Survey Research Center. *Fall Omnibus Instruction Book*. Ann Arbor: Survey Research Center, University of Michigan, 1973. (For other queries about specific questions in text, write to Survey Research Center, Institute for Social Research, University of Michigan, Ann Arbor, MI 48106. Please mention year given in parentheses.)

Survey Research Laboratory, University of Illinois. (Queries about specific questions in text should be addressed to the laboratory, 1005 W. Nevada Street, Urbana, IL 61801. Please mention year given in parentheses.)

Tourangeau, R., Rips, L., and Rasinski, K. *The Psychology of Survey Response*. Cambridge: Cambridge University Press, 2000.

Tourangeau, R., and Smith, T. "Asking Sensitive Questions: The Impact of Data Collection Mode, Question Format, and Question Context." *Public Opinion Quarterly*, 1996, 60, 275–304.

Tulving, E. *Elements of Episodic Memory*. Oxford: Clarendon Press, 1983.

Tulving, E., and Donaldson, W. (eds.). *Organization of Memory*. Orlando: Academic Press, 1972.

Turner, C. F., Lessler, J. T., and Gfroerer, J. C. *Survey Measurement of Drug Use: Methodological Studies*. Washington, D.C.: U.S. Department of Health and Human Services, 1992.

Turner, C. F., and Martin, E. (eds.). *Surveys of Subjective Phenomena*. Report by the Panel on Survey Measurement of Subjective Phenomena, Committee on National Statistics, National Academy of Sciences/National Research Council. (2 vols.) Cambridge, Mass.: Harvard University Press, 1982.

U.S. Bureau of the Census. *Current Population Survey*. Washington, D.C.: U.S. Government Printing Office, Nov. 1976.

U.S. Bureau of the Census. *1997 Economic Census*, Mar. 6, 2001.

U.S. Bureau of the Census. *Current Population Survey, November 2000: Voting and Registration Supplement* [machine-readable data file]. Conducted by the Bureau of the Census for the Bureau of Labor Statistics. Washington, D.C.: Bureau of the Census [producer and distributor], 2001.

U.S. Department of Education. *National Assessment of Educational Progress*. Washington, D.C.: U.S. Government Printing Office, 1972–1974.

U.S. Department of Education. *National Assessment of Educational Progress*. Washington, D.C.: U.S. Government Printing Office, 1972–2003.

Wagenaar, W. A. "My Memory: A Study of Autobiographical Memory over Six Years." *Cognitive Psychology*, 1986, *18*, 225–252.

Wansink, B. "Customer Visits: Building a Better Marketing Focus." *Journal of Marketing Research*, 1994a, *31*, 578–579.

Wansink, B. "Developing and Validating Useful Consumer Prototypes." *Journal of Targeting, Measurement and Analysis for Marketing*, 1994b, *3*, 18–30.

Wansink, B. "Inside Sources of Consumer Insights." In C. Lamb, J. Hair, and S. McDaniel (eds.), *Great Ideas for Teaching Marketing*. (2nd ed.) Upper Saddle River, N.J.: Prentice Hall, 1994c.

Wansink, B. "New Techniques to Generate Key Marketing Insights." *Marketing Research*, 2000a, *12*(2), 28–36.

Wansink, B. "The Power of Panels." *Journal of Database Marketing*, 2000b, 8(3), 190–194.

Wansink, B. "Changing Eating Habits on the Home Front: Lost Lessons from World War II Research." *Journal of Public Policy and Marketing*, 2002a, *21*(1), 90–99.

Wansink, B. "Predicting the Future of Consumer Panels." *Journal of Database Marketing*, 2002b, 9(4), 301–311.

Wansink, B. "Profiling Nutritional Gatekeepers: Three Methods for Differentiating Influential Cooks." *Food Quality and Preference*, 2003a, *14*(4), 289–297.

Wansink, B. "Using Laddering to Understand and Leverage a Brand's Equity." *Qualitative Market Research*, 2003b, 6(2), 111–118.

Wansink, B. *Marketing Nutrition*. Champaign: University of Illinois Press, 2004.

Wansink, B., Cheney, M. M., and Chan, N. "Understanding Comfort Food Preferences Across Gender and Age." *Physiology and Behavior*, 2003, *53*, 459–478.

Wansink, B., and Cheong, J. "Taste Profiles that Correlate with Soy Consumption in Developing Countries." *Pakistan Journal of Nutrition*, 2002, *1*, 276–278.

Wansink, B., and Park, S. "Accounting for Taste: Prototypes that Predict Preference." *Journal of Database Marketing*, 2000a, *7*, 308–320.

Wansink, B., and Park, S. "Methods and Measures that Profile Heavy Users." *Journal of Advertising Research*, 2000b, 40(4), 61–72.

Wansink, B., and Ray, M. L. "Estimating an Advertisement's Impact on One's Consumption of a Brand." *Journal of Advertising Research*, 1992, *32*(3), 9–16.

Wansink, B., Ray, M. L., and Batra, R. "Increasing Cognitive Response Sensitivity." *Journal of Advertising*, 1994, *23*(2), 62–74.

Wansink, B., Sonka, S. T., and Cheney, M. M. "A Cultural Hedonic Framework for Increasing the Consumption of Unfamiliar Foods: Soy Acceptance in Russia and Colombia." *Review of Agricultural Economics*, 2002, *24*, 353–365.

Wansink, B., and Sudman, S. "Building a Successful Convenience Panel." *Marketing Research*, 2002a, *12*(3), 23–27.

Wansink, B., and Sudman, S. "Selecting a Consumer Panel Service." *Quirk's Marketing Research Review*, 2002b, *16*(5), 30–36.

Wansink, B., and Westgren, R. "Profiling Taste-Motivated Segments." *Appetite*, 2003, *21*, 314–317.

Warner, S. L. "Randomized Response: A Survey Technique for Eliminating Error Answer Bias." *Journal of the American Statistical Association*, 1965, *60*, 63–69.

Weinstein, A. *Market Segmentation*. Chicago: Probus, 1994.

Wells, W. D. "Psychographics: A Critical Review." *Journal of Marketing Research*, 1975, *12*, 196–213.

Wells, W. D., and Tigert, D. J. "Activities, Interests, and Opinions." *Journal of Advertising Research*, 1971, *11*, 27–35.

Wentland, E. J., and Smith, K. W. *Survey Responses: An Evaluation of Their Validity*. San Diego: Academic Press, 1993.

Westin, A. *Privacy and Freedom*. New York: Atheneum, 1967.

Willis, G. *Cognitive Interviewing and Questionnaire Design: A Training Manual*. Working Paper Series, No. 7. Hyattsville, Md.: National Center for Health Statistics, 1994.

Glossary

aided-recall procedures Methods for providing one or more memory cues to the respondent when behavior or knowledge questions are asked. Specific procedures include the use of lists, pictures, household inventories, and specific detailed questions.

AIO questions An abbreviation for questions that focus on activities, interests, and opinions. This phrase generally refers to the use of these questions to measure psychographic differences or individual differences in order to predict behavior or develop segments based on the way people think rather than on their demographics.

anonymous forms Questionnaires (usually dealing with threatening topics) that do not obtain names or other critical identifiers, in order to assure respondent confidentiality. For anonymous forms to be effective, the respondent must believe the assurances of anonymity. Self-administered questionnaires in a group setting are the most anonymous form possible. Mail surveys are the next most anonymous. Some respondents, however, may suspect that the researcher will know who they are even if no identifying information is requested. Anonymity is possible even with an interviewer present if the respondent puts the responses to a self-administered form into a sealed envelope.

attitude and opinion questions The terms *attitude*, *opinion*, and *belief* are not well differentiated. In general, *attitude* refers to a general orientation or way of thinking. An attitude gives rise to many specific opinions, a term often used with regard to a specific issue or object. The term *belief* is often applied to statements that have a strong normative component, particularly those having to do with religion or with moral or "proper" behavior.

BARS See *behaviorally anchored rating scale*.

behavior questions Questions that ask about behavior or "facts." Examples are characteristics of people, things people have done, or things that have happened to people that are in principle verifiable by an external observer. Knowledge questions are considered behavior questions.

behavioral intention questions Questions that ask respondents to estimate their future behavior, such as the likelihood they will buy a new car in the next year, or the number of times they plan to exercise in the next month. For infrequently performed behaviors (or narrow time frames), likelihood scales are most accurate, but for more frequently performed behaviors, numerical responses are better.

behaviorally anchored rating scale (BARS) The BARS approach uses graphical rating scales that incorporate specific behavioral descriptions using various points along each scale. (See Figure 7.2.) Each scale represents a dimension or factor considered to be an important part of work performance, and both raters and those being evaluated are typically involved in developing the dimensions and behavioral descriptions.

bias The difference between the value reported and the true value. Sample bias results from the omission or the unequal selection of members of the population without appropriate weighting. Response bias for behavioral reports is the difference between what the respondent reports and the respondent's actual behavior. Response bias for attitude questions is an ambiguous concept. (See also *response effect*.)

bipolar and unipolar questions Bipolar questions are those expressed in terms of either end of a dimension, such as "favor-oppose" or "satisfied-dissatisfied." Unipolar questions are asked only

in terms of one end of a dimension with a neutral or "not-X" point—
for example, "Do you favor X or not?" A bipolar question assumes
that the attitude runs from positive to negative values, with a neutral point in the middle; unipolar questions assume that the attitude
runs from positive to neutral or from negative to neutral but that a
positive view is not necessarily the opposite of a negative view.

bounded recall A procedure for improving a respondent's memory
for dates of events by means of a series of interviews. The initial
interview is unbounded, and data from it are not used. On all subsequent interviews, the respondent is reminded of events reported
previously, and the interviewer also checks to make sure there is no
duplication between events in the current interview and those
reported earlier.

card sorting A procedure for obtaining answers that requires the
respondent to place answers printed on cards into two or more piles.
For example, respondents may be asked to sort a set of threatening
behaviors into two piles, depending on whether they have ever
done them or not. As another example, respondents might be asked
to place a series of future events into nine piles, depending on how
likely they think the events are to occur. The advantages of this
procedure are that it appears to be less threatening than requiring
an oral response to a question, it allows respondents to change their
minds easily by resorting, and it adds variety to the survey.

cards Material the interviewer hands the respondent during the
interview, generally on a cardboard card approximately 5 by 8
inches. The card might contain a list of answer categories when
there are too many for the respondent to remember, or it might
show a picture or diagram to which a reaction is required. Cards are
usually numbered or lettered and placed on a ring so that the interviewer can find the proper card easily.

CATI (computer-assisted telephone interviewing) A telephone
interviewing method in which a printed questionnaire is not used;
instead, the questions appear on a computer screen, and the answers

are entered directly into a computer via a keyboard attached to the terminal. The major advantages of these procedures are that they allow researchers to design questionnaires with very complex skip instructions, to communicate in real time with interviewers if an impossible answer is entered, and to eliminate intermediate steps—which speeds up data processing. The computer is programmed not only to present the next question after a response is input but also to determine from the response exactly which question should be asked next; that is, the computer branches automatically to the next question according to the filter instructions. (See also *skip instructions*.)

closed-ended and open-ended questions Closed-ended questions give the alternative answers to the respondent, either explicitly or implicitly. They may have two alternatives (dichotomous questions), such as "yes" or "no" or "male" or "female," or they may have multiple choices, such as "Democrat," "Republican," or "Independent," or "strongly agree," "agree," "disagree," and "strongly disagree." In contrast, an open-ended question does not provide answer categories to the respondent. An example would be "What do you think is the most serious problem facing the nation today?"

codebook A list of each of the codes used to record the answers to questions in quantitative form on a spreadsheet. Usually codebooks record each item in a location designated by column. (See also *deck, precolumning*.)

coding The processing of survey answers into numerical form for entry into a computer so that statistical analyses can be performed. Coding of alternative responses to closed-ended questions can be performed in advance, so that no additional coding is required. This is called precoding. If the questionnaire is mostly precoded, then coding refers only to the subsequent coding of open questions. (See also *closed-ended and open-ended questions, field coding*.)

context of questionnaire A general term referring to the totality of cues provided that can influence response. These cues may include the announced subject of the study, any instructions provided to the respondent or interviewer, and the questions themselves. Also included would be interviewer behaviors caused by the questionnaire's context (such as nervousness at asking sensitive questions). These cues have a particularly strong influence on responses to attitude questions, but they may also influence responses to behavior questions.

continuation sheets (or supplement) Loose sheets included to obtain information when the number of items, persons, or events varies from household to household. Continuation sheets reduce the size of the main questionnaire, but they increase the complexity of locating the proper form and also increase the possibility that some loose sheets may be lost.

data archives As used in survey research, a library of information stored from previous surveys, primarily in machine-readable form. Information includes question wordings as well as responses, so that archival information is useful in designing new questionnaires as well as in secondary analysis of existing data.

debriefing A meeting of interviewers, supervisors, and research analysts held after the fieldwork or pretest of a study is completed. The purposes of a debriefing are to alert the analyst to possible difficulties respondents had in understanding or answering questions, as well as to improve future questionnaires and field methods.

deck (or worksheet or file) When responses to a questionnaire need to be recorded on more than one worksheet, they must be numbered so that the analysts will know which worksheet goes with which questions. This numbering is usually done by calling each worksheet or file by a "deck" number. Thus, for one respondent, there would be one or more decks of information. The deck and column number would provide each item's location. For example, the sex of the respondent might be recorded in column 10 of deck 1. The Resident Questionnaire (Figure 6.9) might require a larger number of decks in order to record the information. The point at which a new deck (or worksheet or file) is required is predesigned on the questionnaire for ease of keypunching. (See also *precolumning*.)

demographic characteristics The basic classification variables— sex, age, marital status, race, ethnic origin, education, occupation, income, religion, and residence—that characterize an individual or a household.

dependent, independent, and interdependent variables Dependent variables are the behaviors, attitudes, or knowledge whose variance the researcher is attempting to explain. Independent variables are those that are thought to influence the dependent variables. Whether variables such as occupation or income are dependent or independent variables depends on the purposes of the researcher and the model used. Generally, if a trade-off is required, it is more important to measure dependent variables accurately than independent variables. In more complex models, variables may be interdependent; that is, variable A is affecting variable B while variable B is simultaneously affecting variable A. Such interdependent variables should be measured with the same levels of accuracy if possible.

diaries Written records kept by respondents to report events that are difficult to remember accurately at a later time, such as illnesses or purchases of nondurable goods. Diary keepers are requested to make entries immediately after the purchase or other event occurs and are usually compensated with money or gifts for their cooperation.

dichotomous and multiple choice questions See *closed-ended and open-ended questions*.

die-cut pages Pages in a questionnaire that are cut off across the top or on the side so that the interviewer can always see to whom or what the column refers, even when pages are turned. Using die-cut pages eliminates work, too, since the persons or items only need to be recorded once. Pages may be cut with special die-cutting equipment or paper cutters. (See Question 14 in Appendix B.)

"don't know," "no opinion," "undecided," and "no answer" responses A "don't know" answer is given by a respondent to indicate that he or she would be willing to answer the question but is unable to do so due to lack of information. In difficult or sensitive questions about behavior, a "don't know" may also be a polite refusal to answer. A "no opinion" response to an attitude question indicates that the respondent has not yet formed an opinion on the issue. An "undecided" answer indicates that the respondent cannot choose between two or more alternatives to a closed question. A "no answer" typically is caused by a refusal to answer the question or by a respondent's breaking off the interview at some early point. It might also be caused by interviewer error if an interviewer skipped the question. For many research purposes, these categories may be combined, but for some purposes it is useful to have them separated. Thus, for example, on a controversial attitude question, it is useful to separate those who refuse to answer the question from those who are undecided between alternatives and from those who have not formed an opinion. These separate response categories should be read to the respondent, or an additional probe question should be asked.

false positives and false negatives Sometimes respondents will be classified as having an attribute they do not in fact have (false positive). Sometimes they will be classified as not having an attribute when in fact they do have it (false negative). For example, someone who says he voted in the last election but is shown by a record check not to have voted would be a false positive. Someone who said she was not a registered voter but who appeared on the list of registered voters would be a false negative.

field (used in precolumning) The set of columns in which the information is stored on an IBM card is called a "field." A column of an IBM card is a one-column field; hence, more than one column will be required to store a two-digit number. If year of birth is recorded in columns 20–23 of deck 10, columns 20–23 of that deck are the "age field." (See also *deck, precolumning*.)

field coding The coding of open questions by interviewers during the interview. In a field-coded question, the question itself usually is identical to that of an open-answer format. Instead of a blank space for the interviewer to record the respondent's answer verbatim, a set of codes is printed. Interviewers simply check each topic that is mentioned. Field coding should be avoided unless the interviewer records the verbatim response as well, so that the field coding can be checked when the questionnaire is processed.

filter questions Questions asked to determine which subsequent questions (if any) will be asked.

forced-choice questions Questions that require the respondent to choose one alternative among several—even though the respondent might not "like" any of the alternatives. Respondents are usually asked to choose the alternative that is closest to their views, even though no alternative may exactly express their opinion.

form effect A term used to refer to the effect the question's format has on the distribution of responses to questions. For example, differences in response distributions may be caused by use of open-ended instead of closed-ended questions.

free-response format A format that asks respondents to answer questions in their own words, in which interviewers record the answers verbatim.

funneling procedures and inverted funnels Funneling procedures refer to the ordering of questions in a questionnaire so that the most general or unrestricted questions in an area are asked first and are then followed by successively more restricted questions. The major purpose of the funneling sequence is to prevent early questions from providing cues that influence later questions. It is assumed that most respondents have opinions on the issues and can answer the general questions. If most respondents have not formulated opinions in advance, inverted funnels, which ask the specific questions first, may be used. The inversion eliminates the basic advantage of funneling but helps the respondent consider various aspects of a topic before requiring a general opinion.

General Social Survey (GSS) An omnibus nationwide survey conducted by NORC since 1972. It covers a wide variety of topics of interest to social scientists. The data from these surveys are publicly available through the Inter-University Consortium for Political and Social Research at the University of Michigan and are widely used for teaching and research purposes. A codebook giving question wording and response distributions for each year in which the questions were asked is available on line (www.icpsr.umich.edu/GSS/).

group interviews Self-administered questionnaires where a single interviewer provides instructions and may present visual material to multiple respondents in a school classroom, a work place, or some other central location. Interviews with several members of a household would not normally be considered group interviews. The term may also be used to describe focus group interviews, interviews in which six to fifteen people are brought together for a group discussion about a selected topic under the direction of a discussion leader. (See also *self-administered questionnaires*.)

household (or family) composition, household enumeration or listing As most often used, household composition refers to information about the number of household members, their ages, sexes, and relation to one another. This information is obtained from a household enumeration or listing. Initials (or the first names) of household members are usually obtained so that specific questions can be asked about each member individually or so that one or more household members can be selected for further interviewing. A household may consist of only one person or of unrelated individuals. A family consists of two or more related individuals.

individual difference measures These are questions that attempt to differentiate people according to selected psychological variables such as aggressiveness, need for achievement, impulsivity, innovativeness, and so on. These questions typically take the form of standard batteries of questions and are used in psychographic research.

informants Respondents who report information about the behavior or attitudes of relatives, friends, or acquaintances. If the selected respondent is not available, informants may be used to reduce costs or to improve the accuracy of reported behavior for some threatening topics. (See Chapter Six, "Using Key Informants," for the use of the informants in community and institutional settings.)

informed consent A respondent's implicit or explicit agreement to participate in the interview after being informed of the nature of the task. Information provided to the respondent usually includes the purpose of the study, the name of the interviewer and the organization that the interviewer represents, some indication of the time required, and an explicit mention that sensitive questions need not be answered. Most surveys do not require written consent unless additional access to records is required or respondents are minors.

interviewer instructions (or directions) Instructions to interviewers, such as which questions to ask or skip and when to probe, which are included in the questionnaire but not read to the respondent. These directions are put in a different style of type (such as italics or capital letters) so that they can easily be distinguished from the questions. (See also *probes*.)

key informants, community informants Respondents who provide information about the community or institution they are associated with. Key informants are chosen because of their expertise and are usually identified either because of their formal roles (such as political official, officer in a firm or organization, or principal of a school) or because they are identified by other experts as being knowledgeable. Some of the information they provide, however, may reflect their own beliefs. (See also *projective questions*.)

knowledge questions Questions that test the respondent's knowledge about current issues and persons or attempt to measure educational achievement or general ability.

loaded questions Questions worded so that certain desired answers are more likely to be given by respondents. Loaded questions may be legitimately used to overcome a respondent's reluctance to report threatening behavior. The major illegitimate use of loaded questions is in surveys intended for lobbying or other persuasive purposes when the loading of an attitude question is in the direction of the views held by the question writer.

memory error An unintentional error in the reporting of a behavior, caused either by forgetting that the event occurred or misremembering some details of the event. (See also *telescoping* for error in date.)

multiple choice questions See *closed-ended and open-ended questions*.

"no answer" See *"don't know," "no opinion," "undecided," and "no answer" responses*.

nonverbal questions Questions in which either the stimulus or the response is nonverbal, such as a picture, map, piece of music, or physical object. Such questions are most often used as tests of knowledge.

open-ended questions See *closed-ended and open-ended questions*.

opinions See *attitude and opinion questions*.

order effect A change in the distribution (or frequency) of responses to a question, caused either by the order in which the alternative answers are given to the respondent or by the position of the question after earlier questions on the topic. (See also *context of questionnaire*.)

overreporting, underreporting Respondents may report that they have bought more or done something more frequently than they actually have, or they may underreport their activities. Overreporting tends to occur in responses to questions about socially desirable activities, and underreporting tends to be in response to questions about threatening topics.

panel study A data collection procedure in which information is obtained from the sample units two or more times, either by repeated interviews or by diaries. Since panels can track individual changes, they provide more reliable as well as more detailed information over time than independent samples do, but they are more difficult to recruit and maintain. (See also *diaries*.)

PDAs (personal digital assistants) These take the form of a variety of electronic handheld devices that can be used for a wide range of tasks, including data entry.

personal interviews (face-to-face and telephone interviews) Personal interviews are those in which the interviewer both asks the questions and records the answers. Such interviews may be conducted face-to-face or by telephone. Group interviews and self-administered questionnaires are not considered personal interviews even if an interviewer is present.

pilot test, pretest A small field test, primarily of the questionnaire but also of other field procedures, that occurs before the main study is conducted. Pilot tests usually have small samples (ten to fifty cases) and are intended to alert the researcher to unanticipated respondent difficulties. Some organizations use the terms *pilot test* and *pretest* synonymously. Others consider that a pilot test precedes a pretest, and still others consider a pretest to precede a pilot test.

precoding See *coding*.

precolumning The process by which responses to each question or item of identifying information on a questionnaire are assigned to column locations in a series of IBM cards. For example, the sex of the respondent may be located in column 10 of deck 1. This assignment would be indicated on the questionnaire for ease in keypunching. (See also *deck.*)

probability samples Samples of the population from which the sample is drawn (for example, households or individuals) that have a known probability of being included in the sample. In equal-probability samples, each member of the population has an equal probability of selection; in unequal-probability samples, certain types of members of the population are oversampled or undersampled, that is, are given a greater or lesser chance of falling into the sample than their proportion in the population would determine.

probes Questions or statements such as "What do you mean?" or "In what way?" or "Could you explain that a little?" made by the interviewer to the respondent to obtain additional information to a question when the initial answer appears incomplete. Researchers sometimes specify when to use probes and what to say, but use of probes is often left to interviewers' judgment. A key problem for interviewers is to avoid leading probes that put words into the respondents' mouths. Leading probes may start with a phrase such as "Do you mean . . . ?" or "Are you saying . . . ?"

projective questions Questions that attempt to determine indirectly what respondents think by asking their views of what others think. An example of a projective question would be "Do you think people around here would be upset if asked about their sexual activities?" Such questions are intended to reduce the response effect on threatening questions. If the respondent is in a position to know what others think, the projective question becomes a knowledge question. Many answers are combinations of knowledge and projection by the respondent. (See also *response effect, threatening and nonthreatening questions.*)

proxy respondent An individual who provides complete information about another person when the person is unavailable because of illness or for some other reason. Proxy respondents are usually other members of the same household. (See also *informants*.)

psychographic questions Psychographic and "lifestyle" questions are sometimes referred to as AIO (activities, interests, and opinions) research because they generally focus on AIO issues along with behavior. The intent of psychographic questions is generally to provide a means to better predict an individual's preference or behavior or to segment populations to explain why different people behave in different ways. When introduced in the 1960s, the term *psychographics* referred to "the use of psychological, sociological, and anthropological factors, self-concept, and lifestyle to determine how the market is segmented by the propensity of groups within the market—and their reasons—to make a particular decision about a product, person, or ideology" (Demby, 1989, p. 21).

questionnaire The complete data collection instrument used by an interviewer or respondent (or both) during a survey. It includes not only the questions and space for answers but also interviewer instructions, the introduction, and cards used by the respondent. Traditionally, the questionnaire has been printed, but more recently electronic versions are being used on computer terminals. (See also *CATI*.)

random digit dialing (RDD) Selection of telephone samples by random generation of telephone numbers by computer. There are several different techniques for generating RDD samples, the most common of which begins with a list of working exchanges in the geographical area from which the sample is to be drawn. The last four digits are generated by a random procedure. RDD procedures have the advantage of including unlisted numbers, which would be missed if numbers were drawn from a telephone book.

random and nonrandom samples Strictly speaking, a random sample is one type of probability sample, in which the sample is drawn by means of a strict random procedure, such as a table of random numbers. In practice, the term *random sampling* is frequently used to mean any kind of probability sample. The term *nonrandom sample* is most often used to mean any sort of nonprobability sample, such as a quota sample, a convenience sample, or a haphazard sample.

randomized response A method that ensures respondent anonymity on questions dealing with socially undesirable or illegal behavior. The procedure involves asking two questions, one threatening and the other completely innocuous, both of which have the same possible answers (for example, "yes" or "no.") The respondent decides which question to answer on the basis of a probability mechanism (such as a box of red and blue beads with a window in which a single bead appears). Since the interviewer does not know what question is being answered, the response is completely anonymous, although some respondents may not believe this. By knowing the distribution of responses to the innocuous question (such as "Were you born in April?") and the probability mechanism, the researcher can estimate the response to the threatening question.

recall question A question asking about behavior that occurred in the past. Recall questions are subject to memory error. (See also *memory error*.)

records Documents used to reduce memory error on behavior questions. Examples include bills, checkbook records, canceled checks, titles and leases, and other financial records. (See also *memory error*.)

redundancy effect One type of order effect hypothesized to result from asking related questions in such a way that respondents interpret them as excluding reference to information given in previously asked questions.

reliability, reliability checks In the technical sense, as used in psychology and survey research, the degree to which multiple measures of the same attitude or behavior agree. These multiple measures may be used over time or at the same point in time. If repeated in the same questionnaire, the same item should not be asked in exactly, or nearly exactly, the same way, since this irritates the respondent and distorts the estimate of reliability.

response effect A generalization of response bias to include different responses to attitude questions that are caused by question wording, context, and method of administration where no external validity criteria are possible. For behavior questions, response effect is synonymous with response bias. (See also *bias, validity*.)

response set The tendency of some respondents to answer all of a series of questions in the same way, regardless of the differences in content of the individual questions. For example, a respondent who answered the first of a series of questions "Yes" or "Agree" might answer all remaining questions the same way, particularly if the items were ambiguous or not salient.

salience The importance of the topic or question to the respondent, as indicated by the thought that has been given to it by the respondent prior to the interview. Personal and family concerns are generally more salient than public issues.

sample A portion of a larger population selected by some principle. If the selection is done so that the probability of selection is known, it is a probability sample. Inferences about the population can be made, then, according to the principles of statistical inference. If the sample is a nonprobability sample, the kinds of inferences you can make about the population are open to question, because there is no accepted theory of inferences about populations based on information from nonprobability samples.

screening A questioning process, usually short, used to determine whether respondents or households have certain characteristics that would make them eligible for a full-scale interview. Examples would be screens for given ages, incomes, or racial or ethnic groups or for persons with large medical expenses.

sealed envelope or ballot See *anonymous forms*.

self-administered questionnaires Questionnaires that require respondents to read or answer the questions themselves. These are almost all paper-and-pencil forms currently, but computer use should increase in the future. Note that the form is considered to be self-administered even if an interviewer is present to hand it out, to collect it, and to answer questions. (See also *personal interviews*.)

skip instructions Instructions given to the interviewer (and, less commonly, on self-administered forms to respondents) indicating what question to ask or answer next, based on the answers to the question just asked. Skip instructions make it possible to use a single questionnaire for many different types of respondents and to ask only those questions that are relevant. Respondents cannot be expected to follow complex skip instructions accurately. Skip instructions are not required on CATI systems where the skipping is programmed into the computer. (See also *CATI*.)

social desirability, social undesirability The perception by respondents that their answer to a question will enhance or hurt their image in the eyes of the interviewer or the researcher. Desirability is closely related to the sociological term *mores*—the ways of thinking or acting that have ethical significance in a social group and, thus, have the force of law, even if the law is unwritten. Examples of socially desirable behavior are being a good citizen, being well informed, and fulfilling moral and social responsibilities. Examples of socially undesirable behavior include using alcohol and drugs, participating in deviant sexual practices, and violating traffic regulations.

split ballot The use of an experimental design to determine effects of question wording or placement. Alternate forms or placements of questions are randomly assigned to portions of the sample. Usually each half of the sample gets one of two forms or placements of the split questions, but the technique can be expanded to accommodate a larger number of experimental treatments, where each form or placement of the question is considered a treatment.

structured and unstructured questionnaires Structured questionnaires, used in survey research, specify the wording of the questions and the order in which they are asked. Unstructured questionnaires list the topics to be covered but leave the exact wording and order of questions to the interviewer's discretion. Unstructured questionnaires are more likely to be used by anthropologists or psychologists and in clinical settings.

symmetrical distribution A distribution that is symmetrical around the midpoint. The most common example is the normal distribution.

telescoping Misremembering the date when a behavior occurred—particularly, remembering it as having occurred more recently than it did and falling into the period referred to in the question, rather than in an earlier period for which information is not being obtained.

threatening and nonthreatening questions Threatening questions make the respondent uneasy and include as a subgroup questions about socially desirable and undesirable behavior. In addition, some respondents will be threatened by questions dealing with financial or health status, since these topics usually are not discussed with strangers. Nonthreatening questions, in contrast, are those that do not make the respondent uneasy. Questions dealing with drug use, for example, are likely to be threatening to users but not to nonusers. Note that threat depends on perceptions. (See also *social desirability, social undesirability.*)

transitional phrases and questions Words or questions used in questionnaires to alert the respondent that the topic of the questions is about to change. Used to help the respondent understand the logical order being followed.

validation The process of obtaining outside data to measure the accuracy of reported behavior in surveys. Validation may be at either an individual or a group level. Examples include using financial or medical records to check on reporting of assets or illness costs. Unless public records are used, validation at the individual level requires the consent of the respondent. In survey research, validation also has the special meaning of recontacting the respondent to determine whether the interview was actually conducted.

validity A valid measure is one that measures what it claims to and not something else. The concept is clearest with respect to behavioral questions, where an outside validation source is possible. Nevertheless, various researchers have proposed validity measures for attitudinal items. Validity is a continuous concept and refers to the distance between the measure and a completely valid measurement. It is the converse of response bias. (See also *bias*.)

VALS (from *values and lifestyles*) One of the more widely known psychographic segmentation research programs. It is conducted by SRI Consulting and attempts to show more general psychographic segments that are relevant and can be used across a wide number of people and topics. Their psychographic approach sorts people into one of eight different groups. (See Chapter Eight.)

variability, variance As used with a population, variability refers to differences between individuals or groups in the population, usually measured as a statistical variance or simply by observing the differences between the measurements for the group. As used with attitudes, variability refers to the sensitivity of responses to differences in question wording or context. For samples, variance or variability refers to differences between repeated samples selected from the same population using the same survey procedures. For statistical definitions of variance, see any statistics textbook.

variables See *dependent, independent, and interdependent variables*.

Index

Appendix A

List of Academic and Not-for-Profit Survey Research Organizations

Alabama

Institute for Communication Research
College of Communication
University of Alabama
Box 870172
Tuscaloosa, AL 35487-0172
Phone: 205-348-1235
Fax: 205-348-9257
E-mail: jbryant@icr.ua.edu
http://www.icr.ua.edu/

Survey Research Laboratory
Center for Governmental Services
Auburn University
2236 Haley Center
Auburn University, AL 36849-5225
Phone: 334-844-1914
Fax: 334-844-1919
E-mail: cgs@cgs.auburn.edu
http://www.auburn.edu/cgs/srl.html

Capstone Poll
Institute for Social Science Research
University of Alabama
P.O. Box 870216
Tuscaloosa, AL 35487-0216
Phone: 205-348-6233
Fax: 205-348-2849
E-mail: dmccallu@bama.ua.edu
http://bama.ua.edu/~issr/

Arizona

Maricopa County Research and Reporting
111 W. Monroe St., Suite 1010

Phoenix, AZ 85003-1797
Phone: 602-506-1600
Fax: 602-506-1601
E-mail: kandersen@maricopa.mail.gov
http://www.maricopa.gov/res_report/default.asp

Social Research Laboratory
Northern Arizona University
P.O. Box 15301
Flagstaff, AZ 86011-5301
Phone: 928-523-1515
Fax: 928-523-6654
E-mail: Fred.Solop@nau.edu
http://www4.nau.edu/srl/

Survey Research Laboratory
Arizona State University
P.O. Box 872101
Tempe, AZ 85287-2101
Phone: 480-965-5032
Fax: 480-965-5077
E-mail: srl@asu.edu
http://www.asu.edu/clas/sociology/srl/index.html

Arkansas

Arkansas Household Research Panel
Marketing and Transportation Department
University of Arkansas
Fayetteville, AR 72701-9980
Phone: 479-575-4055
Fax: 479-575-8407

Institute for Economic Advancement
Survey/Business Research Group
University of Arkansas at Little Rock

Library Building, #506
2801 South University Ave.
Little Rock, AR 72204-1099
Phone: 501-569-8519
Fax: 501-569-8538
E-mail: apvibhakar@ualr.edu
http://www.aiea.ualr.edu/

California

Cooperative Institutional Research Program
Higher Education Research Institute
University of California, Los Angeles
P.O. Box 951521
Los Angeles, CA 90095-1521
Phone: 310-825-1925
Fax: 310-206-2228
E-mail: heri@ucla.edu
http://www.gseis.ucla.edu/heri/cirp.html

Social Science Research Laboratory
College of Arts and Letters
San Diego State University
5500 Campanile Dr.
San Diego, CA 92182-4540
Phone: 619-594-6802
Fax: 619-594-1358
E-mail: ssrlhelp@mail.sdsu.edu
http://ssrl.sdsu.edu

Survey Research Center
Institute for Social Science Research
University of California, Los Angeles
P.O. Box 951484
Los Angeles, CA 90095-1484
Phone: 310-825-0713

Fax: 310-206-4453
E-mail: efielder@issr.ucla.edu
http://www.sscnet.ucla.edu/issr/src/

Survey Research Center
University of California, Berkeley
2538 Channing Way, #5100
Berkeley, CA 94720-5100
Phone: 510-642-6578
Fax: 510-643-8292
E-mail: info@src.berkeley.edu
http://srcweb.berkeley.edu

RAND Survey Research Group
RAND
1700 Main St.
P.O. Box 2138
Santa Monica, CA 90407-2138
Phone: 310-451-7051
Fax: 310-451-6921
E-mail: sandra_berry@rand.org
http://www.rand.org/methodology/srg/

CATI Unit
Public Health Institute
1700 Tribute Road, Suite 100
Sacramento, CA 95815-4402
Phone: 916-779-0338
Fax: 916-779-0264
E-mail: srg@ccr.ca.gov
http://surveyresearchgroup.com/

Applied Research and Evaluation
California State University, Chico
Chico, CA 95929-0201
Phone: 530-898-4332
Fax: 530-898-5095

E-mail: srcsurv@csuchico.edu
http://www.csuchico.edu/surv/

Ludie and David C. Henley Social Science Research Laboratory
Chapman University
One University Drive
Orange, CA 92866
Phone: 714-997-6610
Fax: 714-532-6079
E-mail: smoller@chapman.edu
http://www.chapman.edu/hssrl/index.html

Connecticut

The Center for Survey Research and Analysis
University of Connecticut
Box U1032, 341 Mansfield Road
Storrs, CT 06269-1032
Phone: 860-486-6666
Fax: 860-486-6655

Delaware

Center for Applied Demography and Survey Research
University of Delaware
282 Graham Hall
Newark, DE 19716
Phone: 302-831-1684
Fax: 302-831-2867
E-mail: ratledge@udel.edu
http://www.cadsr.udel.edu

District Of Columbia

Gallaudet Research Institute
Gallaudet University

800 Florida Ave., N.E.
Washington, DC 20002-3695
Phone: 202-651-5729
Fax: 202-651-5746
E-mail: gri.offices@gallaudet.edu
http://gri.gallaudet.edu/

National Center for Education Statistics
1990 K Street N.W., Room 9501
Washington, DC 20006
Phone: 202-502-7303
E-mail: Marilyn.Seastrom@ed.gov
http://nces.ed.gov

Florida

Institute for Public Opinion Research
Biscayne Bay Campus
Florida International University
3000 NE 151st St.
North Miami, FL 33181
Phone: 305-919-5778
Fax: 305-919-5242
E-mail: gladwin@fiu.edu
http://www.fiu.edu/orgs/ipor

Bureau of Economic and Business Research
University of Florida
P.O. Box 117145
Gainesville, FL 32611-7145
Phone: 352-392-0171
Fax: 352-392-4739
E-mail: info@bebr.ufl.edu
http://www.bebr.ufl.edu/

Survey Research Laboratory
College of Social Sciences
Florida State University
Tallahasse, FL 32306-2221
Phone: 800-933-9482
E-mail: mstutzma@mailer.fsu.edu
http://www.fsu.edu/~survey#

Florida Government Performance Research Center
Florida State University
421 Diffenbaugh Building
Tallahassee, FL 32306-1531
Phone: 850-644-2159
Fax: 850-644-2180
E-mail: bsapolsk@mailer.fsu.edu
http://comm2.fsu.edu/programs/comm/fgpsrc

Georgia

A. L. Burruss Institute of Public Service
Kennesaw State University
1000 Chastain Road, Box 3302
Kennesaw, GA 30144-5911
Phone: 770-423-6464
Fax: 770-423-6395
E-mail: burruss@kennesaw.edu
http://www.kennesaw.edu/burruss_inst/

Survey Research Center
Institute of Behavioral Research
University of Georgia
1095 College Station Road
Athens, GA 30602
Phone: 706-425-3031
Fax: 706-425-3008

E-mail: jbason@arches.uga.edu
http://src.ibr.uga.edu

Survey Research Center
Savannah State University
P.O. Box 20243
Savannah, GA 31404-9703
Phone: 912-356-2244
Fax: 912-356-2299
E-mail: src@savstate.edu
http://www.savstate.edu/orsp/src/about.html

Illinois

Survey Research Office
University of Illinois at Springfield
One University Plaza
Springfield, IL 62703-5407
Phone: 217-206-6591
Fax: 217-206-7979
E-mail: Schuldt.Richard@uis.edu
http://sro.uis.edu

National Opinion Research Center (NORC)
University of Chicago
1155 East 60th St.
Chicago, IL 60637
Phone: 773-256-6000
Fax: 773-753-7886
E-mail: norcinfo@norcmail.uchicago.edu
http://www.norc.uchicago.edu

Survey Lab
Judd Hall
University of Chicago

5835 S. Kimbark Ave.
Chicago, IL 60637
Phone: 773-834-3843
Fax: 773-834-7412
http://socialsciences.uchicago.edu/survey-lab

Public Opinion Laboratory
Northern Illinois University
148 N. Third St.
DeKalb, IL 60115-2854
Phone: 815-753-9657
E-mail: publicopinionlab@niu.edu
http://www.pol.niu.edu

Center for Business and Economic Research
Bradley University
1501 W. Bradley Ave., Baker 122
Peoria, IL 61625
Phone: 309-677-2278
Fax: 309-677-3257
E-mail: bjg@bumail.bradley.edu
http://www.bradley.edu/fcba/cber

Metro Chicago Information Center
360 N. Michigan Ave., Suite 1409
Chicago, IL 60601-3802
Phone: 312-580-2878
Fax: 312-580-2879
E-mail: mcic@mcic.org
http://www.mcic.org

Survey Research Laboratory
University of Illinois at Chicago
412 S. Peoria St., Sixth Floor
Chicago, IL 60607-7069

Phone: 312-996-5300
Fax: 312-996-3358
E-mail: info@srl.uic.edu
http://www.srl.uic.edu

Indiana

Center for Survey Research
Indiana University
1022 E. Third St.
Bloomington, IN 47405
Phone: 812-855-8380
Fax: 812-855-2818
E-mail: csr@indiana.edu
http://www.indiana.edu/~csr/

Indiana University Public Opinion Laboratory
Indiana University
719 Indiana Ave., Suite 260
Indianapolis, IN 46202
Phone: 317-274-4105
Fax: 317-278-2383
E-mail: IGEM100@iupui.edu
http://felix.iupui.edu

Iowa

Institute for Social and Behavioral Research
Iowa State University
2625 N. Loop Drive, Suite 500
Ames, IA 50010-8296
Phone: 515-294-4518
Fax: 515-294-3613
E-mail: shhuck@iastate.edu
http://www.isbr.iastate.edu

Social Science Institute
University of Iowa
123 N. Linn St., Suite 130
Iowa City, IA 52242
Phone: 319-335-2367
Fax: 319-335-2070
E-mail: mike-ohara@uiowa.edu
http://www.uiowa.edu/~issidata/

Survey Section
Statistical Laboratory
Iowa State University
220 Snedecor Hall
Ames, IA 50011
Phone: 515-294-5242
Fax: 515-294-2456
E-mail: nusser@iastate.edu
http://www.statlab.iastate.edu/survey/

Center for Social and Behavioral Research
University of Northern Iowa
221 Sabin Hall
Cedar Falls, IA 50614-0402
Phone: 319-273-2105
Fax: 319-273-3104
E-mail: lutz@csbr.csbs.uni.edu
http://csbsnt.csbs.uni.edu/dept/csbr/

Kansas

CATI Laboratory
School of Family Studies and Human Services
Kansas State University
1700 Anderson Ave.
Manhattan, KS 66506-1403

Phone: 785-532-5510
Fax: 785-532-5505
E-mail: schumm@humec.ksu.edu
www.ksu.edu/humec/fshs/fshs.htm

Survey Research Center
Policy Research Institute
University of Kansas
1541 Lilac Lane
607 Blake Hall
Lawrence, KS 66044-3177
Phone: 785-864-3701
Fax: 785-864-3683
E-mail: pri@ku.edu
http://www.ku.edu/pri

Kentucky

Urban Studies Institute
Survey Research Center
University of Louisville
426 W. Bloom St.
Louisville, KY 40208
Phone: 502-852-8151
Fax: 502-852-4558
E-mail: bgale@louisville.edu
http://www.louisville.edu/cbpa/usi

Survey Research Center
University of Kentucky
304 Breckinridge Hall
Lexington, KY 40506-0056
Phone: 859-257-4684
Fax: 859-323-1972
E-mail: langley@uky.edu
http://survey.rgs.uky.edu/

Louisiana

Survey Research Center
Department of Political Science
University of New Orleans
New Orleans, LA 70148
Phone: 504-280-6467
Fax: 504-280-3838
E-mail: unopoll@uno.edu
http://www.uno.edu/~poli/unopoll/

Maine

Survey Research Center
Edmund S. Muskie School of Public Service
University of Southern Maine
P.O. Box 9300
Portland, ME 04104-9300
Phone: 207-780-4430
Fax: 207-780-4417
E-mail: leighton@usm.maine.edu
http://muskie.usm.maine.edu/src/SRCoverview.html

Maryland

Centers for Public Health Research and Evaluation (CPHRE)
Battelle
CPHRE Business Development Office
505 King Ave.
Columbus, Ohio 43201
Phone: 614-424-6424
E-mail: solutions@battele.org
http://www.battelle.org/hhs/cphre/default.stm

Center for the Study of Local Issues
Anne Arundel Community College
101 College Parkway
Arnold, MD 21012
Phone: 410-777-2733
Fax: 410-777-4733
E-mail: ddnataf@aacc.edu
http://www.aacc.cc.md.us/csli

Institute for Governmental Service
University of Maryland
4511 Knox Road, Suite 205
College Park, MD 20740
Phone: 301-403-4610
Fax: 301-403-4222
E-mail: jb128@umail.umd.edu
http://www.vprgs.umd.edu/igs/

Massachusetts

Center for Business Research
University of Massachusetts Dartmouth
285 Old Westport Road
North Dartmouth, MA 02747-2300
Phone: 508-999-8446
Fax: 508-999-8646
E-mail: nbarnes@umassd.edu
http://www.umassd.edu/cbr

North Charles Research and Planning Group
875 Massachusetts Ave., 7th Floor
Cambridge, MA 02139
Phone: 617-864-9115
Fax: 617-864-2658
E-mail: wmcauliffe@ntc.org
http://www.ntc.org

Communication Research Center
Boston University
704 Commonwealth Ave.
Boston, MA 02215
Phone: 617-358-1300
Fax: 617-358-1301
E-mail: elasmar@bu.edu
http://crc.bu.edu/

Center for Survey Research
University of Massachusetts Boston
100 Morrissey Blvd.
Boston, MA 02125-3393
Phone: 617-287-7200
Fax: 617-287-7210
E-mail: csr@umb.edu
http://www.csr.umb.edu

Michigan

Center for Urban Studies
Survey Research
Wayne State University
Faculty Administration Building
656 W. Kirby, Room 3040
Detroit, MI 48202
Phone: 313-577-2208
Fax: 313-577-1274
E-mail: CUSinfo@wayne.edu
http://www.cus.wayne.edu

Survey Research Center
Institute for Social Research
University of Michigan
P.O. Box 1248

Ann Arbor, MI 48106-1248
Phone: 734-764-8365
Fax: 734-764-5193
E-mail: srchr@isr.umich
http://www.isr.umich.edu

Office for Survey Research
Institute for Public Policy and Social Research
Michigan State University
302 Berkey Hall
East Lansing, MI 48824-1111
Phone: 517-355-6672
Fax: 517-432-1544
E-mail: hembroff@msu.edu
http://www.ippsr.msu.edu

Minnesota

Minnesota Center for Survey Research
University of Minnesota
2331 University Ave. S.E., Suite 141
Minneapolis, MN 55414-3067
Phone: 612-627-4282
Fax: 612-627-4288
E-mail: armso001@umn.edu
http://www.cura.umn.edu/programs/mcsr.html

Wilder Research Center
Amherst H. Wilder Foundation
1295 Bandana Blvd. N., Suite 210
St. Paul, MN 55108
Phone: 615-647-4600
Fax: 615-647-4623
E-mail: research@wilder.org
http://www.wilder.org/research

Mississippi

Survey Research Unit
Social Science Research Center
Mississippi State University
P.O. Box 5287
Mississippi State, MS 39762-5287
Phone: 662-325-7127
Fax: 662-325-7966
E-mail: Wolfgang.Frese@ssrc.msstate.edu
http://www.ssrc.msstate.edu

Missouri

Public Policy Research Center
University of Missouri-St. Louis
362 SSB
8001 Natural Bridge Road
St. Louis, MO 63121
Phone: 314-516-5273
Fax: 314-516-5268
E-mail: pprc@umsl.edu
http://pprc.umsl.edu/

Center for Social Sciences and Public Policy Research
Southwest Missouri State University
901 S. National Ave.
Springfield, MO 65804
Phone: 417-836-6854
Fax: 417-836-8332
E-mail: cssppr@smsu.edu
http://cssppr.smsu.edu/

Nebraska

Bureau of Sociological Research
University of Nebraska-Lincoln

731 Oldfather Hall
Lincoln, NE 68588-0325
Phone: 402-472-3672
Fax: 402-472-6070
E-mail: bosr@unl.edu
http://www.unl.edu/bosr

Nevada

Center for Applied Research
College of Human and Community Sciences
University of Nevada, Reno
Reno, NV 89557-0017
Phone: 775-784-6718
Fax: 775-784-4506
E-mail: calder@sabcar.unr.edu
http://www.sabcar.unr.edu

Cannon Center for Survey Research
University of Nevada, Las Vegas
P.O. Box 455008
Las Vegas, NV 89154-5008
Phone: 702-895-0167
Fax: 702-895-0165
E-mail: lamatsch@nevada.edu
http://www.unlv.edu/Research_Centers/ccsr

New Hampshire

Survey Center
University of New Hampshire
Thompson Hall
105 Main St.
Durham, NH 03824
Phone: 603-862-2226

Fax: 603-862-1488
E-mail: Andrew.Smith@unh.edu
http://www.unh.edu/ipssr/survey-center/

New Jersey

Survey Research Center
Princeton University
169 Nassau St.
Princeton, NJ 08542-7007
Phone: 609-258-5660
Fax: 609-258-0549
E-mail: efreelan@princeton.edu
http://www.wws.princeton.edu/~psrc/

Eagleton Institute of Politics
Rutgers University
Wood Lawn-Neilson Campus
191 Ryders Lane
New Brunswick, NJ 08901-8557
Phone: 732-932-9384
Fax: 732-932-6778
E-mail: eagleton@rci.rutgers.edu
http://www.eagleton.rutgers.edu

New Mexico

Institute for Public Policy
Department of Political Science
University of New Mexico
1805 Sigma Chi Road, NE
Albuquerque, NM 87131-1121
Phone: 505-277-1099
Fax: 505-277-3115
E-mail: instpp@unm.edu
http://www.unm.edu/%7Einstpp/index.html

New York

Marist College Institute for Public Opinion
Marist College
3399 North Road
Poughkeepsie, NY 12601
Phone: 845-575-5050
Fax: 845-575-5111
E-mail: maristpoll@marist.edu
http://www.maristpoll.marist.edu

Center for Social and Demographic Analysis
University at Albany, SUNY
1400 Washington Ave.
Albany, NY 12222
Phone: 518-442-4905
Fax: 518-442-4936
E-mail: s.south@albany.edu
http://www.albany.edu/csda/

Paul F. Lazarsfeld Center for the Social Sciences
Columbia University
420 W. 118th St., 8th Floor
New York, NY 10027
Phone: 212-854-3081
Fax: 212-854-8925
E-mail: psb17@columbia.edu
http://www.cc.columbia.edu/cu/isetr/css.html

Department of Sociomedical Sciences
Mailman School of Public Health
Columbia University
722 W. 168th St., 9th Floor
New York, NY 10032
Phone: 212-305-5656

Fax: 212-305-6832
E-mail: cgh1@columbia.edu
http://chaos.cpmc.columbia.edu/newsms/Flash/Index.asp

Division of Basic and Applied Social Sciences
Keuka College
Keuka Park, NY 14478
Phone: 315-536-5370
Fax: 315-279-5216
E-mail: bass@mail.keuka.edu
http://www.keuka.edu/academic/bass/index.html

Social Indicators Survey Center
School of Social Work
Columbia University
622 W. 113th St.
New York, NY 10025
Phone: 212-854-9046
Fax: 212-854-0433
E-mail: siscenter@columbia.edu
http://www.columbia.edu/cu/ssw/projects/surcent/

The Stony Brook Center for Survey Research
Department of Political Science
SUNY at Stony Brook
Social and Behavioral Sciences Building, 7th Floor
Stony Brook, NY 11794-4392
Phone: 631-632-4006
Fax: 631-632-1538
E-mail: survey_research@sunysb.edu
http://ws.cc.stonybrook.edu/surveys/

Survey Research Institute
B12 Ives Hall

Cornell University
Ithaca, NY 14853
Phone: 607-255-3786
Toll free: 888-367-8404
Fax: 607-255-7118
E-mail: cast@cornell.edu
http://www.sri.cornell.edu

North Carolina

Survey Research Unit
Bolin Creek Center
University of North Carolina
730 Airport Road, Suite 103, CB#2400
Chapel Hill, NC 27599-2400
Phone: 919-843-7845
Fax: 919-966-2221
E-mail: sruinfo@unc.edu
http://www.sph.unc.edu/sru/Home.html

Social and Statistical Sciences
Research Triangle Institute
3040 Cornwallis Road
P.O. Box 12194
Research Triangle Park, NC 27709-2194
Phone: 919-541-7008
Fax: 919-541-7004
E-mail: rak@rti.org
http://www.rti.org

Howard W. Odum Institute for Research in Social Science
University of North Carolina at Chapel Hill
Manning Hall, CB#3355
Chapel Hill, NC 27599-3355
Phone: 919-962-3061

Fax: 919-962-4777
E-mail: bollen@email.unc.edu
http://www2.irss.unc.edu/irss/home.asp

Center for Urban Affairs and Community Services
North Carolina State University at Raleigh
P.O. Box 7401
Raleigh, NC 27695-7401
Phone: 919-515-1300
Fax: 919-515-3642
E-mail: yevonne_brannon@ncsu.edu
http://www.cuacs.ncsu.edu

Ohio

Institute for Policy Research
University of Cincinnati
P.O. Box 210132
Cincinnati, OH 45221-0132
Phone: 513-556-5028
Fax: 513-556-9023
E-mail: Alfred.Tuchfarber@uc.edu
http://www.ipr.uc.edu

Survey Research Laboratory
Kent State University
227 Merrill Hall
Kent, OH 44242-0001
Phone: 330-672-2562
Fax: 330-672-4724
E-mail: bmcdonal@kent.edu
http://dept.kent.edu/cati

Center for Policy Studies
University of Akron

225 South Main St.
Akron, OH 44325-1911
Phone: 330-972-5111
Fax: 330-972-2501
E-mail: jmarquette@uakron.edu
http://www3.uakron.edu/src/

Center for Survey Research
College of Social and Behavioral Sciences
The Ohio State University
3045 Derby Hall, 154 North Oval Mall
Columbus, OH 43210-1330
Phone: 614-292-6672
Fax: 614-292-6673
E-mail: kosicki.1@osu.edu
http://www.csr.ohio-state.edu/

Communication Research Center
Department of Communication
Cleveland State University
2001 Euclid Ave.
Cleveland, OH 44115-1121
Phone: 216-687-4630
Fax: 216-687-5435
E-mail: k.neuendorf@csuohio.edu
http://www.csuohio.edu/com/crc.htm

Center for Human Resource Research
The Ohio State University
921 Chatham Lane, Suite 100
Columbus, OH 43221-2418
Phone: 614-442-7300
Fax: 614-442-7329
E-mail: usersvc@postoffice.chrr.ohio-state.edu
http://www.chrr.ohio-state.edu/

Oklahoma

Bureau for Social Research
Oklahoma State University
306B Human Environmental Services
Stillwater, OK 74078-6117
Phone: 405-744-6701
Fax: 405-744-3342
E-mail: chrisaj@okstate.edu
http://www.okstate.edu/hes/bsr/

Oregon

Oregon State University Survey Research Center
Department of Statistics
Oregon State University
44 Kidder Hall
Corvallis, OR 97331-4606
Phone: 541-737-3584
Fax: 541-737-3489
E-mail: lesser@stat.orst.edu
http://osu.orst.edu/dept/statistics/src/

Oregon Survey Research Laboratory
University of Oregon
5245 University of Oregon
Eugene, OR 97403-5245
Phone: 541-346-0824
Fax: 541-346-0388
E-mail: osrl@uoregon.edu
http://osrl.uoregon.edu

Pennsylvania

University Center for Social and Urban Research
University of Pittsburgh

121 University Pl.
Pittsburgh, PA 15260
Phone: 412-624-5442
Fax: 412-624-4810
E-mail: ucsur@pitt.edu
http://www.ucsur.pitt.edu

Center for Survey Research
Penn State Harrisburg
777 W. Harrisburg Pike
Middletown, PA 17057-4898
Phone: 717-948-6336
Fax: 717-948-6754
E-mail: pasdc@psu.edu
http://pasdc.hbg.psu.edu

Center for Opinion Research
Millersville University
P.O. Box 1002
Millersville, PA 17551-0302
Phone: 717-871-2375
Fax: 717-871-5667
E-mail: Berwood.Yost@millersville.edu
http://muweb.millersville.edu/~opinion/

Institute for Survey Research
Temple University
1601 N. Broad St.
Philadelphia, PA 19122
Phone: 215-204-8355
Fax: 215-204-3797
E-mail: lenlo@temss2.isr.temple.edu
http://www.temple.edu/isr

Rhode Island

A. Alfred Taubman Center for Public Policy and American
    Institutions
Brown University
P.O. Box 1977
Providence, RI 02912
Phone: 401-863-2201
Fax: 401-863-2452
E-mail: thomas_anton@brown.edu
http://www.brown.edu/Departments/Taubman_Center/

Taubman Center/John Hazen White Sr. Public Opinion
    Laboratory
Center for Public Policy
Brown University
67 George St., Box 1977
Providence, RI 02912
Phone: 401-863-1163
E-mail: Darrell_West@brown.edu
http://www.brown.edu/Departments/Taubman_Center/
    pubopin.html

South Carolina

Survey Research Laboratory
University of South Carolina
1503 Carolina Plaza
Columbia, SC 29208
Phone: 803-777-4566
Fax: 803-777-4575
E-mail: oldendick@iopa.sc.edu
http://www.iopa.sc.edu/srl/

South Dakota

Business Research Bureau
School of Business
University of South Dakota
414 E. Clark St.
Vermillion, SD 57069
Phone: 605-677-5287
Fax: 605-677-5427
E-mail: rstuefen@usd.edu
http://www.usd.edu/brbinfo/

Tennessee

Social Science Research Institute
University of Tennessee at Knoxville
209 UT Conference Center Building
Knoxville, TN 37996-0640
Phone: 423-974-2819
Fax: 423-974-7541
E-mail: pa106528@utkvm1.utk.edu
http://web.utk.edu/~ssri/

Texas

Center for Community Research and Development
Baylor University
P.O. Box 97131
Waco, TX 76798-7131
Phone: 254-710-3811
Fax: 254-710-3809
E-mail: larry_lyon@baylor.edu
http://www.baylor.edu/~CCRD

Earl Survey Research Laboratory
Texas Tech University
Box 41015
Lubbock, TX 79409-1015
Phone: 806-742-4851
Fax: 806-742-4329
E-mail: brcannon@ttu.edu
http://www.ttu.edu/~esrl

Survey Research Center
University of North Texas
P.O. Box 310637
Denton, TX 76203-0637
Phone: 940-565-3221
Fax: 940-565-3295
E-mail: paulr@scs.cmm.unt.edu
http://www.unt.edu/src/

Survey Research Program
George J. Beto Criminal Justice Center
Sam Houston State University
Huntsville, TX 77341-2296
Phone: 936-294-1651
Fax: 936-294-1653
E-mail: icc_drl@shsu.edu
http://www.shsu.edu/cjcenter/College/srpdex.htm

Office of Survey Research
University of Texas
3001 Lake Austin Blvd.
Austin, TX 78703
Phone: 512-471-4980
Fax: 512-471-0569
E-mail: survey@uts.cc.utexas.edu
http://communication.utexas.edu/OSR/

Public Policy Research Institute
Texas A & M University
H. C. Dulie Bell Building, Suite 329
College Station, TX 77843-4476
Phone: 979-845-8800
Fax: 979-845-0249
E-mail: ppri@tamu.edu
http://ppri.tamu.edu

Utah

Social Research Institute
Graduate School of Social Work
University of Utah
395 S. 1500 E., Room 111
Salt Lake City, UT 84112-0260
Phone: 801-581-4857
Fax: 801-585-6865
E-mail: nharris@socwk.utah.edu
http://www.socwk.utah.edu/sri/aboutsri.asp

Virginia

Survey and Evaluation Research Laboratory
Virginia Commonwealth University
921 W. Franklin St.
P.O. Box 843016
Richmond, VA 23284-3016
Phone: 804-828-8813
Fax: 804-828-6133
E-mail: srl@vcu.edu
http://www.vcu.edu/srl/

Center for Survey Research
University of Virginia

P.O. Box 400767
2205 Fontaine Ave., Suite 303
Charlottesville, VA 22904-4767
Phone: 434-243-5232
Fax: 434-243-5233
E-mail: surveys@virginia.edu
http://www.virginia.edu/surveys

Center for Survey Research
Virginia Tech
207 W. Roanoke St.
Blacksburg, VA 24061-0543
Phone: 540-231-3676
Fax: 540-231-3678
E-mail: vtcsr@vt.edu
http://filebox.vt.edu/centers/survey

Washington

Collaborative Data Services
Survey Research and Technical Development Units
Fred Hutchinson Cancer Research Center
P.O. Box 19024, MP-647
Seattle, WA 98109
Phone: 206-667-7387
Fax: 206-667-7864
E-mail: kkreizen@fhcrc.org

Social and Economic Sciences Research Center
Washington State University
Wilson Hall, Room 133
P.O. Box 644014
Pullman, WA 99164-4014
Phone: 509-335-1511
Fax: 509-335-0116

E-mail: sesrc@wsu.edu
http://survey.sesrc.wsu.edu/

West Virginia

Institute for Labor Studies and Research
West Virginia University
711 Knapp Hall
P.O. Box 6031
Morgantown, WV 26506-6031
Phone: 304-293-4201
Fax: 304-293-3395
E-mail: scook3@wvu.edu
http://www.wvu.edu/~exten/depts/ilsr/ilsr.htm

Wisconsin

Survey Center
University of Wisconsin
2412 Social Science Building
1800 University Ave., Room 102
Madison, WI 53705
Phone: 608-262-1688
Fax: 608-262-8432
E-mail: stevenso@ssc.wisc.edu
http://www.wisc.edu/uwsc

Institute for Survey and Policy Research
University of Wisconsin-Milwaukee
P.O. Box 413
Milwaukee, WI 53201
Phone: 414-229-6617
E-mail: akubeze@uwm.edu
http://www.uwm.edu/Dept/ISPR

Wyoming

Survey Research Center
University of Wyoming
College of Business Building, Room 1
P.O. Box 3925
Laramie, WY 82071-3925
Phone: 307-766-4209
Fax: 307-766-2040
E-mail: burke@uwyo.edu
http://uwyo.edu/src

Canada

Population Research Laboratory
Department of Sociology
University of Alberta
1-62 HM Tory Building
Edmonton, Alberta T6G 2H4, Canada
Phone: 780-492-4659
Fax: 780-492-2589
E-mail: donna.fong@ualberta.ca
http://www.ualberta.ca/PRL/

Institute for Social Research
York University
4700 Keele St.
Toronto, Ontario M3J 1P3, Canada
Phone: 416-736-5061
Fax: 416-736-5749
E-mail: isrnews@yorku.ca
http://www.isr.yorku.ca

England

National Centre for Social Research
35 Northampton Square
London EC1V OAX, United Kingdom
Phone: 44-20-7250-1866
Fax: 44-20-7040-4900
http://www.natcen.ac.uk

Germany

Zuma-Center for Survey Research and Methodology
P.O. Box 122155
68072 Mannheim, Germany
Phone: 49-621-1246-0
Fax: 49-621-1246-100
E-mail: zuma@zuma-mannheim.de

Appendix B

Illinois Liquor Control Commission: College Student Survey

**PLEASE CIRCLE ONE CODE NUMBER FOR EACH QUESTION
UNLESS OTHERWISE SPECIFIED.**

1. What is your age?
   Under 18 . . . . 1 ∧(Skip to Q.22.)
   18 2
   19 3
   20 4
   21 or over . . . . 5 ∧(Skip to Q.22.)

2. Have you ever had a drink of any type of alcohol? (By "drink" we mean
   a glass of beer or wine, a can or bottle of beer, a wine cooler, a shot or
   jigger of hard alcohol, etc. Do not include sips that you might have taken
   from another person's drink.)
   Yes. 1
   No . . . . 2 ∧(Skip to Q.16.)

3. How old were you the first time you drank alcohol? (Do not include sips
   from another person's drink.)
   _____ years old

4. Did you drink alcohol while you were in high school, even once?
   Yes. 1
   No . . . . 2 ∧(Skip to Q.7.)

5. How often did you typically drink alcohol during your senior year
   in high school?
   Two or more times a week 1
   Once a week. 2
   One to three times a month 3
   Less than once a month 4
   Never during senior year . . . . 5 ∧(Skip to Q.7.)

6. On the days when you drank during your senior year, about how many
   drinks did you consume on average?
   _____ drinks per day

7. In what month and year did you graduate from high school?
   _____ Month   _____ Year

8. Since you graduated from high school, have you drunk any alcohol?
   Yes. 1
   No . . . . 2 ∧(Skip to Q.16.)

9. During the *past 30 days,* have you had at least one alcoholic drink?
   Yes. 1
   No . . . . 2 ∧(Skip to Q.16.)

10. During the past 30 days, on how many days did you drink any alcoholic
    beverages?
    _____ days

11. On the days when you drank, about how many drinks did you consume on average?

    _____ drinks per day

12. In the past 30 days, where did you drink alcohol? *(Circle all that apply.)*
    My apartment/dorm 1
    Home/apartment/dorm of friend
        or acquaintance 2
    At the home of my parent(s) 3
    Fraternity/sorority house 4
    Bar/restaurant 5
    Other *(Please specify)* 6   _____

13. a. On the *most recent occasion* when you drank, did you drink at more than one location?
       Yes 1
       No . . . . 2 ∧*(Skip to Q.14.)*

    b. On that occasion, at how many locations did you drink?
       Two 1
       Three 2
       Four 3
       Five or more 4
       Not sure 8

    c. On that occasion, at what locations did you drink? *(Circle all that apply.)*
       My apartment/dorm 1
       Home/apartment/dorm of friend
           or acquaintance 2
       At the home of my parent or parents . 3
       Fraternity/sorority house 4
       Bar/restaurant 5
       Other *(Please specify.)* 6   _____

    d. On that occasion, at what location did you take your first drink?
       My apartment/dorm 1
       Home/apartment/dorm of friend
           or acquaintance 2
       At the home of my parent or parents . 3
       Fraternity/sorority house 4
       Bar/restaurant 5
       Other *(Please specify.)* 6   _____

    e. On that occasion, at what location did you take your last drink?
       My apartment/dorm 1
       Home/apartment/dorm of friend
           or acquaintance 2
       At the home of my parent or parents . 3
       Fraternity/sorority house 4
       Bar/restaurant 5
       Other *(Please specify.)* 6   _____

14. Who purchased the alcohol that you drank during the *past 30 days*?
(Circle all that apply.)
I did 1
Friend or acquaintance under 21 did. . . . 2
Friend or acquaintance 21 or over did. . . 3
Sibling under 21 did 4
Sibling 21 or over did 5
Parent(s) did 6
Alcohol supplied at party—don't know
who purchased 7
Other *(Please specify.)* . . . . 8 _____

15. a. In the past 30 days, have you had other people buy alcohol for you in
your college town?
Yes 1
No . . . . 2 ∧*(Skip to Q.16.)*

b. In the past 30 days, who have you had purchase alcohol for you in
your college town? *(Circle all that apply.)*
Friend or acquaintance under 21 1
Friend or acquaintance 21 or over . . . 2
Sibling under 21 3
Sibling 21 or over 4
Parent(s) 5
Stranger. 6
Other *(Please specify.)*. . . . . 8 _____

16. Have you ever purchased alcohol, either for yourself or for others?
Yes. 1
No . . . . 2 ∧*(Skip to Q.18.)*

17. a. Have you purchased alcohol *in your college town* in the past 30 days,
either for yourself or for others?
Yes 1
No. . . . . 2 ∧*(Skip to Q.18.)*

b. In the past 30 days, where have you purchased alcohol in your college
town? *(Circle all that apply.)*
Bar/restaurant 1
Retail liquor store 2
Gas station/convenience store 3
Grocery store. 4
Other *(Please specify.)*. . . . . 5 _____

c. In the past 30 days, where have you *most often* purchased alcohol in
your college town?
Bar/restaurant 1
Retail liquor store 2
Gas station/convenience store 3
Grocery store. 4
Other *(Please specify.)*. . . . . 5 _____

d. In the past 30 days, what is the most common way you have purchased alcohol in your college town? (If more than one way, choose the *most frequent way.*) *(Circle only one.)*
   Used fake or altered ID. 1
   Used older friend's/sibling's ID 2
   From friend/acquaintance who sells alcohol. . . 3
   Frequented establishments that do not card. . . 4
   Took a chance I wouldn't be carded 5
   Other *(Please specify.)*. . . . . 6 _____

18. What is your alcoholic beverage of choice? *(Circle only one.)*
    Beer 1
    Wine. 2
    Hard liquor. 3
    Mixed drinks 4
    Other *(Please specify.)* . . 5   _____
    Don't drink. 8

19. How old do you have to be to enter a bar in your college town?
    18 1
    19 2
    20 3
    21 4
    Don't know. 8

20. a. Have you been in a bar in your college town in the past 30 days?
      Yes 1
      No. . . . . 2 ∧*(Skip to Q.21a.)*

    b. What did you drink when you were in the bar?
      Alcohol 1
      Non-alcoholic beverage 2
      Both alcoholic and non-alcoholic beverages . . . 3
      Nothing 4

21. a. Have you been exposed to or participated in any alcohol awareness/ education programs on your campus this semester?
      Yes 1
      No. . . . . 2 ∧*(Skip to Q.22.)*

    b. Have you been exposed to or participated in any alcohol awareness/ education programs that dealt *specifically* with underage drinking on your campus this semester?
      Yes 1
      No. 2

22. What is your gender?
    Male. 1
    Female 2

23. What racial/ethnic background do you consider yourself?
    American Indian or Alaskan Native 1
    Black/African American, not of Hispanic origin . . . 2
    White, not of Hispanic origin 3
    Hispanic/Latino(a) 4
    Asian or Pacific Islander 5
    Other *(Please specify.)* . . . . 6 _____

Thank you very much for your assistance!

Please return your completed questionnaire
in the postage-paid envelope provided to:

The University of Illinois at Chicago
Survey Research Laboratory (M/C 336)
Box 6905
Chicago, IL 60680

Your answers are completely anonymous. Please put the enclosed postcard in the mail at the same time as your questionnaire. In this way we will know that you have returned your questionnaire and will not bother you with a follow-up mailing.

Appendix C

Faculty Retention Survey

Faculty Retention Survey December 2002

Listed below are some factors that may or may not have been significant in your decision to leave the University of Illinois at Chicago or one of its branches. The columns on the left allow you to note how important the factor is to you and your work; the columns on the right allow you to note how important the factor was in your decision to leave UIC.

Please circle the number in each set of columns that best rates the factor's importance. If a factor is not applicable, circle "1" (not at all important).

On a scale from 1 – 5:

1 = Not at all important   2 = Not too important   3 = Somewhat important   4 = Very important   5 = Extremely important

1. Organizational Culture, Policies, and Practices

Important to you and your work Not at all / Not too / Somewhat / Very / Extremely							*Important to your departure* Not at all / Not too / Somewhat / Very / Extremely				
1	2	3	4	5	a.	Organizational culture of the University	1	2	3	4	5
1	2	3	4	5	b.	Sense of community at the University	1	2	3	4	5
1	2	3	4	5	c.	Departmental culture	1	2	3	4	5
1	2	3	4	5	d.	The fit between you and the organization and its mission	1	2	3	4	5
1	2	3	4	5	e.	Amount of research expected	1	2	3	4	5
1	2	3	4	5	f.	Amount of teaching expected	1	2	3	4	5
1	2	3	4	5	g.	Nonresearch/teaching responsibilities and involvement	1	2	3	4	5
1	2	3	4	5	h.	Communication/feedback/support within your department	1	2	3	4	5

	Not at all	Not too	Somewhat	Very	Extremely		Not at all	Not too	Somewhat	Very	Extremely
i. Communication/feedback/support within the University	1	2	3	4	5		1	2	3	4	5
j. Policies on promotion and tenure	1	2	3	4	5		1	2	3	4	5
k. That the University values your field of study	1	2	3	4	5		1	2	3	4	5
l. That your department values your work	1	2	3	4	5		1	2	3	4	5
m. Confidence in University leadership	1	2	3	4	5		1	2	3	4	5
n. Confidence in departmental leadership	1	2	3	4	5		1	2	3	4	5
o. Mentoring opportunities/programs	1	2	3	4	5		1	2	3	4	5
p. Networking opportunities/programs	1	2	3	4	5		1	2	3	4	5
q. Compensation—level of annual salary	1	2	3	4	5		1	2	3	4	5
r. Compensation—benefits	1	2	3	4	5		1	2	3	4	5
s. Opportunities for consulting work (outside the University, for pay)	1	2	3	4	5		1	2	3	4	5
t. Opportunities for consulting work (at the University, for pay)	1	2	3	4	5		1	2	3	4	5
u. Working in a culture that values diversity	1	2	3	4	5		1	2	3	4	5
v. Working in a culture that values and affirms equity	1	2	3	4	5		1	2	3	4	5
w. Safety within the working environment	1	2	3	4	5		1	2	3	4	5
x. Other *(Please specify)* _____	1	2	3	4	5		1	2	3	4	5

2. Professional Life

Important to you and your work						Important to your departure				
Not at all	Not too	Somewhat	Very	Extremely		Not at all	Not too	Somewhat	Very	Extremely
1	2	3	4	5	a. Being able to accomplish meaningful professional work	1	2	3	4	5
1	2	3	4	5	b. Feeling of having a voice regarding your work	1	2	3	4	5
1	2	3	4	5	c. Your course teaching assignments	1	2	3	4	5
1	2	3	4	5	d. Your advising assignments	1	2	3	4	5
1	2	3	4	5	e. Quality of student population	1	2	3	4	5
1	2	3	4	5	f. Opportunities to participate in governance	1	2	3	4	5
1	2	3	4	5	g. Opportunities for professional advancement in career	1	2	3	4	5
1	2	3	4	5	h. Opportunities for professional development	1	2	3	4	5
1	2	3	4	5	i. Rewards/recognition for your research	1	2	3	4	5
1	2	3	4	5	j. Rewards/recognition for your teaching	1	2	3	4	5
1	2	3	4	5	k. Rewards/recognition for doing service	1	2	3	4	5
1	2	3	4	5	l. Clarity and equity in performance reviews (P&T, salary)	1	2	3	4	5
1	2	3	4	5	m. Hours and schedule of work	1	2	3	4	5
1	2	3	4	5	n. Level of stress in your work	1	2	3	4	5
1	2	3	4	5	o. Desire for new professional challenges	1	2	3	4	5
1	2	3	4	5	p. The realization of your expectations upon coming to the University	1	2	3	4	5
1	2	3	4	5	q. Other (Please specify) _____	1	2	3	4	5

3. University Facilities/Services/Resources

Important to you and your work (Not at all / Not too / Somewhat / Very / Extremely)						Important to your departure (Not at all / Not too / Somewhat / Very / Extremely)				
1	2	3	4	5	a. Sufficient support of grants and contracts	1	2	3	4	5
1	2	3	4	5	b. Availability of resources to enable you to do your work	1	2	3	4	5
1	2	3	4	5	c. Adequate support staff	1	2	3	4	5
1	2	3	4	5	d. Adequate graduate student assistance	1	2	3	4	5
1	2	3	4	5	e. Material environment (e.g., offices, classrooms, parking)	1	2	3	4	5
1	2	3	4	5	f. Quality of library facilities	1	2	3	4	5
1	2	3	4	5	g. Quality of laboratory facilities	1	2	3	4	5
1	2	3	4	5	h. Other (Please specify) _____	1	2	3	4	5

4. Environment

Important to you and your work							Important to your departure				
Not at all	Not too	Somewhat	Very	Extremely			Not at all	Not too	Somewhat	Very	Extremely
1	2	3	4	5	a.	The environment of research on your campus	1	2	3	4	5
1	2	3	4	5	b.	The environment of research in your department	1	2	3	4	5
1	2	3	4	5	c.	The environment of teaching on your campus	1	2	3	4	5
1	2	3	4	5	d.	The environment of teaching in your department	1	2	3	4	5
1	2	3	4	5	e.	The environment of service on your campus	1	2	3	4	5
1	2	3	4	5	f.	The environment of service in your department	1	2	3	4	5
1	2	3	4	5	g.	Reputation of your employer as a Research I institution	1	2	3	4	5
1	2	3	4	5	h.	Reputation of your college	1	2	3	4	5
1	2	3	4	5	i.	Rapport with your department head	1	2	3	4	5
1	2	3	4	5	j.	Reputation of colleagues in your department	1	2	3	4	5
1	2	3	4	5	k.	Camaraderie with colleagues	1	2	3	4	5
1	2	3	4	5	l.	Congeniality of colleagues	1	2	3	4	5
1	2	3	4	5	m.	Diversity of colleagues	1	2	3	4	5
1	2	3	4	5	n.	Intellectual dialogue with students	1	2	3	4	5
1	2	3	4	5	o.	Other (Please specify) _____	1	2	3	4	5

5. Individual Considerations

Important to you and your work

Important to your departure

Important to you and your work						Important to your departure				
Not at all	Not too	Somewhat	Very	Extremely		Not at all	Not too	Somewhat	Very	Extremely
1	2	3	4	5	a. The city in which your campus is located	1	2	3	4	5
1	2	3	4	5	b. Travel and commute time	1	2	3	4	5
1	2	3	4	5	c. Social opportunities in local community	1	2	3	4	5
1	2	3	4	5	d. Diversity of local population	1	2	3	4	5
1	2	3	4	5	e. Availability of cultural opportunities	1	2	3	4	5
1	2	3	4	5	f. Quality of local school system	1	2	3	4	5
1	2	3	4	5	g. Quality of housing available	1	2	3	4	5
1	2	3	4	5	h. Child care availability	1	2	3	4	5
1	2	3	4	5	i. Partner's career opportunities	1	2	3	4	5
1	2	3	4	5	j. Geographic climate of your city	1	2	3	4	5
1	2	3	4	5	k. Proximity of family (yours, partner's)	1	2	3	4	5
1	2	3	4	5	l. Other *(Please specify)* _____	1	2	3	4	5

Appendix D

Kinko's:
Open-ended Service
Satisfaction Survey

You are a valued customer. What you have to say is important to us. Please take a moment to let us know how we are doing by filling out this card, by calling Customer Service at 1–800-xxx-xxxx, or by visiting our Web site.

Overall, how satisfied were you with your experience with us today?
(Circle one)

Extremely							*Extremely*	
Dissatisfied							*Satisfied*	
1	2	3	4	5	6	7	8	9

What do we do well? _____

_____

What should we change? _____

_____

What can we do to serve you better? _____

_____

Additional comments? _____

_____

Date of visit: _____   Time of day: _____

Name: _____

Address: _____

City/State/Zip: _____

Area Code: _____ Telephone: _____

Occupation: _____

Thanks for your patronage.

CPSIA information can be obtained at www.ICGtesting.com
Printed in the USA
BVOW01n1044180716

455732BV00001B/1/P